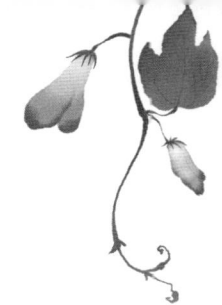

Easier to See *Jeong* (Love) Leaving than Arriving

드는 정은 몰라도 나는 정은 안다.

100 Korean Proverbs Vol. II
[영어로 만나는 한국속담 100편]

Moo-Jung Cho
조 무 정
(C. Bonaverture)

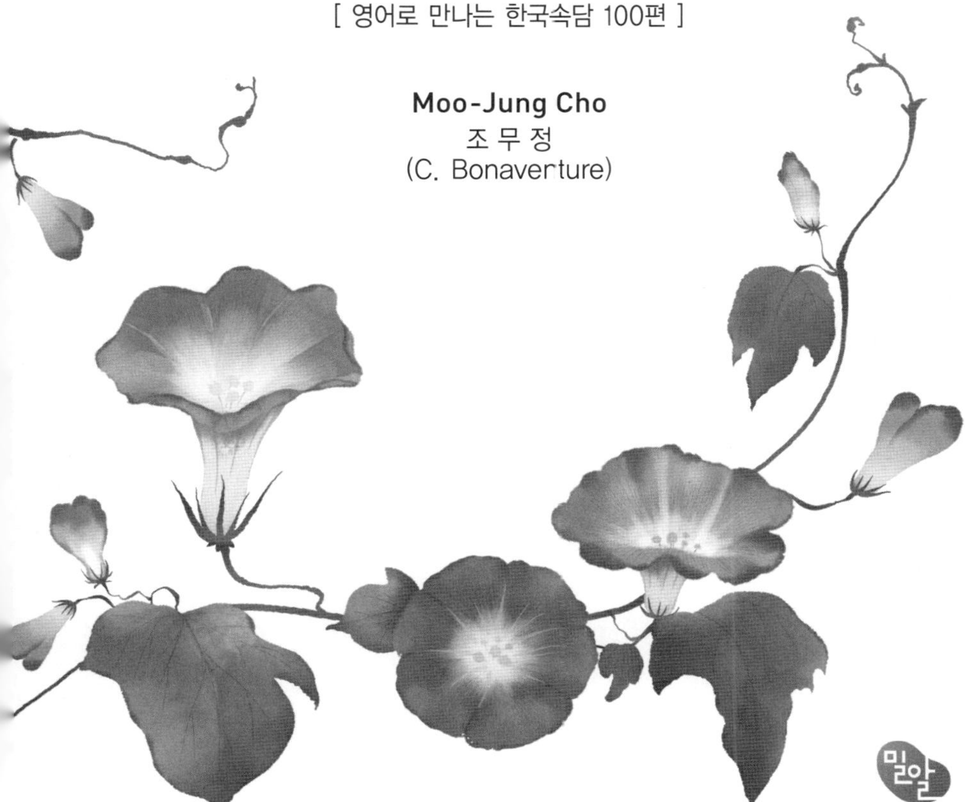

The contents of this work, including, but not limited to, the accuracy of events, people, and places depicted; opinions expressed; permission to use previously published materials included; and any advice given or actions advocated are solely the responsibility of the author, who assumes all liability for said work and indemnifies the publisher against any claims stemming from publication of the work.

Easier to See *Jeong* (Love) Leaving than Arriving

All Rights Reserved
Copyright © 2020 by Moo-jung Cho

No part of this book may be reproduced or transmitted, downloaded, distributed, reverse engineered, or stored in or introduced into any information storage and retrieval system, in any form or by any means, including photocopying and recording, whether electronic or mechanical, now known or hereinafter invented without permission in writing from the publisher.

To

June (주영),
Who has well tolerated yet another
"fishing expedition" on my part,

My Phoenix sister, Choon-Kyung (춘경),
who originally inspired these essays,

My Brother, Deuk-Jung (득정) in Seoul,
Who has encouraged the publication in Korea,

And

Our Korean ancestors, who have continuously
refined these proverbs over centuries.

Easier to See *Jeong* (Love)
Leaving than Arriving

초판인쇄 2020년 3월 16일
초판발행 2020년 3월 16일

지은이 조무정

펴낸이 조병성
기 획 박미희
펴낸곳 밀알
등록번호 2009-000263
주소 서울시 강남구 광평로 295 동관 207호
전화 02.3411.6896
팩스 02.3411.6657

편집/인쇄 도노디자인 (02 2272 5009)

ISBN 979-11-966743-5-9
값 13,000원

*파본 및 잘못된 책은 바꿔드립니다.

CONTENTS

FOREWORD ⋯ 017
ACKNOWLEDGEMENT ⋯ 018
INTRODUCTION ⋯ 020

101. Even the monkey can fall down from trees. ⋯ 026
    원숭이도 나무에서 떨어진다.

102. Ignorance is medicine. ⋯ 028
    모르는게 약이다.

103. It's spilt water. ⋯ 030
    엎질러진 물이다.

104. "No way" can kill you. ⋯ 032
    "설마"가 사람 잡는다.

105. Fastening a bell on the neck of a cat. ⋯ 034
    고양이 목에 방울 달기.

106. The mountain and the river get deeper as you enter. ⋯ 036
    산은 오를수록 높고 물은 건널수록 깊다.

107. Spitting while lying on your back. ⋯ 038
    누워서 침 뱉기.

108. Licking fingers after pulling a dried pollack. ⋯ 040
    북어 뜯고 손가락 빤다.

109. You cannot see your own eyebrow. ⋯ 042
    가까운 제 눈썹 못 본다.

110. No one can go to the bathroom or heaven's gate on your behalf. ⋯ 044
    저승길과 변소 길은 대신 못간다.

111. My cousin buys land, I have a bellyache. ⋯ 046
사촌이 땅을 사면 배가아프다.

112. Brag about spending, not making money. ⋯ 048
버는데 자랑말고 쓰는데 자랑했다.

113. Use a shovel for a job for *homee*? ⋯ 050
호미로 막을 것을 가래로 막는다.

114. A one-day old puppy isn't afraid of a tiger. ⋯ 052
하룻강아지 범 무서운 줄 모른다.

115. The pot calls the kettle black. ⋯ 054
똥 묻은 개가 겨 묻은 개 나무란다.

116. The crayfish sides with crabs. ⋯ 056
가재는 게 편이라.

117. There is no field free of any weeds. ⋯ 058
풀 없는 밭 없다.

118. A thirsty man digs a well. ⋯ 060
목마른 놈이 우물 판다.

119. Don't drink water in front of a child, lest he gets drowned. ⋯ 062
아이 보는데서는 찬물도 못 마신다.

120. Stab and spoil a persimmon you don't want to eat. ⋯ 064
못 먹는 감 찔러나 본다.

121. No investment is worthier than children's education. ⋯ 066
황금 천 냥이 자식 교육만 못하다.

122. Bread is better than the song of birds. ⋯ 068
금강산도 식후 경

123. A dress is like feathers of a bird.   ⋯ 070
     옷이 날개라.

124. Burning a house down to get rid of bedbugs.   ⋯ 072
     빈대가 밉다고 집에 불을 놓는다.

125. Blood is thicker than water.   ⋯ 074
     피는 물보다 더 진하다.

126. One wishes to become a monk while in a Buddhist temple.   ⋯ 076
     절에 가면 중 노릇 하고 싶다.

127. A bad wife is better than a good son.   ⋯ 078
     악처가 효자보다 낫다.

128. We sidestep feces because it is filthy not out of fear.   ⋯ 080
     똥이 무서워서 피하나, 더러워서 피하지.

129. No fish survives in distilled water.   ⋯ 082
     물이 너무 맑으면 고기가 안 모인다.

130. Eat slowly, even ripe persimmon.   ⋯ 084
     무른 감도 쉬어 가면서 먹어라.

131. A rich man in a ravine is poorer than a dog on a shore.   ⋯ 086
     산골 부자가 해변 개보다 못하다.

132. Even a dog is allowed peaceful meals.   ⋯ 088
     먹을때는 개도 안 때린다.

133. An old dog does not bark for nothing.   ⋯ 090
     늙은 개는 공연히 짖지 않는다.

134. A mediocre carpenter complains about tools.   ⋯ 092
     서투른 목수 연장 탓만 한다.

135. No one believes *meju* is from soybean. ⋯ 094
콩으로 메주를 쑨다 해도 곧이 듣지 않는다.

136. People will swallow even TSP, if it is free. ⋯ 096
공짜라면 양잿물도 마신다.

137. Nails resist a light hammer's head. ⋯ 098
망치가 가벼우면 못이 솟는다.

138. Startled by a turtle and now by a caldron lid. ⋯ 100
자라 보고 놀란 가슴, 솥뚜껑 보고도 놀란다.

139. Like kites tangled on a jujube tree⋯. ⋯ 102
대추나무에 연 걸리듯⋯.

140. Parents can take care of their ten children, but not vice versa. ⋯ 104
한 부모는 열 자식을 거느려도 열 자식은 한 부모를 못 돌본다.

141. One feels a splinter under a finger nail, but not a troubled heart. ⋯ 106
손톱 밑에 가시 드는 줄은 알아도, 염통 곪는 줄은 모른다.

142. A mad dog can kill a tiger. ⋯ 108
미친개가 호랑이 잡는다.

143. Everybody sheds dusts when brushed up. ⋯ 110
털어서 먼지 안 나는 사람 없다.

144. Buy and slaughter a cow on credit. ⋯ 112
외상이면 소도 잡아 먹는다.

145. Thread follows the needle. ⋯ 114
바늘 가는 데 실 간다.

146. Quitting is worse than never starting. ⋯ 116
가다가 중지하면 아니 간 만 못하다.

147. Old tigers go home to die.   ⋯ 118
　　호랑이도 죽을 때는 제 집을 찾는다.

148. Looking for tofu in a soybean field.   ⋯ 120
　　콩밭에 가서 두부 찾는다.

149. My cousin buys land, I have a bellyache (second version).   ⋯ 122
　　사촌이 땅을 사면 배가 아프다.

150. The arm holding a shot of sake bends only one way.   ⋯ 124
　　잔 잡은 팔이 밖으로 휘지 못한다.

151. No son is good enough for the long-term care of parents.   ⋯ 126
　　긴 병에 효자 없다.

152. Ordering to plant soybean here, red bean there.   ⋯ 128
　　콩 심어라 팥 심어라 한다.

153. Easier to see *jeong* (love) leaving than arriving.   ⋯ 130
　　드는 정은 몰라도 나는 정은 안다.

154. One thief outsmarts ten sentries.   ⋯ 132
　　지키는 사람 열이 훔치는 사람 하나를 못 당한다.

155. The butcher looks down on ordinary people.   ⋯ 134
　　저는 잘난 백정으로 알고 남은 헌 정승으로 안다.

156. A tiger appears at the fun party in a valley.   ⋯ 136
　　재미나는 골에 범 난다.

157. Use krill for baiting carps.   ⋯ 138
　　새우 미끼로 잉어를 낚는다.

158. Are siblings treasure or foe?   ⋯ 140
　　형제는 잘 두면 보배, 못 두면 원수.

159. All is well in fine clothes.   ⋯ 142
    못 입어 잘난 놈 없고, 잘 입어 못난 놈 없다.

160. Plant an acorn to build a pavilion.   ⋯ 144
    솔 심어 정자 짓는다.

161. Looking for one particular Kim in Seoul.   ⋯ 146
    서울 가서 김서방 찾기

162. Hunger is the best appetizer.   ⋯ 148
    시장이 반찬이다.

163. When a hen crows, the whole household collapses.   ⋯ 150
    암탉이 울면 집안이 망한다.

164. Liquor brings jaundice, wealth brings a corrupt mind.   ⋯ 152
    술은 얼굴을 누르게 하고, 황금은 마음을 검게한다.

165. Encountering a foe on a log bridge.   ⋯ 154
    원수는 외나무 다리에서 만난다.

166. The head of a rooster is preferred to the tail of a dragon.   ⋯ 156
    용 꼬리보다 닭 머리가 낫다.

167. Flapping wings under a blanket.   ⋯ 158
    이불 속에서 활개 친다.

168. Earth hardens after rain.   ⋯ 160
    비 온 뒤에 땅이 굳어진다.

169. A tree with deep roots survives drought.   ⋯ 162
    뿌리 깊은 나무는 가뭄 안 탄다.

170. A woman's curse brings June frost.   ⋯ 164
    여자가 한을 품으면, 오뉴월에도 서리가 내린다.

171. When dirt poor, burglary looks appealing. ··· 166
가난하면 마음에 도둑이 든다.

172. Neither a flamingo nor a phoenix. ··· 168
학도 아니고 봉도 아니다.

173. Listen to the elder, rice cake will come to you. ··· 170
어른 말을 들으면 자다가도 떡이 생긴다.

174. My ax injures my foot. ··· 172
믿는 도끼에 발등 찍힌다.

175. Oil droplets on water. ··· 174
물 위에 뜬 기름과 같다.

176. Rest when you fall. ··· 176
넘어진 김에 쉬어 간다.

177. Get the land, then build the house. ··· 178
터를 잡아야 집을 짓는다.

178. Fish evaded is always bigger than the fish caught. ··· 180
놓친 고기가 더 크다.

179. Save a penny, or *pun*(푼), to lose a fortune? ··· 182
한 푼 아끼다가 백 냥 잃는다.

180. Straight words from tilted mouth. ··· 184
입은 비뚤어져도 말은 바로 해라.

181. Fists are closer than the law. ··· 186
법은 멀고 주먹은 가깝다.

182. Having kimchi juice before the rice cake served. ··· 188
김치국부터 마신다.

183. Praying for another rainy day during monsoon season.   ⋯ 190
   백일 장마에도 하루만 더 왔으면 한다.

184. Acupuncture onto a pumpkin.   ⋯ 192
   호박에 침 주기

185. Begging for mercy can melt steel.   ⋯ 194
   비는 데는 무쇠도 녹는다.

186. Lose a tooth while chewing tofu.   ⋯ 196
   두부 먹다 이 빠진다.

187. Cracking noise from a demon munching rice seeds.   ⋯ 198
   귀신 씨나락 까먹는 소리.

188. Morning enlightenment is for peaceful evening death.   ⋯ 200
   아침에 도를 들으면 저녁에 죽어도 좋다.

189. Lend the money and lose a friend.   ⋯ 202
   돈 빌려주면 돈도 잃고 친구도 잃는다.

190. Plant trees if you wish to watch birds.   ⋯ 204
   새가 보고 싶거든 나무를 심어라.

191. The very ghost at your home will carry you away.   ⋯ 206
   집안 귀신이 사람 잡아간다.

192. Water to lower ground, criminals to jail.   ⋯ 208
   죄는 지은 데로 가고 물은 트는 데로 흐른다.

193. A wooden roller thrusts out in the dark.   ⋯ 210
   아닌 밤중에 홍두깨.

194. Messengers on a one-way journey.   ⋯ 212
   함흥차사.

195. True stories from a drunken man.   ⋯ 214
　　　취중에 진담 나온다.

196. A watermill never freezes.   ⋯ 216
　　　부지런한 물방아는 얼 새도 없다.

197. None of fingers is alike.   ⋯ 218
　　　한날한시에 난 손가락도 길고 짧다.

198. Can you fly even without hair?   ⋯ 220
　　　털도 안 난 것이 날기부터 하려 한다.

199. Speak louder, win the argument.   ⋯ 222
　　　남대문 본 놈과 안 본 놈이 다투면, 안 본 놈이 이긴다.

200. Flexibility over rigidity.   ⋯ 224
　　　꺾이느니 보다 차라리 굽히는 편이 낫다.

　　　INDEX (in essay number)   ⋯ 226

FOREWORD

In this day and age when the fingertip on a smartphone would trigger everything in a heartbeat, it is indeed refreshing to see that there are still Renaissance men who believe in a fundamental approach to cultural understanding. Here, quick glorification via digital display is replaced with reading and thinking. How much can one digest foreign culture through sightseeing on a tour bus? How can one learn foreign custom and tradition without speaking their language? Acquiring genuine empathy for foreigners may mandate living with them for years, sharing their warts and all. We are to regurgitate what we have learned til it crystallizes out as our own voice. Then, only then, we can say something.

My dear friend, Cho Moo-jung (조무정 with penname, C. Bonaventure) lived his first 25 years in Korea and the subsequent 50 or so in various parts of the United States: Vancouver, Canada (where we met as graduate students); Lawrence, Kansas; Kalamazoo, Michigan; Chicago, Illinois; Chapel Hill, North Carolina (where he taught at a university); and now finally retired to Las Vegas, Nevada, for earnest writing. By training he is a pharmaceutical chemist. And yet, he has developed a keen interest in dynamics between different cultures and their influence on world peace. This is far beyond facile political swerves involved in short-term national interests. It is all about people and their wisdom.

His thesis has been that empathy-based cultural understanding is the only way to long-lasting world peace. To this end, he introduces Korean proverbs to English-speakers. Wisdom embedded in these old sayings not only tell the world where Koreans have been but also helps extrapolate them to the future. If his first volume, *The Tongue Can Break Bones,* is any indication, this book, *Easier to See Jeong* (Love) *Leaving Than Arriving,* will equally enlighten readers on Korea and her people.

Hagen Koo, PhD
Professor Emeritus of Sociology
University of Hawaii
September 15, 2019

ACKNOWLEDGEMENT

There are many people for whom I ought to express my gratitude at various stages of this book's development. First and foremost, my sister sent me *Thousand Korean Proverbs* in loose pages in late 1960s. Choon-Kyung (조춘경) didn't say why she was sending them to me, for I didn't have any time to do anything about it. I was then a student whose every minute was dedicated to studying. Deep in my mind though, I knew I would write my own interpretation of the proverbs. It took more than 40 years to introduce the first 100 to English speakers. *The Tongue Can Break Bones* came out in the Spring of 2018. It has taken for a few decades but is better than never. *Easier to See* Jeong(*Love*) *Leaving than Arriving* is a sequel of the first volume, once again dealing with another 100 proverbs.

Writing is a lonely endeavor. No one glances over my shoulder to see every word I am writing. When I revealed to a few friends my plan to write essays on Korean proverbs, it was Han-Duck Kwan (권한덕) who sent me two children's books on Korean proverbs from Seoul, as if the first thousands I was consulting was not enough. Now, I had a bottomless source of materials. Then, other friends would sporadically ask if I know this or that. Choon-Taek Chun (전준택) of Las Vegas and Won Kim (김원) of Seoul not only introduced me to proverbs #136, #170 and #187, but also suggested me what angle I ought to take in my interpretation. As they say, the next move of a chess game is a lot easier for bystanders to see.

Long before I embarked on the project, I had asked myself who the readers of these books should be. The primary target was the second generation of Koreans in this country and Americans who may be interested in Korea. Because the essays are written in English, publishing them in Korea was not the original intention. But, then, I realized that many foreigners reside in Korea nowadays, for whom these proverbs should provide some historic and cultural backdrops of their present whereabouts. In addition, the books would benefit Koreans also as I heavily quoted happenings in the U.S. and the world. Unlike my generation of Korean, many young Koreans seem to read and speak English quite well.

Deciding to have them published in Korea was one thing but how to go about the business was something I was not ready to deal with. I am greatly indebted to my immediate older brother Deuk-Jung (조득정) in arranging Mil-Al Publishing Company for the publication. I would also like to acknowledge the fine job of my Editor, Paul Kim of San Diego, California. But for his thorough editing and suggested re-writing, the essays herein would still have shown rough edges here and there. Those are all mines, never his neglects. Finally, but not in the least, I am most grateful for the help I received from Ms. Mi-Hee Park (박미희) of Mil-Al, particularly her patience during our long-distance communications with my broken Korean and her kind guide through the unfamiliar map of book production in Korea.

Since this book is a continuation of *The Tongue Can Break Bones*, the first entry begins with #101. The third volume will start with #201. Since each essay is only two-page long, INDEX is in entry number. As before, I dug out the primary references from Wikipedia as well as NAVER whenever a research of a given topic was warranted.

INTRODUCTION

The beauty of proverbs lies in their simplicity. Spoken and written in plain language, any child can memorize them as soon as he or she learns to speak. However, the deep-rooted meaning of these idioms evolves as we age. Most likely, children hear a given proverb for first time from an older, and thus wiser, person who relates it to one occasion, and then, they hear the same proverb spoken later by others in slightly different situations. Soon, these proverbs become children's own.

At least, that was how I acquired the essence of Korean proverbs. There was no class at school, neither at the elementary school nor at the university, where we learned what Korean proverbs are all about. Now sitting here, several thousand miles away from Korea, without any reputable references or teachers to consult with, I am trying to present what I believe to be the true element of the Korean proverb. Even if there were books and articles written about the topic, I would probably not have read them lest they should affect my own understanding, thoughts, and feelings.

If there is one unique feature in Korean old sayings, it would be gentleness, often with a humor derived from the everyday lives of average citizens. They are as if the sharp edges have been worn down through continuous use over many years. They are rolling hills under the blue sky peppered with lazy white clouds, never the Alps or the Himalayas under a windy snow storm. They are small, gentle streams and the peaceful sound of a lullaby, never the deafening thunder of Niagara Falls. Many Korean proverbs end with a question mark. Instead of stating outright, "The first spoonful of food will never give you satiety," one asks "Would the first spoonful of food bring about satiety?" You will come up with the same conclusion in the end, but it asks you with some level of subtlety. The gentleness and subtleness that I identify Korean proverbs with must be from the people's life as well as the geographic and terrestrial surroundings of Korea. Describing these two factors alone will take up a tome, and I will instead let these proverbs speak themselves.

And the wisdom therein! The oral history of Korea goes back for 5,000 years. The traceable history for the two millennia preceding the 15th century has been recorded in Chinese characters and in our own alphabets since then. Although many idioms were thus written in Chinese, especially those four-letter phrases in Chinese characters, I suspect that they could not have been very popular among our ancestors, since most of them were simply illiterate in Chinese. The class division itself, between learned men, or 양반 (*yang-ban*), and the ordinary citizens, or 서민 (*seo-min*), has been a popular subject among the latter, sprinkled with their own ridicule and wit. These ordinary people, who shared barely-won happiness as well as various adversities in their lives, invented and used the proverbs. They are the collective consciousness of Korean people, which defines who we are now.

Some 40 years ago, my sister who lived in Phoenix, Arizona, sent me *One-Thousand Korean Proverbs* in several loose pages. I do not know where they were originally from, but I knew that one day I would try to interpret them for English-speakers. I have kept them in a drawer for all these years. As I tried to translate a few of them in English just to gauge the scope of the job, I immediately encountered the difficulty of keeping alive those rhymes that are perfect in Korean language, which has survived for decades, if not centuries. They are poetries. I do not know how to translate them into English. All I can say is that I did my best. In some fortunate cases, however, there are some English versions that are almost mirror images of Korean proverbs. I hurriedly copied them in this book. If there is an English version that is similar in its implication to a Korean proverb, I introduce it in the text.

As to the implied content of a proverb, I take my own prerogative: others may interpret it in different ways. The proverb may talk about an earthworm or spider, but I am more interested in learning about what their behaviors teach us about human interaction and interactions among institutions, communities, or even nations. I will be the first to admit that my thought in the interpretation process tends to drift widely and wildly. Japanese kamikaze pilots appear in a story involving tiger cubs. The story about smoke from a chimney introduces those cheaters in contemporary baseball. Quite often, I find a great pleasure in submitting my own opinion on various topics as I have not yet had opportunities to do so. Be it cynical or sounding ridiculous, the writing is, to the truest sense, my own voice: good as well as bad that have been accumulated during my life of over 70 years.

Language is a culture, which leads to the next problem of how to take care of the stark differences between the two cultures. I naively thought that I should be in good position to address this issue since I have, after all, lived approximately one third and two thirds of my life in Korea and the United States, respectively. It was once again my own guesswork to determine to what extent I ought to cover cultural background in these essays. I apologize in advance if I have too many superfluous words or too little on the Korean culture.

Then, there are many words with different nuances and meanings: krill and shrimp are completely different from each other, but we Koreans call them both 새우, or *saewoo*. Tangerine and orange are both 귤, or *gule*. Since the topic of proverbs varies widely and since there is no framework for sorting them in some rational manner, I list them completely at random. As far as I can tell, the *One-Thousand Korean Proverbs* that I received many years ago does not appear to have any discernable order either. I simply present them in a chronological order with the date of write-up at the end of each entry. I have tried to avoid discussing ongoing events: instead I cited time-tested, well-established historical accounts. However, I could not let the episodes involving the 45th President of the U.S. just pass by unnoticed. He has provided an immeasurabl eamount of priceless examples of how one should not lead the nation and its citizens. I am thus thankful for his contribution.

The most impressionable and formative period of my life in Korea was just after Korean War (1950-1953). There was a large contingent of American soldiers in the country. Whether we liked or not, their presence offered us a great deal of exposure to the American culture. We read Hemingway and Steinbeck, followed the fights of Cassius Clay (Mohammad Ali since then), admired Mickey Mantle's career at Yankees, hummed along with Beatles, watched American films like *From Here to Eternity,* and even monitored closely what was happening in the political arena of the United States. At night, my ears were glued to the AFKN (American Forces Korea Network) radio station, which carried songs requested by the loved ones back at home for the American soldiers in Korea, largely what I later realized was country music. My poor English did not allow me to fully understand what the lady announcer was saying, but I figured it was all about boosting troop morale. I still vividly remember the alluring voice she spoke in. As I look back now, I understood America far better than they did about Korea.

Imbalance in cultural understanding between nations has undoubtedly added fuel to ongoing animosity, often igniting a full-blown war. Even at that tender age, I found myself wondering how many Americans knew anything about Korea, exception being Korean War and our cold winter. Years later, I discovered that the Peace Corps campaign by the Kennedy administration was to help Americans understand the culture of developing countries. I just hope that this book could also similarly contribute to the understanding of Korean culture among English-speakers. It is one tiny grain of sand on the vast oceanic beach, but is better than nothing.

Having been a scientist, it has become a habit to always reveal the source of a given piece of information in my writing. Here, I am greatly indebted by Wikipedia and NAVER. Even with these online encyclopedias, whenever warranted, I went back to the primary literature to confirm that what I was writing is indeed correct. My Korean is no longer what it used to be when I was a college kid in Korea. Inevitably, I had to consult Korean-English as well as English-Korean dictionaries, both by Dong-A Publishing and Printing Company. To my delight, they often introduce an English version of a Korean proverb. These occasions were like finding a few coins between the cushions on a sofa.

I used a pseudonym, C. Bonaventure, as the author of the first volume, *The Tongue Can Break Bones*. It was published in the U.S. in June, 2018. As writing essays has never been my profession, my real name would not mean anything. Bonaventure was the Christian name given to me when I was baptized as a Catholic. There is neither more nor less significance associated the pseudonym. Just accept it as is. Now that both the first book and *Easier to See* Jeong (*Love*) *Leaving than Arriving are* coming out in Korea, there is no reason not to use the name given to me when I was born. Some of my old Korean friends may still recognize the name.

I immensely enjoyed writing these essays. It is my hope that readers find this collection somehow meritorious and enjoy reading as much as I did with my writing. (adopted from *The Tongue Can Break Bones:* 11/12/19)

Easier to See *Jeong* (Love) Leaving than Arriving

드는 정은 몰라도 나는 정은 안다.

100 Korean Proverbs Vol. II
[영어로 만나는 한국속담 100편]

Moo-Jung Cho
조 무 정
(C. Bonaventure)

Even the monkey can fall down from trees.
원숭이도 나무에서 떨어진다.

[101]

Almost all species of monkeys are tree-dwelling. For them, traveling through the dense foliage of trees must be equivalent to people walking on the ground or driving on inter-state freeways. As extraordinary as it may sound, they can fall from the trees: so says the above proverb. A straightforward interpretation may well be that we cannot always be free from mistake or accident in what we do routinely. I suppose that's what makes us human. However, what is not stated explicitly is that in such a rare occasion, the consequence can be quite devastating or tragic. Is there an inverse relationship between the rarity of incident and the severity of its outcome? How often would one get struck by lightning and be killed? Can a monkey fall down from a tree, right into the open mouth of a Burmese python?

Once upon a time, there lived a world-renown astronomer. He would spend all of his waking hours in the darkness of the night, studying stars in the sky. He attended trivial chores of domestic life only during the daytime, in-between fretful sleeps. Come dusk, he was off to various hill tops, with long field glasses, trained toward a small section of the starry sky. The dedication to his vocation was absolute. Gazing at stars was his life and religion. His dedication was such that he could not take his eyes off the stars, even while walking. One night, the astronomer tripped over a small exposed rock and stumbled down to the ground. His head broke open when it hit the solid rock surface of a boulder, and he died right there and then. He was found holding his dear binoculars and notebook onto his chest, rather than keeping his body away from the boulder. I don't remember who told me this story, when I was a child, but the ending was so shocking that I still remember the lesson we were to learn: this learned man who knows every constellation, far away in the universe, failed to notice a small piece of rock protruding from the ground.

The deadly thing just sat there, less than six feet below his eyes.

Mistake is the key component in the above stories of the monkeys and astronomer. Had they been more careful in their routine activities, both could have avoided their misfortune. What if an unexpected accident or incident happens to an unsuspecting person, not because of carelessness, but because of dubious will? In 1989, the founder of The PTL (Praise The Lord) Club, Jim Bakker, was found guilty on numerous counts of mail and wire fraud and sentenced to a 45-year prison term (later it was reduced to eight years and he received parole after only five). This whole thing, while sensational and quite entertaining, started with an allegation that he, Jim Bakker, raped his secretary, Jessica Hahn (who later appeared nude in *Playboy* magazine). To silence Hahn, a sum of $279,000 was paid to her. The attempt to cover-up the hush money led to the conviction, and ultimately divorce from his equally fascinating wife, Tammie Faye. What was shocking to us ordinary citizens was Bakker's brazen behavior: he committed adultery, while preaching fidelity at his own church full of followers.

Such episodes are quite common among hypocrites, especially politicians. Wilbur Mills, the chair of the House Ways and Means Committee, had to resign in 1974 because of a silly dalliance with a stripper named Fannie Foxe (oh, what a name). The front runner in the 1987 Democratic primary election, presidential candidate Gary Hart, was forced to quit the race because of a picture with a model on his lap, on a boat named "Monkey Business" (oh, what a name). Newt Gingrich, of the Republican Revolution in the 1990s, admitted he was having an affair with a staffer. This man was spearheading impeachment of Bill Clinton, because the latter had a fling of some sort with Monica Lewinsky. The hypocrite is still hanging around doing cameos on TV. Donald Trump paid $130,000 of hush money to keep Stormy Daniels (oh, what a name) quiet about their encounter. This man is currently our President.

These extra-marital affairs are hardly accidental. They are usually planned in advance, with the help of their third brain in-between their legs. One common thread, in both cases involving the monkey and politicians, is that they must be terribly embarrassed with what they have done. (07/15/18)

Ignorance is medicine.
모르는게 약이다.

[102]

When a man is accused of a crime, his first attempt to establish his innocence or to avoid punishment would be an outright denial, "No! I didn't do it." This approach could work if there is neither clean-cut forensic evidence nor reliable witnesses. It would help further, if a polygraph result is less than concrete. If this plan is not an option, he can claim he did not know that what he had done constituted a crime. The third option would call for temporary insanity: this strategy should circumvent all those hassles involved in the first two approaches, but it can be risky because the jury may not agree with such an assertion. Even without a lawyer, most adults, with reasonable intelligence, could come up with these scenarios and understand their accompanying risks. The second option, claiming innocence by maintaining ignorance, is certainly a compromise, possibly leading to a lenient sentence, if not freedom.

The proverb would be a Korean equivalent to "Ignorance is bliss." The medicine referred to here means the best way of avoiding unpleasant, awkward, embarrassing, painful, or even tragic consequence of a given incident. The word ignorance, or not-knowing, carries a nuance of innocence, albeit passively. Those three wise monkeys, representing "hear no evil, see no evil, and speak no evil," may justify, to a certain extent, your inaction to moral obligation and even legal responsibility, when you encounter impropriety or a crime. However, we will effectively become useless human beings if we claim ignorance all the time and run away from those seemingly inconvenient topics such as moral obligations. "Not getting involved" cannot be one's motto in life. A man, with blood all over his body, torn clothes, and broken bones here and there, was crawling away from his car after being involved in a terrible accident. People rushed to him and asked him to stay still until an ambulance arrived. The guy kept on saying that he just didn't want to get involved. Johnny Carson told this story many years ago.

What would you do if you witnessed the wife of your dearest friend cheating on him? Would you become the bearer of shocking news to your friend? In April, 1995, Timothy McVeigh and Terry Nichols bombed a federal building in downtown Oklahoma City, killing 168 people and injuring more than 680 others. McVeigh's friends, Michael and Lori Fortier, were shown the bombing plan earlier, but they did not warn anyone. Michael was sentenced to 12 years in prison for failing to warn the government. His wife, Lori, received immunity in exchange for her testimony. Between 1978 and 1995, Ted Kaczynski, better known as the Unabomber, killed three people and injured 23, through mail-delivered bombs in a nationwide campaign against technology advancement. After an extensive FBI man-hunt had failed, he was caught primarily by a tip-off from his own brother, David Kaczynski, who recognized Ted's writing style in his manifesto. What could have gone through David's mind when he blew the whistle?

You know for sure that one of your classmates obtained a passing grade in their final by copying someone else's answers. Would you report the incident to your teacher? You were a Catholic bishop and have just learned that a priest in your diocese has been sexually abusing altar boys for several years. Would you go to the police, try to settle with the victims in a monetary term, or ignore it by covering up? If you were the Fortiers in the above story, would you have forewarned the FBI? It could have prevented the Oklahoma City bombing, but it would have sent your friends McVeigh et al. to prison for a very long time. Once, not a long time ago, Congressman Jim Jordan had worked for the Ohio State University wrestling team, as an assistant coach, and is now accused of having known that their team doctor repeatedly molested and assaulted team members, but did not take any action to stop it. Now, it has become an issue of whether or not he was there to witness the sexual harassment.

In all these cases, you really wish that you were not foretold of the coming incident. Yes, ignorance can be indeed bliss. (07/18/18)

It's spilt water.
엎질러진 물이다.

[103]

If something is irreparably broken, there is very little you can do about it. There is only so much super-glue for broken jewels or counselors for your broken heart can do. When you drop and break a bottle of water on the ground, there is no way to get the water back into the bottle. "It's no use crying over spilt milk," that is. Here is a similar Korean proverb: "Play with the penis of your dead son (as much as you wish), or 죽은 자식 불알 만지기," implication being "What good is it?" However one may view it, the loss of a child is truly a devastating tragedy to his parents. This proverb urges the parents to move on with their own lives, instead of just imagining what their son's penis could have brought along.

One ordinary spring day, about 25 years ago, the Law School at the university where I was teaching pharmaceutical chemistry requested that I serve as a translator for a court case involving a young Korean mother. Their senior students were helping her with pro bono work. As it turned out, the mother was arrested for having killed her infant son. The tragic accident happened in a town, about 50 miles from where I lived and was the home of a major U.S. Army installation. The defendant was working at a local bar when the child died. She had married an American soldier, while he was stationed in Korea, and followed him to this town. Somehow, they separated and she was raising their infant son all by herself. On the night of the accident, she meant to tend the bar for only a few hours, just to help a coworker who unexpectedly had to leave early. The critical mistake she made was that she placed her sleeping son in the top drawer of a chest of drawers. After all, she thought, she would be back in a few hours. While she was away, the furniture fell forward to the floor and the child died of a head injury. She had left the drawer ajar so that the child could breathe. As the son slept, he must have moved to the front of the half-opened drawer, causing it to tip over and fall forward.

According to the transcript submitted by the police investigators, she admitted her crime repeatedly in the midst of wailing, beating her own chest with fists and pulling her hair out. Obviously, a Korean was present at the first interrogation to translate her cry, "It's all my fault. Just let me die with my son. I killed him!" I could easily envision her crying and shouting, "내 탓이요, 내 탓이요…. 내가 내 자식 죽였어요. 날 죽여줘요!" A direct translation of these words was what I read in the transcript. It was a natural cry from a Korean mother, or any mother really, under such duress: their cries are pure, honest, confessional, and the most honorable words any mother would have uttered. I explained as best as I could such nuance embedded in Korean mothers to four law school students present. They immediately understood me and developed a defense strategy accordingly. Meg Wolitzer's recent novel, *The Female Persuasion,* introduces a mother who accidentally kills her own nine-year old son. It happened when she drove her car backward on the driveway, without noticing her son lying on his belly playing with his pet box turtle. The son was run over by her car. No, the mother didn't go to jail but she suffered from mental agony for the rest of her life.

When seemingly trivial mistakes we make or the lukewarm efforts we invested in a pending task lead to an irretrievable, tragic consequence, we may beat our chest in deep regret and stamp our feet in self-loathing. That was what I did, with much remorse and guilt, immediately after I learned that I failed to pass the college entrance exam. It must have been in 1960. We know that wrongs, once done, cannot be undone, no matter how much you regret them. The only thing we can do is repent for our sins for the rest of our lives as honestly as we can. We hope for forgiveness, from whomever we believe in, so that our existence in the next world would be guilt- and regret-free. The early life of St. Augustine (354–430) or St. Ignatius of Loyola (1491 - 1556) was full of missteps with women, and yet their influence in Christianity and Western philosophy is immeasurable to this day. Likewise, the main character in *The Carnal Payer Mat,* a Chinese novel of erotica, by Li Yu (1610 - 1681), was a notoriously licentious man in his youth, but in the end he repents for his acts and becomes a Buddhist priest. (07/20/18)

"No way" can kill you.
"설마"가 사람 잡는다.

[104]

When someone predicts a grave event that you do not want to see happen or is telling you some unbelievable story, you'd say, "no way, it's not going to happen." In Korean, we say "*sulma* (설마)." You say it with wide opened eyes, surprised and disbelieving. Partially opening your mouth is an option. In typical gossip, say, your friend tells you that so-and-so is getting a divorce, your immediate reaction would be, "What? What are you saying? No way!" If you were a Korean, you could say "*sulma*. This is a totally unexpected story. In public, the couple always appeared to be enjoying the perfect marriage. The immediate disbelief would then be followed by real juicy stories, perhaps over many cups of coffee. The above proverb is saying that denying what is coming, purely based on your own instinct, can lead you to a big problem down the road, like getting killed! Listen to one of Murphy's Laws: "If anything can go wrong, it will." You'd better believe it and take necessary precautions now.

The U.S. Secretary of State, Mr. Mike Pompeo, at the Senate confirmation hearing for the CIA Director position last year, solemnly declared that the notion of climate change as a national security threat was "ignorant, dangerous and absolutely unbelievable." For a while, I thought he was describing himself with these adjectives. Anyway, we will see how his "no way" to climate change will turn out. At this writing, the State of California is suffering from a wild fire on a biblical scale, and so are the Scandinavian countries. The whole planet seems to be boiling. Korea has just recorded the hottest day-time temperatures in its history. Globally, 2018 is shaping up to be the fourth-hottest year on record. The hotter years were the three preceding years. Note that on June 1, last year, this country just walked away from the Paris Agreement on climate change and its nearly 200 member nations, saying "no way."

Here are a few more questions that had originally received "no way" as an answer, but later turned out to defy the doubters. Could the Chicago Cups win the World Series? Could the U.S. Olympic men's hockey team beat the Russian team? Has it ever occurred to you that a Korean man can win the Boston Marathon? Could the U.S. Women's National Soccer team win the World Cup? Likewise, who would have ever thought it possible that the Japanese women's national soccer team win the Cup? Any sporting event where the underdog unexpectedly wins the title, especially overcoming many adversities, would qualify for the above list. A political upset, such as the recent victory of Alexandria Ocasio-Cortez over ten-term incumbent Congressman Joseph Crowley, was unthinkable to many Democrats in the New York 14th District primary election. What about the outcome of this country's presidential election in 2016? In these instances, people said *"sulma."*

Any Cinderella story, like the fable of *Choon-hyang*(춘향), will also make the list. The story develops in the late Joseon Dynasty (1392 - 1897). At the tender age of 16, Choon-hyang fell in love with a son of a prominent village chief. When his father was re-appointed and had to move to Seoul, Choon-hyang couldn't follow her Romeo, as she was the daughter of *gi-seng,* someone socially much lower in status. For the time being, let's just say that her mother was a concubine. Amidst this devastating farewell, the young man promised her that he would come back, after passing the government-sponsored exam, known as *gwa-go*(과거), and getting an appointment as a civil servant. As it turned out, the new village chief was quite a lecher. Upon hearing how pretty Choon-hyang was, he demanded bedding with her, which Choon-hyang adamantly refused. In retaliation, the lecher put her in jail. At his birthday party, this Don Juan was about to force his way into deflowering Choon-hyang, but at the nick of time, her Romeo appeared as a secret King's commissioner, with almighty authority and responsibility. Choon-hyang did not recognize him, when he was testing her fidelity by asking her to attend his chamber. Choon-hyang told him that she had already committed herself to her "fiance." This, of course, pleased the young man immensely. The story consists of a series of *sulma* events, but with a happy ending for a change. (07/21/19)

Fastening a bell on the neck of a cat.
고양이 목에 방울 달기.

[105]

Once upon a time, there was an annual convention of mice colonies. The main theme of that year's convention was Homeland Security. There were numerous symposia, addressing various topics like mandatory service of female mice in military forces, and poster sessions dealing with a disparity of subjects, ranging from the effect of aged Swiss cheese on juvenile mice to the liability of albino mice during the night-time sentry service. Just like any other convention, however, the formal conference schedule was one thing, but the real reason of the gathering was, well, just that: getting together and having a good time with old friends. The climax was the Friday night banquet: the male mice all dressed up in tuxedos, with dolled-up wives or girlfriends in evening dresses, hooked in elbow, proceeded to assigned tables with their names on a folded cardboard. They were there indeed to see and to be seen. Wine was flowing aplenty and cigars were almost a prerequisite after dinner. Laughter from one table was followed by even louder laughter at another table, as if they were competing for the noisiest atmosphere. There was laughter, at the exaggerated misfortune of their children, good natured, self-depreciation humor; gossip involving lost tails, even rehashed old stories of their long-gone teachers, and so on and so forth. Indeed, they were having a great time in red face, with a trace of sweat in spite of the chilly autumn night outside.

    Then, from the head table, came the clangs of an empty wineglass lightly banged with a fork. "OK, ladies and gentlemen, attention please." It took some time for the room to become reasonably quiet. The speaker on the mic introduced the president of the association for a final remark on the convention. By that time, most of the participants ran out of topics for chit-chat anyway, and were coming back from the restrooms with hitched-up pants and re-applied lipstick. The president delivered a rather somber address: in essence, he reported that many law-abiding, good citizens from respectful families, have disappeared this year, presumably attacked and killed, if not devoured, by this one particular nasty cat in the neighborhood. The president solemnly pronounced the name of each individual mouse missing, a total of about a half dozen. There was a dead silence, followed by a low murmuring noise, with gathered but bowed heads, over the dining tables. It was the harsh reality check in an otherwise gay and joyful night. The upshot of the concluding remark by the president was soliciting ways or ideas to prevent such tragic episodes in the upcoming New Year.

Now the floor was open to anyone for suggestions or recommendations. Ideas varied widely, ranging from using some apps on smartphones, establishing a special military unit, developing 24-hour surveillance teams, ditching a deep trap on the ground, to outright assassinating the cat, etc. One particular suggestion that attracted everyone's approval was that the cat needed a bell around his neck so that whenever he approached a mouse, his advance would be detected early on by the sound of the bell. It was a brilliant idea that every mouse regretted not having thought of himself. It was one of those eureka moments that justified an eruption of loud cheers for celebration, erasing the preceding solemn mood a few minutes earlier. They emptied all the wine bottles, right there and then. The gleeful moment of jubilation lasted for a while, till a smart mouse stood up to quiet the conventioneers and ask, "Alas, who will place the belt around the neck of this beast?" Dead silence descended upon the convention hall at lightning speed. So the meeting ended on a sour note, and the mice slowly disappeared into the darkness of the night.

It is often said that "tons of rhetoric weigh less than a gram of deed." To obtain a quick but agreeable outcome of the matter at hand, we may say anything that will please listeners at the very moment. Possible consequences may not be our immediate concerns. As we discussed earlier in Entry #42, "Good medicine is usually bitter," flattering words always agree with you, while harsh but well-thought advice hurts your ears. It is just human nature. (07/22/18)

The mountain and the river get deeper as you enter.
산은 오를수록 높고 물은 건널수록 깊다.

[106]

A full translation may read as: "The mountain is getting higher as you climb up, while the water is getting deeper as you wade into the river." At first glance, the proverb appears to give us a warning and to demand our respect for nature. Rightly so. Just last week, a duck boat capsized on a lake near Branson, Missouri. As many as 17 vacationers, out of 31 people on board, drowned, nine of which were from one family. A duck boat is essentially a military truck used during the Korean War, which was modified to float on water as well as to run on the ground. This re-born amphibian can reach a land speed of 50 MPH (80 km/hr) and 6.3 MPH (10 km/hr) on water. It is shielded water-tight, in 1/8 inch (3.2 mm)-thick sheet metal. Its seemingly powerful and invincible appearance is, however, in contrast to its questionable stability in water, perhaps as questionable as the gliding ability of a helicopter. On the day of accident, Branson was under a severe thunderstorm warning. About 30 minutes after the warning was issued, and within a few minutes after it began taking on water, the duck boat sunk.

About seven years ago, I hiked the Appalachian Trail from Erwin, Tennessee to Harpers Ferry, West Virginia, approximately 600 miles, or 960 km, in two months total. The passage was, on average, three-to-five feet wide, often a dark tunnel, with a dense canopy of foliage, but opening up once in a while. It was full of turns, twists, switchbacks, or simply straight ups and downs. The ground usually had protruding rocks, dead leaves, or exposed tree roots. On some occasions, it was covered with pine needles or small broken twigs, like the softest carpet one could imagine. When the trail skirted the side of a mountain, the ground tilted sideways adopting the slope of the mountain and thus one misstep could cause some serious downfall. It was nerve breaking when the exposed tree root and dead leaves were wet and slippery on rainy days. An emergency whistle was the only comfort I had.

What I still remember vividly, was the endless bends near the top of any peak. Small, open sky always appeared as if I were very close to the top, or the edge of the mountain. To my dismay, there would be another bend or another twist. The mountain, indeed, seemed to be getting higher with every step. I do not think I had ever been to the top of a mountain; rather, we skirted around or passed through the gaps between mountains. The second part of the proverb deals with a river. When we timidly wade into a river for the first time, we don't know how deep the middle can be. All we know for certain is that the river is getting deeper with water running faster.

So, what would these natural observations all mean? For some reason, which could be beyond your control, a job you've just embarked on becomes more complicated, time-consuming, labor-intensive, expensive, and encountering unfortunate misfortunes. These are much more than you estimated during the planning stage. As the planner of the project, you knew all along that you had to "expect the best, plan for the worst, and prepare to be surprised." You also knew Murphy's Law: "If anything can go wrong, invariably it will." But still, they are a rude awakening.

A metaphoric interpretation may well be that, as we try to understand the nature of things in this universe and in our lives, we will become more confused and the only thing that we will clearly realize is how ignorant we are. This is, in spite of the rapidly advancing scientific knowledge and technological breakthroughs of our time, in such fields as molecular biology as applied to genetics, the so-called big-bang theory of an ever-expanding universe, as well as computer science and engineering. In Entry #16, "The head bows when grain matures," I even implied that "Knowing is not-knowing," and that what we know is minuscule compared with what we do not know.

As we enter the forest on a huge mountain or wade into a wide river, they seem to become more awesome than when we saw them from a distance. Likewise, as we live a long life and try to understand the meaning or goal of life more clearly, what we in fact realize is how impossible it is to answer those fundamental questions. (07/23/18)

Spitting while lying on your back.
누워서 침 뱉기.

[107]

This is not a complete sentence. It is a phrase one can use as in: "Your behavior is like spitting while you lie on the back." If one does, where does the saliva, possibly full of nasty phlegm, go? Right on your face, is where it will end up. However one may look, spitting is an ugly behavior. It is considered rude in many cultures. The 2008 Summer Olympic Games were held in Beijing. This was the first time that modern China made a debut with a big event on the international stage. To promote a favorable impression of the country, there were a series of collective efforts to modify citizen's behavior that might be frown upon by foreign visitors. Of the various things citizens were asked not to do, urinating on a street in broad daylight and spitting in public were at the top of the list.

One typical instance, where one can use the above expression, would be where one speaks ill of his own family, community, or even country, to a stranger. Listeners may find the belittling of your own wife or children interesting, and may show you a great deal of empathy and sympathy, but they will probably laugh at you behind your back. "What kind of a man is this guy? How come he cannot keep his own domestic matters in order?" Not to "spit onto your own face" is such a common and basic virtue that nobody needs to point it out to you.

And yet, that is exactly what President Trump did at the July 16, 2018 press conference, subsequent to the Helsinki Summit with his Russian counterpart Vladimir Putin. His own Justice Department, intelligence community, and both chambers of Congress unanimously concluded that the Kremlin had interfered in the 2016 presidential election. But Trump was saying, "I will tell you that President Putin was extremely strong and powerful in his denial today." Effectively, he refused to believe and respect what his own "family" had been telling him for many months. This strange and extraordinary behavior was so utterly unbelievable that people began to wonder if it was indeed true that Putin had some serious dirt on Trump. This Helsinki press conference was preceded by a series of insults to generations of our World War II allies at a most personal level: heads of Germany, Canada, France, and U.K. were all subject to Trump's ridicules. Talking about spitting onto one's own face, this was at its best.

It is said that immigrants are most patriotic to their motherland soon after they land on the foreign country of their future life. This is perhaps an unconscious effort to avoid "spitting onto one's own face." News from Korea in the late 1960s, when I left the country, was generally bad: infiltrators from North Korea engaging in a gun battle in the vicinity of the Presidential Palace, attacking an umpire after a boxing match at the 1988 Seoul Summer Olympics, physical confrontation of Korean assemblymen, the assassination of President J.H. Park, and the collapses of a bridge over the Han River, etc. They were all pathetic incidents and we, then graduate students in the United States, criticized among ourselves, many domestic affairs in Korea. We seldom, however, said bad things about Korea, in the presence of non-Korean folks. The former is a reflection of patriotism, while the latter is like not revealing family troubles to neighbors. On July 7, 1972, I even wrote a letter to then President J.H. Park, supporting his resolution to unify the Korean peninsula without any interference from any third parties, like the United States. It was a small gesture of patriotism on my part.

Fast forward to the 2010s, I am proud of being, or having been to be exact, a Korean as the commercial products from Korea are successfully competing with any other imported products here in the U.S. They may include; cars, smart phones, televisions, household appliances such as washing machines and refrigerators. Likewise, when Psy's Gang-Nam Style arrived here in 2012, my class of over 150 students asked me to show them the dance steps involved. How proud I was then! Just last month, K-pop boy band BTS's "Fake Love" won a 2018 Billboard Music Award. After all these years of residing in this country, I am still patriotic to my motherland Korea, far from being "spitting on my own face." (07/25/18)

Licking fingers after pulling a dried pollack.
북어 뜯고 손가락 빤다.

[108]

During the winter time, the fishing villages along the east coast of the Korean Peninsula harvest plenty of walleye pollack (명태). They are hung and dried, right on the beach, just like laundry. The cold-temperature and low-humidity sea-breeze is perfect for the drying. Thawing and freezing cycles, under the brilliant winter sunlight and re-freezing over night, somewhat resemble the so-called lyophilization or freeze-drying process, commonly used in the food and pharmaceutical industries. The resulting product, pale yellow in color, covered with wrinkled gray skin, and rough but bristling in texture, is called *boog-eoh* (북어). It can be stored or transported, without any synthetic preservatives, until they are processed to foods such as a soup or side dish. I do not know how *boog-eoh* (북어) became a traditionally essential item to be placed on the table at rituals for remembering one's ancestors, *jesa* (제사).

Drinking soju calls for something to munch on, if not a formal meal: dried cuttlefish, *o-jing-eo* (오징어), or *boog-eoh* serve the purpose quite well, especially when they are broiled right at the table on an open charcoal fire. They are slightly salty and chewy. When hot, the dried fish is much softer and one can tear them to a bite size much more easily. The above proverb asks us what we have after the dried fish was pulled apart by hand. Is there any discernable taste afterward on your finger? Act-wise, it's similar to licking your fingers after you eat, say, pizza or Buffalo wings. After we finish some sticky dishes using our hands, in the absence of a finger bowl or wet towel, we tend to lick our fingers to clean them or to go for the after-taste. I suppose one can always clean fingers on one's pants, but the point here is you may not have anything left on your finger after dealing with dried stuff. A similar Korean expression is: "A dog has just come back from a boulder," or "개 바위 등에 갔다 왔다." What do you expect to see on the sunbaked boulder after the dog visited the place?

One of the most frustrating occasions in life is when you do not have anything to show, after much investment of time, effort, and possibly money: just like a dog failing to make any dent on the boulder or you not having anything on your fingertip after you pull apart the dried fish. Knowing that you have given your best and earnest efforts can offer you only so much self-consolation. Other people may collectively call you a failure. In the late 1990s, I received a research grant from the National Institute of Cancer. The main premise of the proposed studies was to employ the naturally occurring self-defense system we all have, largely in immunity towards invading pathogens, in fighting off abnormal growth of unregulated cells forming solid tumors. The reviewers, called Study Section, liked the strategy and experimental approach in the proposal. The chemistries involved were tough and the animal model we wished to use was not as straightforward as I had thought. In the end, we did not have anything to publish. We learned a lot, but did anybody else also learn anything? Appearance-wise, there was no difference between me and the dog who visited the big boulder on the mountain.

Visiting the DMV (Department of Motor Vehicles) is as dreadful as visiting a dentist office. I did it three times in one week, one unbelievably hot summer in Nevada. The only matter I did achieve was registering my car and getting a new driver's license in this new town. The first time, I did not bring my U.S. passport, which serves as an alternate to a birth certificate. The second time, I failed to bring my original Social Security card. People usually use a driver's license to establish his or her identity, but I forgot I was doing it in reverse order. I was a frustrated dog, barking at a chicken on the rooftop after failing to catch it. Does this reflect my advanced age? My wife went there only once, which made the whole situation even more irritating. If my fingers tasted somewhat salty on that hot summer day, it was not because I had torn up a dried pollack, but because I was sweating. This was what happened and, yes, one could say that my visit to the DMV was like a dog visiting a boulder for a while. (07/27/18)

You cannot see your own eyebrow.
가까운 제 눈썹 못 본다.

[109]

According to Wikipedia, the field of view of an individual human eye, when fixed with a directed gaze, is typically 30° upward and is limited by the brow. When downcast straight, it is about 70°, but interfered by the nose. If one casts their gaze toward the temple, the angle would be about 100°. For both eyes combined, the visual field is 135° vertical and 200° horizontal. If we let the eye move rapidly, the range expands quite significantly. However, no one can see one's own eyebrow completely. I suppose one can argue that we surely can see an eyebrow, or for that matter, any part of face with a mirror. Heck, with two mirrors we can even see the back of our head, but that's not what the above proverb tries to say. An eyebrow is just above the eyes and yet you cannot see it with your own eyes: they are too close to see, just as the truth is often too close to be recognized. It could be the elephant in the room that everyone has failed to see, or looking for a baby on your back. See also Entry #141, "One feels a splinter under a finger nail, but not a troubled heart."

Although we cannot diagnose our own "troubled hearts," we sure see the faults of other people without much difficulty. If I may generalize, we try to solve other people's problems with a great deal of enthusiasm, while we are seemingly neglecting our own well-being. Moreover, we tend to gauge others based on our own experience and standard. How could I complain about the way my neighbor mows the lawn, decorates their front courtyard, and leaves their cars or boat (!) on their driveway? Who are we to say that democracy and capitalism of this nation would also be most ideal for other countries with different cultural and religious histories? If our being "superior" is not the real reason, why do we pester them constantly with unsolicited advice, often with implicit threats? Is basic humanity and virtue also a subjective concept? How can we find one ideal that fits all? "If you see one fault in a person, remember that you have ten." Aren't we forgetting that the world would be a perfect place to live if every citizen on this planet could take care of themselves first?

The above proverb also reminds us of the limitation in our capability and capacity. Here, the following proverbs seem related: Entry #69, "A knife cannot carve its own handle," "A doctor can't fix his own illness," and "A monk can't shave his own head."

On December 7, 1941, Japan attacked the U.S. Pacific Fleet in Pearl Harbor, forcing the U.S. to engage in World War II. The chief architect of the surprise attack was the Vice Admiral Isoroku Yamamoto, who had earlier spent some years in the U.S. and thus understood the hitherto, unknown potential of industrial America. He, in fact, expressed serious misgivings about the war, with a warning, "We can run wild for six months or maybe a year, but after that, I have utterly no confidence." And yet his opinion was overridden by the Japanese Cabinet in September. Within seven hours of the strike on Pearl Harbor, the Japanese also attacked the Philippines, Guam, Wake Island, the British garrisons in Borneo, Malaya, Singapore, and Hong Kong, each with a spectacular success.

After all, the Japanese military experienced little, or very feeble, resistance when they invaded China. Although China was, at that time, a country that had been torn apart with their own civil war in the 1930s, the arrogance the Japanese acquired from this "smooth sailing" in the vast land of China must have rendered the Japanese military establishment to become over-confident for a quick victory. They were also greatly encouraged by the equally successful war fronts of their counterpart, Western Axis German and Italy. Speaking of "the blind leading the blind," this was it.

Involvement of Americans in Vietnam after the French fled in the 1950s and in Afghanistan in the early 1990s after the Soviet military fled were equally idiotic and arrogant ventures. Americans fully understand that "you can lead a horse to water, but you can't make him drink," and yet behaved as if they were juveniles on high testosterone. Here, the U.S. clearly underestimated the will power of the people in those nations. (07/28/18)

No one can go to the bathroom or heaven's gate on your behalf.

저승길과 변소 길은 대신 못 간다.

[110]

In your life, there are some roads that you will have to walk by yourself. Nobody else can do that for you. According to the above proverb, one is the walk or rush to the bathroom when your bladder is about to burst. Simply put, no one can urinate for your relief. The second road that you will have to walk by yourself is the journey you are taking to the next world when you are departing this world. Dying is an individual undertaking, somewhat a lonely walk, even in a mass suicide. The statement on these two occasions is absolutely true for everyone on this planet, including any billionaire or homeless man: it is an egalitarian thought at its best.

Alexandria Ocasio-Cortez, commonly abbreviated as OAC, is from a Puerto Rican family and is now 28 years old. She was born, and now lives, in the Bronx, New York in a modest one-bedroom apartment. As recently as last year, she was tending tables at a taco place. On June 26th, in the Democratic primary for the 14th Congressional District, she soundly defeated the incumbent, Joseph Crowley, the most powerful politician in Queens County, and the fourth-ranking Democrat in the House of Representatives. He had not faced a primary opponent in the past 14 years, and had become complacent while Ocasio-Cortez was campaigning her tail off. In their first primary debate, Crowley didn't show up. Ocasio-Cortez debated an empty chair with the incumbent's name on it. They were to have a second debate, about a week prior to the election. Crowley was a no-show again. Instead, he sent a substitute, a former city councilwoman, who happened to be another Latino.

I cannot say for sure that Crowley lost the primary because he was absent from those two debates, but it certainly helped his demise as a politician. He simply did not walk the walk that he had to. In the mid-term election this November, if elected, OAC will most likely become the youngest woman ever elected to the U.S. Congress.

Stories of failure are abundant when somebody else is asked to do our "home work." A child was asked by his father to follow a visiting guest to where he was staying so that the father could repay the visit later. When the child came back home, his father asked him how he was going to find the visitor's lodge. The child answered, "It is very easy, father. There was a big bird sitting on the roof of the lodge where he was staying." Here is another story that may involve the same pair of father and son. They were on a small row boat on a lake, and the father accidentally dropped something valuable into the water. The father immediately asked the son to remember where the mistake took place so that he could come back later to retrieve it from the bottom of the lake. The son made a mark on the side of the boat, exactly where it fell off. Later, the father must have scolded his half-witted son as vigorously as he could, but it all could have been avoided, had the father taken the task himself. More abundant are the stories of failure because of lukewarm efforts not because of idiocy. Speaking of myself, I still attribute the failure of the college entrance examination to the tepid effort on my part, almost 60 years ago.

Ulysses S. Grant (1822 - 1885) served as Commanding General of the Army and later the 18th President of the United States, the highest positions in both the military and the government of the U. S. As a soldier, his brave conduct on the battle field is well recorded: see *Grant*, by Ron Chernow. Dwight D. Eisenhower (1890 - 1969) was a five-star general in the United States Army, and served as Supreme Commander of the Allied Expeditionary Forces in Europe, during the Second World War. Later, he also served as the 34th President of the United States, from 1953 to 1961. As a presidential candidate he had declared that he would visit Korea to see the Korean War firsthand. In late 1952, he did go to Korea and witnessed a military and political stalemate. In both cases of Grant and Eisenhower, they indeed walked their walk. As a footnote, in the summer of 1953, an armistice took effect with Korea being divided into two pieces. Whether we liked it or not, the boundary still remain in effect today. (07/29/18)

My cousin buys land, I have a bellyache.
사촌이 땅을 사면 배가 아프다.

[111]

In any culture at any time in human history, purchasing a sizable plot of land is considered an excellent, long-term investment. As such, it speaks volumes as to the financial prowess of the man who has just acquired the land: he immediately becomes a subject of envy and jealousy among his acquaintances. Thus, this proverb says that you don't feel good when you learn your cousin has just bought a piece of valuable land: instead of congratulating and celebrating, jealousy and envy for his financial prowess, cause you to feel sick.

I will be the first to admit that Koreans, especially Korean women, are unduly jealous and envious of other's success. This is a broad, and perhaps unfair, generalization of Koreans, but we Koreans are not generous in praising and congratulating others for their achievements. It could simply be a new pair of shoes your friend is wearing or a new piece of furniture in their home. I honestly do not know why it is as such. After all, it won't cost any money or sacrifice on our part. This tendency, of being a miser, may reflect one's envy and jealousy, which ultimately leads to bellyache. It is the crux of the above proverb. Although some people distinguish between the meaning of these two words, envy and jealousy, here, I would use them interchangeably, with jealousy a bit worse than envy. Other cultures appear to have similar sentiments, as we will see in Entry #149 later.

Many forms of envy and jealousy seem to originate from a lack of self-confidence. Sexual jealousy, for instance, constantly torments one with a suspicion that a wife or girlfriend is guilty of infidelity. Even the slightest flirtation from a wife can lead to a miserable state of agitation, if a husband allows the suspicion to rear its ugly head. Even if he is better looking, more intelligent, making more money, and enjoying a higher social status than the subject of his wife's flirtation, once a man becomes obsessed with suspicion, nothing else matters. Such stories involving a love triangle have flourished throughout history, from Greek tragedies to Italian operas. And tabloid journalism is always sniffing around real, juicy scandals. A tragic ending, like murder, would be the climax of such a story.

Once there lived a peasant who raised a donkey and a goat. He was particularly fond of the donkey, as the animal always worked hard without much complaint. The peasant's affection toward the donkey irked the goat. Thus, said the goat to the donkey, "Can't you see how much hard work you have to endure? Just pretend you've become weak lately by stumbling into the stream whenever you cross. I am sure the master would reduce the burden on your back from then on." Noticing how weak the donkey had become, the farmer hurriedly brought the animal to a veterinarian. The vet told the farmer, after careful diagnosis, that the only way to boost the donkey's stamina was to feed him goat liver. The farmer promptly proceeded to slaughter the goat for his liver.

When my seven siblings and I were growing up, our mother used to tell us, "Right now, you are all brothers and sisters and everything is hunky-dory, but remember this: it won't be as such, unless you all become equally successful or equally poor." Meghan Markle's rift with her father and her half-siblings come to my mind. It all happened only after Meghan married Prince Harry. Her father said how terrified her daughter, now Duchess of Sussex, had been and that Princess Diana would have loathed how he was treated by the British Royal circle. Her half-sister attacked Meghan, whom she hadn't seen for years, through some nasty twitter rants, calling her "Duchess of nonsense." Her half-brother called the Royal wedding the biggest mistake, claiming that Meghan was not the right woman for the Prince. He also called her a "jaded, shallow, conceited woman." Now I can see mother's wisdom quite clearly. According to my ever-wise wife, the closer the people involved, the more serious this jealousy-and-envy business becomes. Both women were right on the money as to the Markles. Fortunately, my seven siblings and I were all in equal footing during our lives. (08/01/18)

Brag about spending, not making money.
버는데 자랑 말고 쓰는데 자랑 하랬다.

[112]

We work to earn a living: that is, to make money so that we can spend it for food, shelter, clothing, education, entertainment, and various services. For most of us, the income is from a job, which varies a great deal. The medical profession seems to be highly sought after in any society. Physicians are respected, as they save lives and relieve pain from suffering people. They are admired as well as envied, since the job comes into being only after many years of professional training. It usually entails a high income. In my utopian world, however, it cannot be a vocation to ask for a fee in return for a service as noble as saving one's life. How could someone ask for money after saving the life of, say, a drowning person? In the same vein, interpreting law for ordinary citizens, who are not well versed in legal jargon, is a matter of charity not a job for hire. Soldiers, whose fundamental function is killing other human beings, cannot be a profession. Along this line of logical elimination, what is left for a decent means of living may well be farmers, fishermen, construction workers, and all other labor-intensive jobs, along with scientists and engineers who contribute to society with new knowledge and technology.

The nature and size of income are pretty much determined by a given job: thus it is said, "Money is money." In contrast, there is a great deal of individual variation, in regards to spending any surplus after acquiring basic needs. I suppose it all depends on an individual's priority. Some are generous towards charity works, while others may prefer saving for rainy days, so-to-speak. This part of money matters are what the above proverb is emphasizing: pay attention to spending rather than making money. It is indeed often stated that how to spend money is more difficult than how to make money. For many, who try to make ends meet and survive from paycheck to paycheck, it may sound like another cliché. However, according to an article by Ken Stern in the April, 2013 issue of *The Atlantic,* in 2011, Americans with earnings in the top 20% of income levels donated cash to charity less than those in the bottom 20%: on average, 1.3% versus 3.2%.

Similarly, another study, published in the August, 2012 issue of *The Chronicle,* pointed out that families making $100,000 or more contribute to charity less than those making between $50,000 and $75,000. This may imply that poor people better empathize with the poor and thus committed to sharing their meager discretionary funds. However, I cannot stop admiring those American billionaires who spend a very significant portion of their wealth to philanthropy. The Bill and Melinda Gates Foundation, comes to my mind. They have $38 billion in assets. George Soros has a net worth of $8 billion, but that is after he donated $18 billion to his philanthropic foundations. Here, I am not speaking of those who lobby lavishly for their own, say, political inclination or others who donate mainly to evade paying taxes. In contrast, I am under the impression that there are few serious charity works proposed and sustained by Korean *chaebols.* To be fair, they seem to offer generous donations, in cases of natural disasters or some man-made, tragic events.

It is not clear why the major stakeholders or the owners of Korean conglomerates are less inclined than their American counterparts in establishing foundations exclusively for charity. As a disclaimer, I have to acknowledge that this statement is based on my own impression and perception, and not based on a reliable data set. As I pointed out in Entry #37, "No need to envy others," Koreans live in a collective society. And yet, Koreans appear to be less forth coming than Westerners, when called for a higher purpose, such as individual freedom and prosperity, climate change, or world peace. Individual sacrifice or charity work by Koreans seems to carry a nuance of "forced volunteering." Church-sponsored volunteer work, albeit noble and admirable, are to be distinguished from the works done by individual, corporate-based foundations. A collective commitment involving individual sacrifices in a self-centered society like America, appears to be worthier and more honorable. Could it be then possible that Koreans are more egocentric, and with some exaggeration, selfish? (08/02/18)

Use a shovel for a job for *homee*?
호미로 막을 것을 가래로 막는다.

[113]

One of the most popular gardening tools in Korea is a small, hand-held hoe called a *homee* (호미). The tool has the bottom of a triangular iron piece connected to a wooden handle, via an iron rod, and is bent in an L-shape. The tip is rather sharp and the main body curves slightly inwardly; perfect for digging the ground on your knees. Since a *homee* is bent 90-degrees, it is best to use the tool in a striking motion, from above, and pull dirt up to plow. Similar to a small hoe, it is commonly used in weeding, harvesting potatoes, and the likes. A *garae* (가래) is a typical shovel. It usually requires the coordinated action of two arms and one foot, not to mention a scooping motion from the whole body. This proverb says that there are many jobs you can complete with a small *homee*, instead of using a big shovel that requires much labor and sweat. The minimalist viewpoint underlying the proverb is rather appealing in our society, where anything big and noisy seems to be the winning way.

I understand that the United States spends on its military, as much as the next nine countries combined. And yet, we don't seem to gain any headway toward world peace or the security of this land. "These Toilet Seat Lids Aren't Gold-Plated, but They Cost $14,000: The Pentagon has to clean up its confusing and wasteful budget." See an opinion column by the Republican senator from Iowa, Charles Grassley, in the December 19, 2018 issue of The *New York Times*. (This story was added later.) The article went on to say, "Over the past few months alone, the Defense Department has had to explain why it's been paying $14,000 (approximately 1,600 만원) for individual 3-D printed toilet seat lids and purchasing cups for $1,280 each. These are just the latest examples on a long list of unacceptable purchases made by the department, including $436 for hammers in the 1980s, and $117 soap dish covers and $999 pliers in the 1990s." In my mind, they should have learned what a *homee* can do first and go from there.

Indeed, if one starts a project at the proper time, then a *homee*, rather than a shovel, can be sufficient. Imagine a small leaky hole in a dike, such as the one we find in the Dutch fable, "A boy who saved the Netherlands." If you recall, a large portion of the Netherlands is below sea level, and one day, a little Dutch boy noticed a leak in the dike that protected the lower land from the sea. Intelligent and civil-minded, he stuck his finger in the seawall to stop the leak, and perhaps saved the country. In this sense it would be equivalent to "A stitch in time saves nine." Many health-related issues can also benefit by practicing the proverb also. Without daily exercise and sensible dieting, we may all end up as a 300-pound, amorphous mass of tofu-texture, glued to the blue rays of a computer monitor all day and all night. Exercise and dieting are small measures one can take every day, and yet many people end up with disastrous consequences, like diabetes or cardiovascular disease.

What *homee* is to gardening is what exercise is to health. Most seniors of my age are under daily medication for lowering blood pressure and cholesterol, possibly until they die. When a side effect appears, physicians may lower dose or recommend an alternative drug. Suing the drug manufacturer could be an option for patients. Just last month, Johnson & Johnson was asked to pay $4.7 billion to 22 women, who developed ovarian cancer. Apparently, there were some epidemiological studies that linked regular use of talcum powder for genital hygiene to ovarian cancer. The lawyers involved are now advertising on TV to recruit more potential plaintiffs so that they can make money.

The longevity of the elderly is said to reflect a subjective assessment of health, rather than an objective one given by physicians. The self-assessment should begin with erasing the notion that modern medicine and medical technologies will cure every disease under the sun. Instead, we will have to invest small but regular steps towards our wellbeing. Then, only then, a *homee* will be all we need when misfortune arrives. (08/05/18)

A one-day old puppy isn't afraid of a tiger.
하룻강아지 범 무서운 줄 모른다.

[114]

What does a one-day old puppy know about anything? As far as he is concerned, anything warm and hairy could be his mother who offers an abundant supply of milk. That would include any animals of prey such as tigers, which the puppy would regard as a dangerous enemy in later life. The puppy has yet to form a concept of fear (to the best of my knowledge, it is not embedded in his DNA). Right now, he is not afraid of anything, just like "no brain, no pain." However, the naivety and gullibility implied here should not and cannot be applied to grown-up people. If one is ill-informed or ignorant of world affairs, the saddest and often scariest part of it is that they are usually not aware of their own ignorance. They are invariably foolish, albeit perhaps innocent.

In "active ignorance," one is seeking new knowledge actively - yes, actively: however, there is a built-in filtering mechanism. The part of "seeking knowledge" is commendable. After all, that's how one educates himself or herself. The latter can be dangerous, since the decision on what to keep as useful and what to discard as useless, inconvenient, or outright wrong, is based on the limited knowledge base and experience of the person. It implies that the person unconsciously believes that he or she knows everything under the sun and behaves accordingly. This exercise, in effect, shuts off a wide spectrum of ideas that one could have accommodated and appreciated. Here is a related maxim: those who read all the time without thinking could become a dull person, while those who think all the time without reading can become a dangerous hypocrite. The ultimate outcome of active ignorance would be bigotry, hatred, intolerance, division, xenophobia, and even misogyny. The world we live in now appears to be full of actively ignorant people. We don't need to look far to see and understand my assertion: just read the tweets from the current President.

There is a finite, but significant, difference between the crimes or wrongdoings committed by those with innocent ignorance and those with active ignorance. We can hardly scold the foolish behavior of a puppy in front of a tiger. The tiger and all other powerful, carnivorous animals are said to thrive on the "smell" of fear among their prey and the one-day old puppy doesn't shed any odor of fear. A mother tiger, with her own pups in tow, may adopt this baby into her family, just like the boy who was raised in the jungle, by wolves, in *The Jungle Book,* by R. Kipling (1894).

Yesterday, August 6, 2018, Apple, Facebook and YouTube all decided to delete much of Alex Jones' "screaming" and divisive materials from their sites. Jones was a radio talk show host, propagating his sermons based on conspiracy theories. Earlier, he had claimed that grieving families of the Sandy Hook Elementary School shooting were faking their pain. "I've looked at it and undoubtedly there's a cover-up, there's actors, they're manipulating, they've been caught lying and they were preplanning before it and rolled out with it." Now, he is facing lawsuits filed by multiple families, victims of the Sandy Hook Massacre. What world do we live in?

The scary part of it all is that there are plenty of followers of, for the lack of better word, crazy leaders. We see it now utterly beyond our comprehension how Adolf Hitler was able to mesmerize and lead a whole nation into World War II and how the good people of Germany let the Holocaust happen. We can say the same thing, with a great deal of lament, about instigators of all wars and atrocities in history. And yet the same tragic human conflicts are happening now in every corner of this planet. Almost a half of the eligible voters of this nation somehow elected Mr. Trump as the president in 2016. According to the November 1, 2017 issue of *Cato at Liberty,* nearly two-thirds of registered Republicans agree that journalists are an enemy of the American people. Menacing journalists has become contagious among Trump supporters to the point that some news networks started to hire security guards for their correspondents. However one may look at these numbers and the trend of hostility, it is frightening. It is also sad that the rest of us must live with these folks harmoniously. They are far from a one-day old puppy without malignant intentions. (08/08/18)

The pot calls the kettle black.
똥 묻은 개가 겨 묻은 개 나무란다.

[115]

This dog, smeared with feces, laughs at and belittles another dog that is stained a little bit with mustard. Note that, here, feces and mustard share a similar color and texture. Pots and kettles are all black from years of use, but the pot claims that the kettle is black, implying he is not. How could this proverb be pertinent in real life? How dare a married man, who has been carrying on a love affair, accuse and humiliate another man who has committed adultery? That was exactly what Republican Congressman from Georgia, Newt Gingrich, did to then President Bill Clinton with the Lewinsky scandal in the late 90s. In fact, Gingrich was not the only congressman who favored Clinton's impeachment while having an extramarital affair: there were; Gary Condit (Democrat from California), Pete Domenici (Republican from New Mexico), Henry Hyde (R-Illinois), Robert Livingston (R-Louisiana), Dan Burton (R-Indiana), Bob Barr (R-Georgia), Steven C. LaTourette (R-Ohio), David Vitter (R-Louisiana), et al. For more juicy stories, see the *List of federal political sex scandals in the United States* in Wikipedia. Didn't these people read the Bible? "He that is without sin among you, let him cast the first stone at her." (John 8:7)

Then, there was a Republican House Representative from Tennessee, who opposed abortion in the sternest fashion, and yet made his ex-wife have two abortions and tried to persuade his mistress, who was also his patient into an abortion as well. Notice that he had been a physician prior to his stint as a politician. Speaking of hypocrites, nobody excels him. We have some more: child-molesting priests, bribery-accepting judges, prosecutors conspiring with defendants, policemen demanding sexual favors from women who were caught speeding, embezzling bankers, teachers concocting grades, etc. According to the above proverb, these people are smeared with feces not mustard.

Admittedly, Bill Clinton allowed his "third leg" to dictate his behavior toward Monica Lewinsky. He was an ordinary man, most likely with an ordinary level of testosterone in his blood, but just couldn't let the "opportunity" slip by. Because of his position, he undoubtedly had more of such chances than most of us. In the end, his "sin" was that he failed to keep the stringent and high standard expected from his position as the president of the most powerful nation on this planet. Otherwise, he was a good president. During his tenure, we enjoyed the longest period of peace and a federal budget surplus for the first time in my memory. John F. Kennedy was equally infamous for his dalliance with beautiful women including Marilyn Monroe. Nonetheless, his progressive political idealism and fair mind to fellow citizens were second to none. He is undoubtedly one of my favorite presidents.

I do not condone the affairs Clinton and Kenney committed. My lenient position towards them reflects the fact that neither of them really went out publically denouncing adulterers. There is a subtle but significant difference between these presidents and those who preach one thing in public but break exactly what they are preaching in their personal life. If we define the worst kind of liars as the people who cheat themselves, they are the ones, hands down. What do they tell themselves at the end of the day? Or don't they talk to themselves? If there was a scale from zero to ten, in assessing them as human beings, my grading would certainly be a negative number: something like -10.

The main reason why we do not seem to care about the "true color" of many public figures is that we have somehow let these people be what they have become. Most of the politicians cited above were re-elected even after they admitted their illegitimate affairs. Do we forgive them in the Christian belief of forgiveness? Or do we judge politicians with a standard that is different from the one we use to value other citizens or even close friends? Indeed we have established, rather unconsciously and based on accumulated experience, what to expect from a person. It largely depends on what the person is: clergy versus car repairman, teacher versus businessman, Democrat versus Republican, politician versus artist, even man versus woman, etc. In an ideal world, we will not have such varying standards. Pots and kettles will not argue who is blacker. (08/10/18)

The crayfish sides with crabs.
가재는 게 편이라.

[116]

Both crayfish and crab are crustaceans with thick exoskeletons and a single pair of claws. In the presence of a totally different third species, they support each other in fighting off invaders, while defending their common interests. That is what the above proverb tells us. Being similar in their appearance and behavior, the proverb sounds reasonable. It would be equivalent to: "Birds of a feather flock together," "Blood is thicker than water," "The arm always bends inwards," or "The enemy of my enemy is my friend." These maxims also appear to adequately describe the pattern of alliance among nations under pressure: the Axis of Germany, Italy, and Japan, against the Allies of Britain, France, and the United States, during the Second World War, or the more recent North Atlantic Treaty Organization (NATO) versus the Warsaw Pact. The resulting balance of power offers a delicate equilibrium of apparent stability. I suppose these separate alliances would disappear to form a united front, just like crayfish and crab, against what could be perceived as a common enemy; say, living creatures on another planet. A perceived threat is what we grown-ups think of upon encountering foreign aliens: remember Steven Spielberg's 1982 movie *E.T.*?

Prior to AD 668, our Korean ancestors had maintained three nations in and around the Korean Peninsula: the Kingdom of *Goguryo* ruled the vast area of land, encompassing the current Manchurian territory in Northeast Asia as well as a half of the Korean Peninsula all the way down to the northern border of what is currently South Korea. The western half of the southern peninsula was occupied by *Bagje*, while the east by *Shilla*. *Goguryo* shared the longest border with the short-lived Sui Dynasty of China (581 - 618). There were a series of battles between these two neighboring nations, eventually leading to the downfall of Sui and the emergence of the Tang Dynasty (618 - 907). With military help from the Tang, *Shilla* was able to unify all three kingdoms in 668, but they lost to Tang the majority of the territory that *Goguryo* had maintained in the north. Just as a financially struggling business will have to pay back later what they borrow from a bank, *Shilla* had to give up the vast territory of Manchuria to Tang. It was the last time Koreans roamed the Manchurian territory.

Fast forward to the end of the 19th Century, Korea had to rely on the military and diplomatic prowess of Japan, in fending off the undue influence of other countries such as France (1866), the U.S. (1871), Britain (1885), Russia (1895), and of course China (1894). At the peak of the then prevailing global imperialism, every nation of power was drooling for Korea, a nation terribly weakened by internal conflicts and corruptions. Korea's "flirtation" to Japan irked third parties and led to the Sino-Japanese War (1894 - 1895) and Russo-Japanese War (1904-1905), both right on the Korean Peninsula. Korea was nothing but a live fish on a cutting board, and everyone was ready to chop its head off with a cleaver. In 1910, Japan finally invaded Korea and ruled her for the subsequent 35 years, until they surrendered to the Allied Force in 1945.

After the crayfish and the crab defeated their common enemy, the stronger of the two might have devoured the other. The fate of Korea was pretty much determined at the Yalta Conference in February, 1945, among the major participants of the Second World War: Franklin D. Roosevelt, Winston Churchill, and Joseph Stalin. During the Korean War (1950 - 1953), the North received much military aid from Communist China, including a 600,000-strong Chinese army. The support was requested by the grandfather of current head, Kim Jong-un. It was almost 70 years ago. The North is still paying their debt to China. Likewise, the South has relied heavily on help from the United States and we are still a "running dog" of the U.S.

In summary, the post-*Goguryo* Korea has continuously suffered from external forces. We have never had a real chance to be completely independent form others during the past millennium. Shall we just shrug it all off, saying it is simply the nature of human race? (08/11/18)

There is no field free of any weeds.
풀 없는 밭 없다.

[117]

We always have one or two trouble makers among close friends, a funny uncle in the family, a few bad apples in a barrel, one or two weirdos in a classroom, an odd sibling in a family, shoes or clothes seldom worn, a bad stock in an investment portfolio, an ugly duckling, etc. So long as we are not robots, we will all have different, individual characteristics: just like a finger print, birth mark, or dental map. By field (밭), the proverb meant crop-producing soil such as a wheat field and the weeds (풀) referred to here is an undesirable element. Examples may include a bad neighbor in a community, sex offenders and criminals in a society, and corrupt or fraudulent organizations in a nation. In other words, according to the above proverb, it is impossible not to have these bad people in any society and that we have to live with them no matter what. It is a sad acknowledgment in resignation.

When we lived in North Carolina, our home was on one-acre of land. Having a perfect lawn was one dream or obsession I had. Centipede grass was my choice as experts say it is one of the toughest grasses that do not need any fertilizers and could fight off weeds such as clover, crabgrass, dandelions, et cetera. It sounded perfect for an ambitious but lazy homeowner. The grass is quite sensitive to chemicals and in fact dies when one applies fertilizer even at a light dose. Because of this sensitivity to chemicals, most of the weed killers in the market also kill centipedes. All said, I liked the idea of not polluting the ground with weed killers. The upshot of it all was, however, that our lawn had every weed one could imagine, among some real centipede grass here and there. The only way to get rid of the weeds was pull them up by hand, complete with their roots. This was labor intensive and painful as I suffer from many allergens, rampant during the spring in North

Carolina. Another option was, of course, to sell the house, along with the troublesome lawn, which we were fortuitously able to do. Here, in Las Vegas, where we live now, many people lay synthetic lawns in their backyards because of the scarcity of water. I just could not lower myself to such a level though. I decided to avoid the whole issue by having pavers. Now, the above proverb has become a non-issue.

In some instances, odd behavior of individuals is simply a publicity stunt for a "15-minute fame," or notoriety. In the 1970s, "streaking" naked on the baseball field during a game was quite entertaining and drew a great deal of amusement from viewers. It was an innocent public prank, daring the police or sporting officials. For a while, the TV relayed those scenes live. This free debut to social media with a massive audience, in turn, encouraged more of them. Nowadays, the streakers, once caught, can be formally charged with indecent exposure. The police would like to attribute the lack of streaking in recent years to this change in law, but the truth is that all TV stations have agreed not to show anymore naked people running around. Collectively ignoring is one of the best ways to kill some silly behaviors people choose to do just for the sake of short-lived notoriety.

Yesterday marked the one-year anniversary of a deadly rally by white supremacists in Charlottesville, Virginia. A demonstration commemorating the event took place near the White House. Prior to the demonstration by a scary group, "Unite the Right," the news media were all hyped up and the Governor of Virginia even declared a state of emergency. There were front-page pictures of the demonstration and its counter-demonstration in addition to their leader's names. Why do the news media pay attention to these seemingly minor events? If we ignore the planned demonstration, it will eliminate any more future events of similar nature. The other day, the great quarterback of the Green Bay Packers, Aaron Roger, said one of the most sensible statements I've heard regarding Trump's displeasure of National Football League players kneeling down during the national anthem: "Let's just ignore whatever he says." Rogers was essentially saying that we cannot have a lawn without any weeds, the latter being no other than own president. (08/13/18)

A thirsty man digs a well.
목 마른 놈이 우물 판다.

[118]

The man who needs water most will be the one who starts to dig a well first. With this proverb, we are saying that people act on their own interest first. Albert Schweitzer (1875 - 1965) has been universally viewed as one of the most unselfish humanitarians that ever lived on this planet, famous for his dedication to the well-being of the aborigines in a remote African nation. However, some pundits argue that his charity work was nothing but his own need for enlightenment of his Christian faith. With this logic, one can say that the life-long sacrifice of Mother Teresa (1910 - 1997) can also be viewed from such an angle. One can present a similar, but terribly misled, argument as to the motifs of sexual predators and random murderers. This discussion is just to show how generic the above proverb can be.

    An interesting word found in the proverb is 놈, pronounced *nom*. I simply used "man" for the word, but more fittingly might be "guy" or even "son of a bitch." The word is used in jest or humor, certainly not malignant or derogatory in purpose. Its use adds some more color to the sentence. As I pointed out on numerous occasions, Koreans are not the most logical people on earth: how can one get drinking water now, when he has just started digging? It may take a while to see water. In contrast, more rational Chinese people used to say, "Dig a well before you are thirsty." I was looking for a similar proverb in other cultures but couldn't find any. A remotely related Dutch proverb says: "Who has no thirst, has no business at the fountain."

    What is the most common interest people act upon? I would say that money, sex, and power are at the top of the list. One's success in this contemporary world is often superficially measured by how much money one has or is making. When I was a young adult, my parents implicitly prodded me to be careful with money and beautiful women. It was the most absurd advice a young man, full of ambition and testosterone, could willingly accept. But it had some persuasive power. First, paper money is literally dirty. We do not know who had it before you. It could be full of germs. Look at the wrinkle at the corner, all worn out and almost discolored. Indeed, I still have this urge to wash my hands thoroughly with soap and hot water after counting paper money. Good thing we no longer use them often nowadays: most transactions are via credit card or mobile phone. While my parents' words have certainly spoiled my appetite and affinity to money, I am also fully aware that money is essential in maintaining a decent life, not only for me but also my wife. Money is to living, as air is to breathing. What my parents meant to say was that I ought to stay away from greed.

So, how much money is enough for one's living? To most of us, the answer may well be "never enough." There is always a new car to buy, a nice vacation to have, fancy restaurants to frequent, nice clothes to wear, a beautiful house to live in, and so on and so forth. The list seems endless. One "hindrance" to achieving these goals, is of course, the fact that we have to work hard, often to the extent of becoming a workaholic or a slave to money. Winning a jackpot in a state lottery is certainly one way to get rich with little effort, but it will never happen to me. I know my luck and the odds in such matters. As far as I can tell, there is no other solution to the "dilemma." We will have to compromise. As they say, "If money be not thy servant, it will be thy master."

Money can "buy" beautiful women and power if one decides to do so, although he may have to struggle with his own moral obligation for a while. See also Entry #97, "How long could deer's tail be?" Interestingly, the latter two cannot bring money unless you are, say, a corrupt politician or a pimp. As to the unsolicited advice from my mother on beautiful women, I think what she meant was just avoid those women of "high maintenance" or with expensive taste. She somehow already knew that I ought to date fun-loving, good-looking Democrats, but marry a Republican who can balance the checkbook and cook a nice meal. Alas, even that advice has become irrelevant at this advanced stage of my life. (08/14/18)

Don't drink water in front of a child, lest he drowns.
아이 보는 데서는 찬 물도 못 마신다.

[119]

By default, children grow up by imitating what they see in adults, especially their parents. Young animals are the same way. When you drink a glass of water in front of a child, the child will also want to drink water, regardless if he is thirsty or not. At the very least, he will want to grab the glass of water. The proverb specifically says "cold" water, but its significance was lost to me. In Entry #20, "A mudfish muddles a puddle," I introduced how the single mother of the great Chinese philosopher Mencius (372 - 289 BC or 385 - 303 or 302 BC) moved around till they settled close to a village school. There, all young Mencius saw was children studying. To Mencius' mother, the environment was important for her son to grow up in: not that her child would have understood and appreciated her efforts. She just provided her son with a subconscious "mirror" so that he can practice what he witnessed day in and day out.

Monkeys are said to imitate the behavior of human beings quite readily. I was told we can capture a monkey by taking advantage of this trait. Here is how. Disembark on the bank of a lake, where monkeys often visit to drink water. Leave a bottle of liquor (a cheap one but the stronger, the better) along with a bundle of sturdy rope. Go back to your boat and wait. When the curious monkeys descend from the nearby forest, and come upon the liquor bottle you left earlier, you and your buddy open your own bottle of Johnny Walker Blue and start to drink (but don't get too drunk, or better yet, just pretend to drink or drink plain water). Monkeys will do the same and will have a great time in drunken stupor (you can dance on the boat if you wish to see them also dancing on the ground). Now, you have your friend tie you on the mast of your boat, with your own rope, as tight as he can (make sure your friend will release you later on). Monkeys will do the same, with one of them on a tree trunk (if they are good sports, they may even tie two of them). Then, paddle your boat to land (and you know what to do next).

Imitation, as a conscious behavior, entails a component of admiration of their object by the imitator. The above story of monkeys may, or may not, involve conscious admiration of the behavior of you and your buddy on the boat. If you urinate into the open water of the lake, would the monkeys do the same? If not, do they have a higher standard of civility than you do? In adult life, imitation is all from envy and admiration, as they say that imitation is the sincerest form of flattery. Young adults, in their most impressionable age, mimic whatever their idols do: their gesture, body language, facial expression, haircut, clothes, shoes, words, political inclination, etc. The tendency seems more common among teen-aged girls. More often than not, the desire of imitating a celebrity is limited by insufficient financial means. How could you afford a Porsche when you admired the coolest of the cool actors, James Dean (1931- 1955)? But his gestures were free to take on.

Importing a foreign culture and their language is a form of imitation at a national level. How and when Chinese characters became part of the Korean written words is something that happened so a long time ago that we don't even think about such questions anymore. How English words have nowadays been imbedded, irreversibly, into daily Korean language was discussed in Entry #58, "Frogs don't remember they were once tadpoles." As to cultural invasion among the nations, see Entry #83, "A drizzle still can wet your clothes." If I may generalize, culture seems to flow from one country to another, in the direction of powerful nations to weak, in terms of, say, military power, economic prosperity, justice, education, political systems, etc. When Korea was an underdeveloped country (the politically correct word would be "developing" country), not many nations knew about Korea. Through the Korean War (1950 - 1953), the nation was known for its cold winter; however, such an image was more than compensated by subsequent economic prosperity and a flourishing democracy. Through the 1988 Korean Summer Olympics, and the ever-popular K-pop and electronic gadgets of recent years, Korea has now become a nation one ought to reckon with. It is no longer a nation of "morning tranquility" but a highly sophisticated, "developed" country. (08/15/18)

Stab and spoil a persimmon you don't want to eat.
못 먹는 감 찔러나 본다.

[120]

Once there lived a narrow-minded miser who loved apples. Each time he went to market, he noticed that the price of an apple had been continuously creeping up. Cursing under his breath, he mumbled to himself, "Why didn't I think of growing an apple tree myself, right in the front yard?" He brought one home and planted it in the fall. The tree, albeit small, developed sturdy roots and survived the winter quite well, all thank to his devotion to watering and fertilizing the tree. Come spring, sure enough, it began to show a promising crop of apples for the fall. He was quite pleased with his decision to have an apple tree right at home and the efforts he invested for promising outcome. As the hot summer yielded to dry autumn days, the apples were getting mature and soon to be harvested.

One day, he came home from work to discover that most of the matured apples were picked over by local, good-for-nothing kids. It was the very day he had planned to taste some of them for the first time. He was terribly disappointed and understandably furious. Had he known who stole his apples, he could have killed them right there and then. In due time, however, he recovered his sense and came up with a new plan: this time, he decided to keep the apple tree deep in the mountain, at a secret place that no one would ever discover or visit. However, because of heavy shade, the tree never had a chance to flourish. It simply died. From this story, children are to learn two independent lessons. One was that we never steal anything from anyone. Just imagine what the poor man had to go through. The second lesson was a bit abstract in concept: had he kept the tree where it was, at least some kids must have enjoyed the apples. Wouldn't it better than no one having any apples at all?

If you are so full in the stomach that you cannot eat any more of anything, like a persimmon (of all things), then at least make sure that you spoil it so that nobody else can have it. This is a twisted, evil mind talking, but obviously there must be such nasty people throughout human history. Another similar Korean proverb is: "pour ash over the steamed rice you don't want to eat, 못 먹는 밥에 재 뿌린다." Honestly, I did not know how cruel Korean people can be. This is nothing like the strategic retreat in a war, where the retreating army makes sure that nothing is left behind, lest it benefit their enemy. In 1950, when North Korea invaded the South with lightning speed, the fleeing South Korean army had to destroy the bridge spanning the Han River just to slow down the advancing army from the North. It entrapped most of the innocent citizens in Seoul, including our family. That was a situation deemed appropriate during a war, but here, why would anyone stop others from benefitting from surplus?

In 2010, President Obama signed off the so-called Affordable Care Act, or Obamacare. Since it came into force in 2014, the percentage of people without health insurance had approximately halved from 2010 to 2016. The Act was developed under the guiding principle that "more participation would translate to more competition, which would drive down premiums and thus make health insurance more affordable." Everyone, including politicians, would agree with the principle involved and the data from the field appeared to support that we were indeed moving towards the goal laid out. And yet, it has faced tremendous opposition from Republicans in recent years. Why do I perceive the opposition as "ruining a persimmon" or "spraying ash over cooked rice" by Republicans? Such silly political games they play make me nauseated.

The new ruling party given more power will do anything to mitigate what the opposition party and their administration have achieved in the past. Add to their ploy prosecutors with unlimited power. It spells the dictatorship in modern democracy. This seeming new norm was what Korea has gone through in recent years: the duly elected President Geun-Hye Park was sent to jail for what amounts to a life-sentence. At this writing, the New York State Governor, Andrew Cuomo, is about to sign a bill that will establish an independent, publicly accountable commission that would investigate prosecutorial misconduct. Now, that is something Koreans may wish to adopt, instead of trying to jab a persimmon they do not want to eat. (08/16/18)

No investment is worthier than children's education.
황금 천 냥이 자식 교육만 못하다.

[121]

In Entry #99, "All fields are fertile to diligent farmers," we learned how much sacrifice Korean parents would endure to secure their children's education: simply, "a lot." I just cannot stress how important the subject is in every Korean household. Here, in this proverb, the same point is emphasized again: "A thousand *nyang* (냥) in gold coins is not as valuable as children's education." Just like other countries in the past, the Joseon Dynasty of Korea (1392 - 1910) used coin-based currency. There were three coinage units: the *nyang* (냥), *jeon* (전), and *poon* (푼), molded in gold, silver, and brass, respectively. Of these, the *nyang* (냥) is of the highest value. "A thousand *nyang* (냥) in gold coins" must have been a large sum of money then: let's say, a million, in today's U.S. dollars. Even if a child inherits this much money, it is simply money: it comes and goes. Education, on the other hand, stays with us throughout our lifetime. Just like once we learn how to ride a bike or swim, we never forget.

At some point in their lives, teenage boys in any place would dream of becoming the next Mick Jagger of the Rolling Stones, or a member of BTS. If a boy is incline to becoming a sports figure, his idol could be Tottenham Hotspur forward Son Heung-min (손흥민), or Tom Brady, quarterback of the New England Patriots. Their fame and wealth is one thing, but the many perks that accompany their celebrity status would be something else altogether. Likewise, ambitious girls may wish to become a trend-setting fashion designer, a fancy artist of some sort, or even the first female president of the United States. However, this kind of daydreaming quickly bursts to a somber and "inconvenient" realization that fulfilling their dreams requires efforts and time, not to mention talent. In due time, most of the youths resign to the truth that their daydream is intangible and start to prepare a college application in a hurry. Blessed are indeed those who doggedly pursue what they enjoy most, with a great deal of zeal and passion, and ultimately succeed in what turned out to be an extension of their hobby. Here, the talent you are born with begets passion, and eventually wins the fierce competition involved.

In this day and age, to be professionally successful, one must have an educational background in a given field relevant to the job. It is a minimally required, seldom sufficient condition. Other supplemental requirements may include experience, performance at the job, and luck in some cases. Although one may appear to have a suitable education in a given field, the specific program or college one has attended plays a role in getting a position in highly competitive fields. At the PhD level, one is often asked about his or her pedigree: the potential employer may look into who the research advisor was. Even with this conventional career path, there are some dangers lurking over a young man in every corner. Here is one I used to witness quite often: if we keep telling a student with only marginal talent and ability how good he is, he may convince himself that it is indeed the case. In the same vein, we should not discourage a youth with constant criticism either.

The last thing any parents want to see is their young adult son or daughter coming home penniless and all beaten up by the highly competitive real world. The parents cannot say, out of sympathy and empathy, "I told you so. You should have listened to us. The other day, I saw a help-wanted sign at this corner restaurant." How to avoid this situation is the crux of the above proverb. Now here is the dilemma: if you give up a dream too early, you may live the rest of your life with the lingering question of "what-if?" If you pursue a dream too late, you may be too old to start a new career.

Then, which way should one follow; the heart full of passion or the brain full of cold reality? And when do you decide? So, the real education seems to take place not in the classroom, but within yourself, through the interactions with others: parents and siblings at home, teachers at school, or friends and peers at after-hour beer sessions. Even if you are not terribly good at anything, there is no reason to give up on yourself. After all, they say, "Short flax makes long thread." (08/18/18)

Bread is better than the song of birds.
금강산도 식후경

[122]

Kumgang-san (금강산) is one of the most famous mountains in Korea for its natural beauty. It is located only about 30 miles north of the current border between North and South Korea, on the *Taebaek* mountain range (태백산맥) that runs along the eastern coast of the Korean Peninsula. Its beauty is such that four different names are given to each of the four seasons, although it is generally known as "Diamond Mountain." Here, *Kumgang* (금강) and *san* (산) mean diamond and mountain, respectively. In scale, it is not like Mount Fuji in Japan or Kilimanjaro in Tanzania: instead, it is most charming and possesses delicate details. For Koreans trekking *Kumgang-san* likens to the pilgrimage to Mecca for Muslims and the Holy Land for Christians. Seeing *Kumgang-san* is literally a once-in-a-lifetime dream. Because the mountain is currently located in North Korean territory, we cannot visit the place. I am not sure if I will be able to see the mountain in my lifetime either.

If we are to list the basic physiological needs in the order of importance, food would be at the top. It may be followed by sleep, safety including clothing and shelter, and sex. Far at the end, we may add entertainment including vacations and tourism. Without food, we simply cannot survive, and the rest of the needs become a moot point. The above Korean proverb combines these two seemingly unrelated subjects to tell us that one would visit even the famous *Kumgang-san* only after having a full stomach. When you are dying of starvation, nothing is agreeable. The proverb simply emphasizes the importance of food in our daily survival. An English equivalent may well be: "A loaf of bread is better than the song of many birds."

Although the Battle of Stalingrad during the Second World War lasted for less than six months (August, 1942 - February, 1943), it was one of the bloodiest battles in human history: approximately two million were killed or wounded. The city of Stalingrad was completely encircled by the Soviet Red Army. After house-to-house combats, the exhausted German soldiers eventually surrendered to the Soviets. After the defeat, as many as 100,000 prisoners of war were sent to Siberia. The majority of them died there within a few months of arrival. Some of them survived. Because they were so hungry and underfed, it was later learned that many committed cannibalism. For these German prisoners, and those Jewish Holocaust survivors we see in archival pictures, wishing to see any of the Seven Wonders of the World would be the last thing they would dream about. The raw instinct for survival was so strong, their hunger dispelled the basic notion of decency, not to mention morality.

In the so-called "1965 Northeast Blackout," human error caused the electric power to be cut off for 13 hours. Affected areas included New York City as well as towns in Ontario, Canada. It happened on an early November evening. Nine months later, there was a burst of newborn babies. The same phenomenon happened in 2012, after hurricane Sandy hit the eastern shores of New Jersey and New York, causing a power outage. What do these events, almost 50 years apart, tell us? There was no entertainment that required electricity. People simply went to bed early.

The birth rate among developed countries, where man-made entertainment is a main stay of daily life, appears to be lower than among developing countries where the main nightly activity could well be what people do in bed. In a given country, the birth rate has steadily decreased as the society enjoys more options for entertainment. Various, readily available entertainment may not be the sole reason for the low birth rates, but it must help people diversify night activities. The 1990s were the last decade in Japan, where the birth rate exceeded the death rate. Korea has been facing the same trend of negative population growth. The human race, as a whole, would be extinct without a means of propagation, and yet sex often receives less priority than entertainment, as the above episodes involving power outages attest to. (08/20/18)

A dress is like feathers of a bird.
옷이 날개라.

[123]

Pretentious and wealthy people tend to be keen about their attire. For the former group, fancy clothes can compensate for whatever is lacking in a person. The latter group can simply afford expensive clothes. Average citizens envy those rich folks who, at fancy restaurants, hand over the keys to their Porsche to a valet attendant. Conversely, we may also assume that others would look us up if we wore fancy clothes and owned a nice, recent model car. This pretense of being rich seems particularly prevalent in Korean society. Here in the U.S., most young people have two sets of clothes, one for winter and one for summer: you wear either a hooded, well-padded fleece of some synthetic fabric, or a t-shirt with a pair of short pants. No, never in Korea, especially for ladies with means: they must have at least four sets of clothes, for each of the four seasons. When you go out, you dress as best as you can lest others assume that you are a dirt poor peasant.

Numerous proverbs contain words like dress, coat, clothes, etc. Listed below are some which share meaning, similar to the above proverb. See

https://www.bartleby.com/89/index1.html

- A smart coat is a good letter of introduction.
- Clothes or the tailor make the man.
- Good clothes open all doors.
- When a man's coat is threadbare it is easy to pick a hole in it.
- In your own country your name, in other countries your appearance.

The followings seem to carry a nuance of cynicism.

- It is not the gay coat that makes the gentleman.
- More goes to the making of a fine gentleman than fine clothes.

- He that is proud of his fine clothes gets his reputation from his tailor.
- A well-formed figure needs no cloak.
- Everyone sees his smart coat; no one sees his shrunken belly.
- An affectation in dress implies a flaw in the understanding.
- Fine linen often conceals a foul skin.
- No fine clothes can hide the clown.

Other proverbs appear to plainly contradict what others are saying.

- The coat does not make the man.
- The gown does not make the friar or monk.
- That suit is best that best fits me.

Americans tend to wear clothes that simply make them comfortable. Casual dress is subtly encouraged and some employers set Fridays as a dress-down day. What seems behind the trend is the implication that a self-confident person does not need to pay attention to how his appearance is portrayed to other people. Appearance can indeed be deceiving, as seen in the prologue of Kevin Kwan's *Crazy Rich Asians*. Three extremely wealthy and well-connected Chinese women have just arrived at one of the most famous hotels in London, wearing rain-soaked clothes, with their kids in tow. The snobbish manager refuses to admit them to the most spacious suite of the hotel, which they had reserved for four nights. "I'm afraid I'm going to have to ask you to leave the premises," says the manager. "Can we just use your telephone?" Eleanor pleads to no avail. She finally makes a phone call to her husband in Hong Kong. Fuming, the husband makes a few phone calls to buy the hotel out right. The hotel owner, some knighted royalty, personally shows up at the hotel lobby, escorting the Chinese family to ensure an all happy ending. Before everyone heads to the much awaited hotel suite, escorted by none other than Lord Ruper, now the previous owner of the hotel, the head of the Chinese family says to the manager, "I'm afraid I'm going to have to ask you to leave the premises." (08/21/18)

Burning a house down to get rid of bedbugs.
빈대가 밉다고 집에 불을 놓는다.

[124]

One can over-react in response to a misfortune. In this proverb, one tries to burn down a whole house just to kill a few bedbugs (빈대), most likely out of fury. This type of irrational behavior may originate from frustration, anger, revenge, hatred, and so on and so forth, but certainly in hot temper or out of stupidity. No one, with reasonable intelligence, would try to kill a fly with a sledge hammer, send a police SWAT (Special Weapons and Tactics) team to recover an overdue library book, separate infant children from parents because of national security reasons, issue a ticket to a little girl with a lemonade stand because she violated a city ordinance, or call an ambulance because of chronic constipation, etc. These things happen, however idiotic they may sound. People involved may later say that they did so simply because they could, but the fact of the matter lies in the solemn reality that we live under paranoia to potential threats. We tend to take extreme measures to right the wrong, even when subtle diplomacy could have worked out nicely.

During the Korean War, our house was infested with bed bugs. As a child, I remember killing them between two thumb nails. As their bodies get busted, they make a tiny popping noise and an obnoxious smell! As we complained of itching, they gave us DDT (dichloro-diphenyl-trichloroethane) powder to be spread inside our clothes. It worked like a charm. This was the 1950s. Since then, in the early 1970s, DDT was completely banned in agricultural use because of its harmful impact on the environment. The bed bug population has considerably declined since then, till several years ago when guests of some hotels in major cities started to complain about the bug. Apparently, once established, bed bugs are extremely difficult to abolish. High heat (113° for an hour), if applicable, is considered an ideal way, but definitely not recommended is burning down the whole house.

There is nothing magical about winning over adverse obstacles with a large excess of resources such as an army, money, labor, etc. There is nothing you cannot buy with money, for instance, or burning down a house to kill bed bugs. However, when one avoids a disaster with a minimalistic approach, it can make a headline in the news media, and will be heralded as a miracle or heroic. In Entry #78, "Three shoemakers outsmart Einstein," I introduced *Jegal-liang* (제갈량), also known as *Jegal-gongmyung* (제갈공명). This man was a highly intelligent "prime minister" in one of the three nations in ancient China, approximately two millennia ago. His cleverness in battle strategy and loyalty to his emperor are legendary to not only the Chinese but also to Koreans. The nation he was serving, *Chok-han* (촉한), was the weakest of the three and yet, thanks to the clever strategies of *Jegal-gongmyung*, most of the time they managed okay. Introduced below are two such episodes.

One time, *Chok-han's* army had to retreat deep inside a mountain. Complete defeat was looming over these fleeing soldiers, but not *Jegal-gongmyung*. He instructed his soldiers to sprinkle lime powder into a stream, to mimic the appearance of the water after rinsing rice, prior to cooking. As they fled up the valley, he ordered his soldiers to reduce incrementally the amount of lime powder dumped into the stream. The general of his enemy was smart enough to notice the change, and concluded that a significant contingency of *Chok-han's* army was now left behind, hidden for a certain ambush. They stopped chasing right there, and the general self-congratulated himself for the smart decision he made.

Another time, a fort of *Chok-han's* army was completely surrounded and outnumbered by enemy soldiers. An unconditional surrender seemed inevitable. However, *Jegal-gongmyung* ordered his men to change clothes to a most unremarkable white garment and sweep the ground after they widely opened the fort gate. An advanced scout of his enemy reported this strange and unexpected scene to his general, who immediately recognized something very fishy. He had heard about the wicked tricks of *Jegal-gongmyung* so much, he became scared and ordered his men to quickly retreat. Now, this must be the type of trick we need to defeat bed bugs. (08/22/18)

Blood is thicker than water.
피는 물보다 더 진하다.

[125]

There is an old Korean saying, "The smaller pepper is hotter." See Entry #50. Both water (H2O) and oxygen (O2) are one of the smallest molecules there is, with molecular weights of only 18 and 32, respectively, and yet they are essential to the survival of all forms of live animals and plants. Water seems abundant, occupying almost 70 percent of the surface of the earth, and yet does not seem available when and where we need it most. Approximately 70 percent of the human body is water, present in not only blood but also tissues and organs. Surface water, like that from oceans and rivers, provide important means of transportation for cargo as well as travelers. Like the sun, however, we do not appreciate its ready availability until, for one reason or another, we run out of water.

Although we use water all the time, we do not fully understand its behavior at the molecular level. Its unique properties and strange behaviors are largely attributed to extensive as well as intensive self-association, caused by so-called hydrogen bonding. At a given moment, we do not have free, or unassociated, single water molecules floating around. They are all bound to one another. A theoretical analysis indicates that aggregates of four molecules are the most abundant species we would find. Here, "binding" should be understood as facile with reversible association, not like objects attached together for good with super-glue. It is the only liquid which expands in volume upon freezing, able to burst a water pipe exposed to cold weather rendering ice to float. Water is heaviest at 4°C (39°F), explaining why a lake freezes on the surface first. Likewise, water becomes viscous, or thicker, as the temperature decreases. Eighteen grams of water, about 0.6 ounces, contains 6×10^{23} individual molecules and occupies a volume of 18 milliliters, or 0.02 quarts. When the same amount of water becomes steam, its volume increases more than 1,000-fold to

22.4 liters (5.9 gallons). The phenomenon was the basis of the steam engine and the first industrial revolution. In summary, water is a very strange liquid.

Blood delivers nutrients and oxygen gas to various parts of our body. Blood flows because the heart pumps it out. When the heart fails, the blood stops and we simply die. It is the legal definition of death. Blood is red because it contains a large number of erythrocytes, or red blood cells. These cells are red because they keep inside an iron-containing, red-colored protein called hemoglobin. Oxygen gas is not soluble in blood and thus gets carried throughout the body bound to hemoglobin, inside red blood cells. In the tissue that needs the gas, the bound oxygen is released from the red blood cell. They pick up oxygen when they pass through the lungs, where freshly inhaled air is available. This gas exchange occurs in a cooperative manner, involving the hemoglobin molecule.

Some nutrients are also insoluble in blood, and thus get carried after latching onto other circulating proteins such as albumin. Cholesterol, and its chemical derivatives are bound to special carriers called lipoprotein particles such as HDL (high-density lipoprotein) and LDL (low-density lipoprotein). To the dismay of any learned people, these are referred to simply as good cholesterol and bad cholesterol, respectively. Because of these substances, as well as red and white blood cells, blood is quite thick. In the order of fluidity, in reciprocal to viscosity, we can perhaps list bodily fluids as follows: saliva, runny nose, tears, sweat, urine, lymph, pus, blood, and semen.

When people say, "Blood is thicker than water and the arm always bends inwards," what they signify is the importance of blood relations in human interactions. See also Entry #116, "The crayfish sides with crabs." I will side with my wife, children, siblings, and friends, when required. I will defend my neighbors in a dispute. I would root for the Korean soccer team, the basketball teams of the U.S. and the university I used to be a professor of, and the American teams or athletes in the Olympics. This pretty much sums up what the above proverb tries to convey. Then, there is another expression, "Semen is thicker than blood." This is also a correct statement in terms of viscosity involved, however, I have not yet formulated my interpretation of its meaning. (08/23/18)

One wishes to become a monk while in a Buddhist temple.
절에 가면 중 노릇 하고 싶다.

[126]

Early one autumn morning, a man late sixtyish in age, was standing in a waiting line at the Seoul, Gang-nam bus terminal. He had a simple daypack on his back, and was holding a Styrofoam coffee cup in his right hand. He was dressed for hiking. It was a chilly morning, and a faint hint of steam shot up, straight from the coffee cup. His left hand was inside his pant pocket, keeping company with his bus ticket. Brisk, not cold, he tried to convince himself. An unfocused stare was cast at some distance, as a group of hikers gathered at the same queue, breaking the quiet morning. Once on board, he grabbed a window seat, with his face leaning against the widow. He watched the passing scenery without much seeming interest. A solid three hours later, he got off the bus. The hiking club of young people also left the bus. Obviously, they were all heading for the same Buddhist temple, deep and high in the mountains. At a dime store at the bus stop, he lingered for a few minutes, letting the boisterous hiking group take off first. He walked slowly and the noise from the group soon faded away.

It was a bit too early for the trees to change color, although they showed a promising fall soon coming. The morning chill yielded a hot sun on his back, and now he began to taste the salty skin around his mouth as he kept climbing up the narrow trail to the temple. He took a break in the shade, munching on a granola bar he had bought earlier at the bus stop. The absence of any noise was deafening. The stillness was disrupted only by cars on a rural road far below: seeing a car moving and hearing its noise a bit later. A shadow of a big bird was passing by him quickly, wakening him from a stupor. As a breeze erased the sweat from his forehead, he all of a sudden realized that he had not uttered a single word all morning. He liked that. A smile appeared to affirm his appreciation for tranquility.

The yard, just in front of the main hall with a Buddha sitting hands together, is loitered with visitors: families with children, young couples, a group of seniors, and single individuals like him. They were just milling around, admiring pagodas, and touching the old wooden pillars of the temple, all stained in red and cracked with age. Some were reading the history note board, enjoying the view of the valleys below, and the flat rice field far away. The hiking club of youth was not there. He figured they must have gone through this place already and gone to other smaller chapels scattered around. He also headed toward a small stream, some distance away from the main attractions. He sat on a rock and dipped his feet into the stream. It was cool at first but then became too cold. He dried his feet and laid down on the ground beside the stream, then closed his eyes under the hat he was wearing all morning.

Now that he had retired, nothing was really holding him in the big city of Seoul any more. Two sons had all grown up and married to start their own families. Both of them were, in fact, doing much better than he did when he was their age. They had been flatly ignoring any subtle gestures from him for any financial support. He was grateful for their independence, but thought it may change once they start to have their own babies. His wife had been dead for at least a decade and so had some dear friends. He had shared with a lady friend his plan of trading the noisy and crowded city life for a Buddhist temple, particularly this one. She seemed to fully understand and appreciate his thoughts and feelings about the remaining days of his life. He would definitely set up a bank account for her. Then, what else is there to take care of? Do I need to catch up with what is happening in this country or world affairs? Why would I? Hasn't the time arrived to examine myself more inwardly?

His tomorrow was to begin at 3 AM, a session for magnanimity, following on foot the chief priest with a wooden gong. A divine service of adoration would begin at 4 AM in front of Buddha. Breakfast, walking the perimeter for meditation, calisthenics, and a break would follow. At 9:30 AM, he was to see the chief priest. For this interview, he was ready to answer two questions: "Why do you wish to join the priesthood?" and "isn't the decision rather selfish?" (08/24/18)

A bad wife is better than a good son.
악처가 효자보다 낫다.

[127]

Married couples call each other, say, for attention in Korean, *eobo* (여보) or *dang-sin* (당신). These are roughly equivalent to "darling" or simply "hey" in English. *Eobo* (여보) means "like a jewel," while *dang-sin* (당신) stands for "like my own body." These original meanings have all been forgotten by now, like we say "good morning" even on a morning of nasty weather and foul mood. With his friends, a man refers to his wife as *manura* (마누라) or *eo-pyun-ne* (여편네). These words are somewhat self-effacing, but never with any malicious intent. I understand that these words originated from "lie down facing each other (마주 보고 누워라)" and "stay by me (옆에 있네)," respectively. The hidden, implicit meaning of these words, which we never consciously regurgitate, is that married couples are a treasure to keep "till death do us part."

Now, as an old man, I recall that people who make me comfortable are the ones whose company I have cherished the most. Their wealth, education, or standing in society did not matter much, so long as they were simple-minded and honest. In the interactions with me, they did not have any specific reason, purpose, calculus, or prerequisites. Their yesterday, to me, is the same as our today, like a constant flow of water in a stream. It will be the same tomorrow. With time, however, friends, neighbors, relatives, teachers, clerics, students, and even my children will leave me for their own lives. Or they might have already departed this world. People at a funeral are largely guests of the deceased's children, whereas many wedding guests are friends of parents. It just reflects a change in generation. They are the crowd we keep closely, by necessity but not necessarily by choice. Then, who will stay with me till the end?

The above Korean proverb says that there is no bad wife. It is a statement in default, as everyone, except a wife, will eventually move away. However your children may adore you, they will soon have their own spouses and children to support and tend to. Why does the proverb compare a bad wife with a good son? In Korean tradition, a good son, or *hyo-ja* (효자), is the one who lives with his parents even after he marries and has his own children, offering much happiness to his aged parents. Even under this sort of most ideal family arrangement, there is an undeniable tension between the mother and her daughter-in-law: see Entry #80, "A mother dislikes her daughter-in-law's heel."

In those old pictures, taken when we were a young couple, the wife tends to lean on the husband, often holding his arm. Many years later, when we become much older, the pictures show an old man hanging onto his wife, often an arm thrown over his wife's shoulder, possibly for support. In spite of, or maybe because of, all the shortcomings each of us has, the squabbles we have had, and the adversities we have gone through together, it is the wife who will stay with each of us till the end.

The bond that keeps a Korean couple together is *jeong* (정), which may be best translated into love in English. According to a Korean-English dictionary, the word would mean: love, feeling, emotion, affection, sentiment, passion, human nature, compassion, sympathy, etc. For the present case, it suffices to say that the word *jeong* is love. But it is far from love "at first sight," because *jeong* develops and solidifies with time. See Entry #153, "Easier to see *jeong* (love) leaving than arriving." Once established, *jeong* becomes an irreversible and permanent presence. You cannot just brush it off casually as many discontent young couples seem able to do. Indeed, the *jeong* established between an old couple may well be the best example of love. See Entry #86 "The squabble of a married couple is like cutting water with a knife."

As Socrates once said, "By all means, marry. If you get a good wife, you will be happy. If you get a bad one, you will be a philosopher." Indeed there is no bad wife. What else can we say? (08/28/18)

We sidestep feces because it is filthy not out of fear.
똥이 무서워서 피하나, 더러워서 피하지.

[128]

While we lived in North Carolina, I used to walk every morning through a wild nature trail nearby our place. It had small rapids, woods, song birds, and other small animals one would expect to see on such a trail: spiders, box turtles, deer, snakes, squirrels, etc. You are not supposed to let dogs loose, but no dogs were leashed and everybody was still happy. Here in Nevada, I walk on a paved sidewalk lined with palm trees and a lot of flowers. The road is in a well-groomed, gated community, accommodating a golf course, with a speed limit of 25 MPH, and all that jazz. Every dog is on a leash and led by owner. The contrast in setting of the two places is remarkable, and yet there is a commonality: dog poop. Dog-walking Carolinians would pick up the mess with the usual plastic bag they brought from home and carry it back home for disposal. I seldom saw a discarded mess on the path. The homeowners association here provides those bags at several places, each with a trash bin. They are strategically placed along the sidewalk. Interestingly, I see more dog poop in this neighborhood than in North Carolina, but that is beside the point. The above Korean proverb is saying that we sidestep the dog poop because it was filthy, not because we are afraid of it.

On August 3rd of this year, President Donald Trump decried in his tweet: "Lebron (*sic*) James was just interviewed by the dumbest man on television (CNN), Don Lemon. He made Lebron look smart, which isn't easy to do. I like Mike (Jordan)!" Both Don Lemon and LeBron James practiced the crux of the above old saying by offering no rebuttal: nothing but a dead silence. Following the long-held tradition, President Trump invited the 2017 NBA Champion, Golden State Warriors to the White House. One of the most productive players on the team, Stephen Curry, told the media that he would not participate in the visit. Their head coach, Steve Kerr, also showed a lukewarm enthusiasm about the invitation. A quick tweet was out from Trump on September 23: "Going to the White House is considered a great honor for a championship team. Stephen Curry is hesitating, therefore invitation is withdrawn!" Once again, a dead silence ensued from both Curry and Kerr. In these episodes, what has the most powerful man on this planet become, as the athletes maintained silence? The answer is in the heading of the proverb.

In many instances, avoiding an unnecessary trouble, because fighting is not worthy of an effort, is a wise thing to do. People wrestling in mud eventually get covered with dirt, regardless of who wins. In the above case, a divisive nature of a public dispute may render some of their ardent fans, who happen to be Trump supporters, to assess their loyalty. The passivity of being quiet could be perceived as surrender or cowardliness; however, it may well turn out to be a win over time. They might have lost a few battles as a strategic retreat, but won the war, so-to-speak.

A series of military warfare strategies in ancient China are well preserved in ten volumes, collectively known as Ten Military Classics, *moo-geong-sip-seo* (무경십서). Some of them are almost three-millennium old. Each book deals with different aspects of warfare and offer specific strategies. The last book, Volume 10, contains as many as 36 strategies in six chapters, each titled in an inscrutable Chinese metaphoric expression. The first strategy of the first chapter reads, for example: "Cross the ocean cheating the sky," no matter what it may mean. The last one, the 36th strategy, suggests, "Run away now but plan for the future." It implies that the best plan, when you face an almighty army of your foe, is to flee for your dear life. Appearance-wise, running away from an enemy with both arms protecting the back of the head is a sure sign of defeat. However, there is an important difference between fleeing in a helter-skelter fashion and a well-planned, bona fide, strategic retreat. For the former, you'd be hard pressed and embarrassed to a third party, but with the latter, you'd appear confident to return later for a decisive victory. I believe that the silence from those basketball players toward Trump's tweeter attacks belongs to the latter case. Wise men they are. (09/01/18)

No fish survives in distilled water.
물이 너무 맑으면 고기가 안 모인다.

[129]

When a person is severely dehydrated for one reason or another, you cannot infuse pure, distilled water directly into his vein. Instead, the patient would receive a Ringer's Solution intravenously. It is basically a 0.9% sodium chloride solution, providing "tonicity" identical to that of the human bodily fluid blood. When suspended in pure water, red blood cells swell and eventually burst open in hemolysis. Conversely, in a very concentrated salt solution, water comes out of the red cell, rendering it to shrink, a phenomenon known as crenation. For the same reason, fish cannot survive in pure distilled water. This is, of course, in addition to the fact that there is no food in distilled water. A direct translation of this proverb is "If water is too clean, fish will not come."

Imagine a perfectionist who is constantly motivated by his own high standards in everything around him and subtly insists upon others to be the same. His work ethics is such that there is no flawed element in job performance. His house is always meticulously maintained, monthly bills paid on time, taxes returned without any cheating, lawns without any weeds, clothes always clean and well ironed, shoes shined, cars clean in and outside, chin shaved clean, and so on. He speaks in precise words, the most appropriate on a given occasion without any superfluous words. He is the type of man who buttons up his shirt all the way to his throat. His face is pale, giving off a nuance of sterility, but body is in good shape, neither overweight nor thin. He has never cheated on his wife, and will not likely have an affair in the remaining days of his life. He does not drink or smoke. However you look, he is the perfect specimen of a human. Why can't we love such a perfect man?

Looks can be deceiving, as in "Judge not a book by its cover." A close scrutiny may reveal that he can be anything but perfect. He could be the "The Great Santini," in the 1979 film of the same name. In the movie, this quite successful marine pilot, played by Robert Duvall, is depicted as a bully to his wife and teen-aged children. Such a man could command much awe and respect, but not affection from others. Why not, indeed? Here is an old Chinese maxim: "emptiness is fullness," implying that there is no reason to show off your steely resolution to others all the time. Display weakness in humble posture, but keep the iron will inside. Playing dumb is often the best strategy on many occasions, as in "playing possum" to save one's own life.

Once there lived a little boy in a village, who always chose a nickel rather than a dime, when both were offered to him. Townsfolk assumed that this less-than-bright child thought the nickel was more valuable because it was bigger in size than a dime. Whenever people gathered around the town center, this rather entertaining episode repeated itself. It always ended with delightful laughter among the bystanders. It never failed: he always grabbed the nickel. One day, an old man cornered the boy after the crowd dispersed and asked, "Hey, young man, don't you know a dime is worth more than nickel?" "Of course, I do," answered the boy. "Then why do you pick the nickel all the time?" questioned the man. The boy replied with an answer that would have made the crowd look silly. "Had I chosen the dime, that would have been the end of this exercise and I wouldn't have been able to earn anything again."

Fables and fairy tales we were exposed to as a child were full of lessons that we should always be humble in behavior to other people. We were continuously taught that arrogance should be avoided at all cost. Bragging about our own perfection in all matters would be shunned by others who practice humility. If you wish to be around people who look at you with only awe, then yes, show them how perfect you are. Once your success tumbles to the ground, those people will be gone in a heartbeat. If you wish to be surrounded by people who will accommodate you with never-ending affection, show them you are also a human being, prone to errors and misfortunes. Most importantly, tell them you live in an ordinary environment, like a regular fish in natural water. (09/14/18)

Eat slowly, even ripe persimmon.
무른 감도 쉬어 가면서 먹어라.

[130]

Unlike here in this country, Asian persimmon is a popular fruit that Korean, Chinese, and Japanese enjoy during the fall and winter. Yellow-orange or red-orange in color, the shiny skin is tough to chew, especially when they are immature. Most people peel off the skin with a sharp knife for further processing as fruit cocktail, etc. Although immature persimmons feel hard, the flesh softens with time so that one can almost scoop it up with a small spoon, like ice cream. There is little to chew with ripened persimmons, except the seeds of course, and one can almost suck the flesh into one's mouth. It could be as good a weapon to pitch at your foe as raw eggs. The flesh is rich in glucose and tastes uniquely sweet. It is the major component of a somewhat spicy fruit punch, known as *su-jeong-gwa* (수정과), which is usually served cold as dessert. It also contains ginger, cinnamon, honey, and is always garnished with pine nuts. Next time you go to a Korean restaurant, ask for *su-jeong-gwa* after dinner. If they do not have it, the place cannot be a good Korean restaurant. It is a good drink that will wake you up from wining and dining. It is much better than hot coffee or cold sorbet.

Unripened persimmons are bitter and astringent in taste, because the fruit contains a high level of tannins. In an acidic environment as in the stomach, tannins precipitate out to form a solid. In chemical terms, these tannins not only undergo polymerization, but also form insoluble molecular complexes with a variety of substances in the stomach to form a mass of almost solid gummy material. When eating unripened persimmons, this is the source of indigestion one would experience. This chemical understanding of the indigestion problem was, of course, not known to people when the above proverb was born. Based on repeated observations and power of deduction, our ancestors knew unripened persimmons were something to avoid. As the fruit matures, the tannin level goes down and the flesh becomes very soft, no longer being a real concern for indigestion. Nonetheless, the above proverb warns you to be careful, even with ripened persimmons, lest you end up with indigestion. What does it imply?

What appears to be an easy job initially may turn out not to be. We all know about the outcome of the Aesop's fable, "The Tortoise and the Hare." If you recall, the tortoise was constantly tormented by the hare who ridiculed his clumsy movement. The tortoise finally had enough and one day challenged the hare to a race. In no time, the tortoise was left far behind in the dust. In fact, he was so far behind, the hare took a nap, still confident that he would win the race. When he woke up, however, the race was over. The slow crawling tortoise was on a steady and patient pace to complete the race ahead of the arrogant hare. Two Sundays ago, the National Football League had season-openers. One game, of which outcome surprised everyone, was the one between the almighty Pittsburg Steelers and the Cleveland Browns. Any casual sport fan would know that the Browns had lost all 16 games they played in the 2017 season, following the 1-15 record the previous season. They tied in overtime 21 to 21. Within an hour after the game, the netizens declared that the Browns effectively won the game. This unexpected event reminded me of the above proverb. No matter how weak your opponent may look, you will have to face them in earnest and with respect, just like you ought to chew carefully and thoroughly, even with mature persimmons.

As pointed out in the previous Entry # 129, pretending with apparent humility that you are nobody is in fact an excellent strategy to get other people around you to relax. Your competitors, like the hare in the fable, may feel they are not threatened. Instead, they may feel sorry for your seeming inability to deal with the job at hand. You may even invoke sympathy and compassion from them. Compare such a man with another, who shows an iron fist whenever warranted and demonstrates the demeanor of a know-it-all. Later, once you become a successful man, you can always practice this "luxury" of becoming humble. (09/17/18)

A rich man in a ravine is poorer than a dog on a shore.
산골 부자가 해변 개 보다 못하다.

[131]

The Korean peninsula, especially its eastern part, is quite mountainous and thus commercial development must have been severely limited when this proverb was in use. Nonetheless, a wealth gap among villagers deep in the mountain must have existed. This proverb tells us that a man living in such a remote hamlet, albeit rich by their own standard, can still be poorer than a dog wandering around the seashore. For one thing, the dog could have enjoyed a variety of fish and seafood that were discarded by street venders, just before they became completely decayed. Let us imagine how a man, who lived on a mountain, would have acquired seafood, and also imagine a dog freely roaming and sniffing around a seaside town. Reflect these images onto the above proverb. However, there must be more to this direct translation, but its hidden message is difficult to decipher. My first attempt is that all things in nature must be spoken of in relative terms, often from a broader perspective than just what appears here and now. One million dollars for most of us is a big sum of money and yet could be trivial to a billionaire, like when you lose a dollar on a card table out of a thousand dollars in your pocket.

In high school, we were given a student ID number based on height: the smallest guy was assigned to the number one and tallest guy with the highest number in the class. This number was used in determining the order of many classroom functions like seat arrangement, cleaning the classroom at the end of the day, vaccination schedule, roll call, lunch services, sitting for a class picture, etc. It was a big deal at that time, although later I realized that the difference in height we noticed among the classmates was in fact minuscule when we are compared with Americans. Just last week, we had a high school class reunion in Los Angeles and I found that we were all same in height! Back then, we were tadpoles in a small pond and were all acorns with no big difference in size. What is the point of measuring and comparing?

The richest and poorest families in a small mountain village are the same when we realize that neither family enjoys seafood as easily as a stray dog on the seashore.

Various phenomena involving light are best explained by considering light as a particle or wave. With the wave model, light is composed of waves, each with different wavelength. The wavelength used in a microwave oven is approximately 10 cm or about 4 inches. The wavelength of colors we see ranges from approximately 380 nanometer (nm) for violet to 780 nm for red. In between, we have those other colors of the rainbow. These are very short waves compared with the microwave used in an oven. Note that 1 nm is only 0.0000001 or 10^{-7} cm. Within the wide spectrum of waves, what we can see with the naked eye is in an extremely narrow portion, only about a span of 400 nm total. Within this range, we also distinguish color and are blind to the rest. Likewise, humans can hear a sound within a certain frequency range. Our smelling ability must bear a similar limitation compared to, say, a dog.

There has existed a palpable tension between the concepts of science and religion throughout human history. Owing to its spectacular success, science as we know now is taken as almost absolute truth. It is a measuring stick of right and wrong in matters of the physical world. To some atheists, such as Francis Crick, science may well be their true religion. See Entry #31, "Dig one well at a time." However, other notable scientists, including Schrodinger, Einstein, and Linus Pauling, all addressed the philosophical aspect of life towards the end of their lives. From their teachings, we can conclude that even science and religion share the core element dealing with the truth of matter as well as soul.

Different opinions and beliefs are desirable for the betterment of society, as novel thoughts and mutual understanding emerge during the accommodation of diverse viewpoints. Democracy occupies a small span in a wide spectrum of political philosophies and practices. Within this tiny range of ideal, on this tiny planet in "an obscure corner of the universe," humans have been fighting tooth and nail throughout the history for no good reason at all. As if this wasn't enough, we now have a president and two political parties that are trying, with their best efforts, to divide the nation and people. Humans often are simply pathetic. (09/24/18)

Even a dog is allowed peaceful meals.
먹을 때는 개도 안 때린다.

[132]

In most states in this country, a death-row inmate facing his imminent fate is allowed a last meal of his choice. I do not know how and when such a practice became a custom. Ted Bundy was certainly one of the most notorious serial killers in American history. He was eventually sentenced to death for rape, necrophilia, and more than 30 homicides. He was executed in the electric chair, at Florida State Prison, in early 1989. Apparently he declined any special meal and thus was given a traditional meal consisting of steak, eggs, hash browns, toast with butter and jelly, milk, and juice. Besides steak, pizza is also popular for the last meal. In French tradition, inmates were given a "little glass of rum" just prior to execution. In the United States, alcohol is not usually offered, but efforts are made such that an inmate can have the last meal in peace. The Louisiana State Penitentiary, known as Angola, is the largest maximum-security prison in the nation. It is said that the Warden Burl Cain, who served there for 21 years till 2016, often joined the condemned prisoner for their last meal.

Why a meal though? Why not a conjugal visit from a loved one, a stroll in a garden, a gaze at the sky on a starry night, or even some sort of entertainment? There is something special about the meal, for the above proverbs also says, "You don't kick a dog when he eats," or "Even a dog is allowed a peaceful meal." Here, I suppose, the gesture might be out of generosity. An immediate thought is that we should not bother anyone who is deeply engaged in a given task, be it studying, planning a long trip, plotting a bank robbery, engaging in gossip, engrossed in reading, praying, or meditating of some kind. "Just leave me alone for a few minutes so that I can finish this job." Or, more to the present case, it would be "Let me finish this meal in peace, and then you can kill me."

Most of us eat three times a day. Of these meals, breakfast is considered the most important. In the 1960s, nutritionist Adelle Davis came up with a phrase that has become a mantra of our time: "Eat breakfast like a king, lunch like a prince, and dinner like a pauper." The logic behind the advice is that morning is when our body needs the most calories for energy, after a long fast overnight. A heavy lunch, especially with a glass of wine, often leads to a sluggish afternoon. In average households, however, dinner is still the major meal of a day, although I have a friend who does not have any dinner at all. Their last meal takes place around 2 PM. Breakfast, during weekdays, tends to be rushed, for everyone in the family is about to take off for work or school. Lunch is generally with colleagues, and is hardly on your own. By default, dinner is the meal one should enjoy with family, but sadly, they say that we should avoid a heavy dinner.

All said, the above proverb must be telling us something more profound than a dog having a peaceful meal. My own interpretation would be that we have to respect the will and opinion of the weak. If you have subordinates at work, taking care of them should be a higher priority than flattering your own boss. Otherwise, you become a tree with no sturdy roots. The most fundamental tenet of democracy is based on "majority rule with minority rights." How to protect the opinion and freedom of the minority is particularly a tricky issue, essentially casting various shades of democracy. North Korea is hardly a democratic nation, in spite of its official name, the Democratic People's Republic of Korea. Similarly, Duterte's current Philippine government is notoriously poor on civil rights. A U.N. human-rights panel claims that the Xi Jinping's Chinese government is currently holding one million members of the mostly Muslim Uighur ethnic minority in secret camps for "re-education." Approximately the same number of Rohingya refugees, once again largely Muslim, have fled Myanmar to Bangladesh in the past few years. For many nations such as Syria that are currently engaged in civil war, protecting individual rights may be beyond our collective, wishful thoughts: however, all could have been avoided had everyone respected others' rights to live peacefully. Why can't we? We even allow a dog to enjoy a peaceful meal. (09/25/18)

An old dog does not bark for nothing.
늙은 개는 공연히 짖지 않는다.

[133]

As a dog ages, he becomes lazier but smarter, and thus barks with discernable enthusiasm only when it is absolutely warranted. Such occasions may include when his owner is being attacked, their home is intruded or on fire, he is ignored unjustifiably no matter how vigorously he wags his tail, an old friend of his master visits with his own dog, a car passes by with empty oil cans attached to the tail bumper, or a cat disturbs his laziness for no obvious reason. Thus, "If the old dog barks, he gives counsel," or "When an old dog barks, look out." Otherwise, the old dog just abides his time, enjoying a dog day afternoon under the shade with his eyes half closed but with nostrils and ears still fully functioning. He just lets the young puppies make noise and run around, thinking that they will learn in due time what a dog's life is all about. A certain smell or noise would remind him of the good old days of chasing squirrels or deer on a trail, ignoring the calls from his master. However, now he does not see the point of it at all.

A one-year old dog is said to be equivalent to a human teenager. It seems to be about right, based on how both of them behave. Ten to 15 years for dogs are equivalent to 60 to 80 years for humans or even 90 years if a dog is large. These old dogs perhaps represent the subject of the above proverb. Two-year old dogs, or approximately 24 year old humans, marks the most impressionable and yet formative age, when our character is being developed in earnest both physically and mentally. As introduced below, young people of about 20 years old or even senior citizens can be as vocal as teenagers but certainly with distinct and noble purposes.

First, a brief history of modern Korea is in order. Just like 9/11 in this country, historically important events in Korea are usually referred to as a three-digit number, corresponding to the date when a given event took place, usually without reference to the year. Korea was effectively freed from 35 years of Imperial Japanese occupation on August 15, 1945, the day they surrendered to the Allied forces, ending the Second World War. It was only a few weeks after two atomic bombs were dropped on Hiroshima and Nagasaki, and only a few years after I was born. On the same day in 1948, the government of the First Republic of Korea was officially established, with Syngman Rhee as its president. For us, these two important events became "indelible in the hippocampus" as 8-1-5, *pal-il-o*. On June 25, 1950, the Korean War broke, and thus it is referred to as 6-2-5, *yoog-yi-o*.

The government, under Rhee, was the first time Korea adopted democracy. This experimental period suffered from much corruption and suppression of civil liberty. The upshot of the continuing economic, social, and political instability was a popular uprising on April 19, 1960. It was led by labor and college student groups. This event was naturally referred to as 4-1-9, *sa-il-goo*. Syngman Rhee had to resign and fled the country to Hawaii, where he eventually died at the age of 91. The Second Republic thus born was a total mess from the start. If I recall, various demonstrations took place almost every day. The economy was at the rock bottom. In the political arena, nepotism and bribery were all but open secrets. Even the military forces, then amassing almost 600,000 men, were in discontent and disarray. On May 16, 1961, General Jeong-hee Park launched a military coup d'etat, known as 5-1-6, *o-il-yoog*. It was the end of the short-lived Second Republic, and effectively the beginning of the autocratic Third Republic of Korea. I was old enough to witness both the 4-1-9 uprising and 5-1-6 coup with my own vocal opinions, just like a two-year old dog.

Fast forward to 2017, President Geun-hye Park, who happened to be General Park's daughter, was impeached and sent to prison for some dubious bribery charges. It was, to most thinking Koreans, a simple political retaliation. My older brother back in Korea sent me a video tape where he was demonstrating against the unfair trial they held against President Park. In June this year, I was in front of Las Vegas City Hall protesting against separating infants from their parents, who had entered this country illegally. Both of us are "old dogs," but we barked. (09/27/18)

A mediocre carpenter complains about tools.
서투른 목수 연장 탓만 한다.

[134]

As a Danish proverb says, "Blame is the lazy man's wages," we all have a tendency to blame someone or something else when things go wrong. When a natural disaster, such as a hurricane, tornado, or tsunami, leaves behind much property damage and human casualties, we will surely find somebody to blame. A convenient target can be the head of the Federal Emergency Management Agency for their slow response and recovery efforts. Gone is the day when a person comes forward to acknowledge his own responsibility for a casualty such as a capsized ship or train wreck. So says the above proverb. If you are unhappy with the woodwork a carpenter just finished, he may state "Gosh, I wish I had a better set of tools." Worse yet, in some instances, the unexpected was exactly what was expected, so the conspirator blames something innocent for the outcome. See Entry #21, "Smoke in the chimney without fire?"

Somebody left our garage door open last night. My immediate thought was that it had to be my wife. Then, I quickly realized it was actually me who had forgotten to close it. Even when I know for certain that I did not leave the backyard porch light on, my wife refuses to admit that she did. She can be dishonest this way. Not long after we moved to this town, and thus everything was new, she was waiting at the wrong terminal at the airport I was flying into. When I called her to say that she had been at the wrong terminal, she was awfully mad because I did not tell her that I was taking a different airline from my outbound one. Of course she had my itinerary.

In Michigan, during the 1980s, they had a so-called "no-fault" auto insurance system. It may still be a state law. One benefit of such a system is that we can avoid time-consuming, and sometimes expensive litigation in the court of law, just to determine who caused a car accident and how much compensation should be awarded, etc. I wonder why we cannot have such a handy ruling system in settling disputes among married couples. If someone develops an App and calls it Domestic Dispute Settler or some such, it could be a best seller. I doubt any man would bring his wife to court because he suspects, or knows for sure as in my case, that his wife forgot to turn off a porch light. Speaking of an frivolous litigation, there was one in 1994 in which a 79-year old woman sued a McDonald's Restaurant for selling too hot coffee (180 - 190° F or 82 - 88° C). She accidentally spilled the coffee over her pelvic area and suffered third-degree burns. Her attorneys argued for approximately $3 million in compensation but eventually the case settled for a confidential sum. I suppose it wasn't frivolous to the victim, but we can always ask, "Who spilled the coffee in the first place?"

Who else but current President Donald Trump best illustrates the blame game? He blames everybody for every bad thing happening now, almost two years after he was sworn in as president. The main target of his complaints is previous President Obama as well as current and former Democratic Congressmen and women and the mass media for what he calls "fake news." As an example, Trump tried to lay responsibility on Democrats, for the separation of children from parents who entered this country illegally at the Mexican border, even though the policy came from his own administration. In May of this year, he told his Home Security Secretary, Kirstjen Nielson, "I know what you're going through right now with families is very tough but those are the bad laws that the Democrats gave us. We have to break up families." The fact is that there is no law that mandates the separation of children from their parents at the border.

Harry S. Truman, the 33rd president of this country adorned his desk in the Oval Office with an emphatic sign: "The buck stops here," saying that it was him who took the ultimate responsibility. See more in Entry #41, "Clean upstream begets clean water downstream." Trump never assumes such responsibility for anything negative that happens as a result of his actions. He is as good as the "ever-excusing" mediocre carpenter in this proverb. (10/01/18)

No one believes *meju* is from soybean.
콩으로 메주를 쑨다 해도 곧이 듣지 않는다.

[135]

Meju (메주) is a brick of dried, fermented soybeans (콩). In appearance, it looks like a block of cheese that is undergoing aging. Late in the fall, fully hydrated soybean is slowly cooked, for several hours, and processed to a thick paste. After being molded into a brick, it is cooled until solid. They are tied with rice-straw and hung to the ceiling of a room for fermentation. In the spring, they are further fermented, beneath a warm blanket and completely dried under the sun. This summarizes the typical procedure that our ancestors adopted to prepare *meju*. I am sure the current industrial method would be quite different, most likely employing purified enzymes, instead of adopting natural fermentation. *Meju*, thus prepared, is finally processed to soy sauce or a brownish paste called *doenjang* (된장), or miso. Just like soy sauce, *doenjang* is not directly consumed but added as a condiment to soup and stew. To make a long story short, yes, every child in Korea would know that *meju* is prepared from soybean, not a red-bean known as *paat* (팥). Yet, as so said by a chronic liar, people would not believe the correct information. The crux of the above proverb is that once you are branded as a liar, no one will believe you no matter what you say under any circumstance.

It is a Korean version of the Aesop's fable, "The boy who cried wolf." One of the earliest philosophers who addressed the issue of lying was supposedly Aristotle, who made essentially the same remark and took it one step further: anybody who advocates for lying cannot be trusted. Most of the philosophers from the subsequent millennia agree that there are no circumstances in which one may ethically lie: that is, one should not lie even when the only way to protect oneself is to lie. On September 18, President Trump claimed that the estimate of 3,000 total deaths by the two hurricanes that hit Puerto Rico was fabricated by Democrats. He also said in June that the crime in Germany was way up, when it was, in fact, the lowest it had been in the past 30 years. One can go through the following website to monitor this man's distorted facts or outright lies. When the head of a nation is not reliable, what is going to happen to the nation, not to mention its citizens? What we see now in this country is unprecedented in history, and so the preceding questions stand on its own merit.

https://www.politifact.com/personalities/donald-trump/statements/byruling/false/?page=2

People lie basically to alter, or hopefully improve, how others see him or her. It is a talent in that lying convincingly is something one can perfect only with practice and experience. Some people elaborate a lie with such a great deal of effort that their lie becomes reality to them. I do not know which is more dangerous, knowingly lying or believing in a lie, but both are bad. In terms of gender, men are said to lie in order to please themselves, which is certainly the case of Trump. Women are more likely to lie to please others. At present, there are two prominent women in the White House: the Counselor to the President, Kellyanne Conway, and the White House Press Secretary, Sarah Huckabee Sanders. Both have been making statements at the borderline of lying: they are quick learners of their boss. Conway provoked "alternative facts," after she concocted a "Bowling Green Massacre." Last year, when James Comey, the previous FBI Director, accused Trump of lying about the circumstances for which he was dismissed, Sanders defended Trump by saying, "I can definitively say the President is not a liar." In my dictionary, a person who lies about another liar, is also a liar. The behaviors of these two women, once again, appear to support the generalization: they indeed behaved just to please their boss, President Trump. Kate Atkinson's most recent novel, *Transcription* introduces a heroine, Juliet Washington, who had to live an alternate life. With the pseudo name, Iris Carter-Jenkins, she was a spy in England, during the Second World War. Her "ethical" lying was justified as her patriotic motive was far greater than the above two women. (10/02/18)

People will even swallow TSP, if it is free.
공짜라면 양잿물도 마신다.

[136]

Our Korean ancestors used to obtain laundry detergent from a natural source. In water, suspend the ash from any wood for a while with occasional stirring. Leave it undisturbed until the upper layer becomes reasonably clear and then collect the layer carefully, with little disruption of the ash sedimentation at the bottom. The solution thus obtained, known as *jaet-mool* (잿물), is highly alkaline. One pours it on to soiled clothes in hot, often boiling, water and stirs them occasionally. It works like a charm in removing stains from clothes, especially white clothes. This is of paramount importance because Koreans used to wear white clothes all the time, to the extent that foreigners would call our ancestors "People of white clothes (백의민족)." Trisodium phosphate, commonly known as TSP, is a sodium salt of phosphoric acid. One can buy this white powder at any hardware store. They sell it as an industrial detergent. When dissolved in water, like *jaet-mool* (잿물), it produces a highly alkaline solution. At such a high pH, greasy substances in typical stains are readily hydrolyzed to produce soap-like detergent molecules. In this essay, *yang-jaet-mool*(양잿물) and TSP are used interchangeably.

If one ingests a highly alkaline solution, unless somehow neutralized quickly, the gastrointestinal tract will be severely damaged. The individual will die in due time, following a period of rather agonizing and extremely painful suffering. And yet, the above proverb says that some people would swallow *yang-jaet-mool* (양잿물) so long as it is free! Obviously it mocks "cheap" people, who are looking for anything free. People, not necessarily only the poor ones, love free stuff. It's not that they've never heard of "no free lunch." They know that somebody must pay for what they are getting free. Still, an interesting question is why the proverb uses the word, "swallow" or "drink," instead of "take" or "keep." This is likely because having proper three meals a day was an important event among our (poor) ancestors for much of their lives: see Entry #44, "Embarrassment lasts longer than poverty."

Availability of basic needs, such as food and individual freedom, as well as a desire for an equitable distribution of wealth have been the major sales pitches during the birth of all new social and political philosophies throughout human history. Citizens accept such changes that are brought about by a new paradigm, often through revolution instead of evolution, and forced adoption instead of friendly persuasion. This seems particularly true when basic human rights are involved. Democratic socialism attempts to appease citizens who find capitalism less than ideal in terms of economic just. Their underlying principle is distinct from that of totalitarian and authoritarian communism in Russia and China. Indeed, several Scandinavian nations appear to be flourishing under their own socialism. In 2016, Bernie Sanders ran in the Democratic primary election under the banner of democratic socialism, and almost succeeded. This year, Alexandria Ocasio-Cortez from the Bronx, New York, won the nomination as a democratic socialist for the U.S. House of Representatives. It would be interesting to see how successful democratic socialists will be in the 2020 general election.

Under President Moon, the Korean government appears to have adopted their own version of socialism, perhaps as shown by their favorable views of North Korea and China. In spite of these recent successes in both the United States and Korea, the other day a friend of mine pointed out, over a glass of beer, that such change will never happen in either country. His reasoning for the prediction was that we, Koreans and Americans, long for free stuff like free TSP solution, too much. On the way back home, I regurgitated what he said, while thinking about what happened to Switzerland in 2016. Their citizens flatly rejected a proposal that guaranteed basic income to everyone, regardless of their employment status. See also Entry #13, "Spiders must build cobwebs to catch prey." Such voting will not happen soon, here in the States or in Korea. Why are then Americans and Koreans different from Swiss citizens? I think we have been overindulged in capitalism for too long and too deeply. (10/05/18)

Nails resist a light hammer's head.
망치가 가벼우면 못이 솟는다.

[137]

One has to exert a sufficient amount of force on a nail head with a hammer to properly complete the job. Nails not completely driven into the wood would come back out after a while, as the attached wooden piece wobbles frequently or becomes slowly warped over time. When the round peen, opposite side of the hammer head, is used in the last bit of banging for achieving a satisfactory finish, it often leaves a dented mark around the nail head. This may not be aesthetically acceptable, but it will not likely be loosened later. So says the above proverb: lightly spiked nails will eventually come back out again, implying that without a firm boss subordinates may be in disarray, or they may even start a mutiny if the boss is too unbearable.

    I have a friend who had to quit smoking because of constant nagging, in the form of bona fide harassment, from his family especially his oldest daughter. Since she and the rest of his family meant well, he did not have a choice but to surrender his bad habit for good. He says he was in an irritable mood for a long time, suffering from nicotine withdrawal symptoms. Years later, however, he now confesses that quitting cigarettes was one of the best things that happened to him in his otherwise uneventful life. Gone are the yellow nicotine stains at the finger tips, a stale smell lingering around everywhere in the house, the ugly ashtray full of cigarette butts, and coughing accompanied by phlegm, shortness of breath, smelly clothes, and so on and so forth. I know exactly what he had gone through, as I did the same myself when I married. My wife-to-be was not vocal about my smoking out of politeness, but there were subtle signs, like the flapping of hands to disperse smoke or feigned coughing. At that time, her implied wish was good enough for my command and I just quit smoking cold turkey.

In an analogy of what happens if a nail is not firmly in place, the early history of the Republic of Korea would show what a nation becomes when the government is unstable for one reason or another. See also Entry # 133, "An old dog does not bark for nothing." In 1948, the Republic was born as a democratic nation for the first time. The subsequent experimental period did not proceed very well, with much corruption and little civil liberty. That was what one would expect from a brand new nation, based on a brand new political philosophy and capitalistic economy. Labor groups and college students initiated a popular uprising in 1960, leading to the Second Republic. It was even worse than the First Republic, with rampant civil unrest and an uncertain future as a whole. Just one year later, on May 16, General Jeong-hee Park successfully launched a military coup d'etat: it was the beginning of the Third Republic of Korea. Park was ruthless, like a forceful hammer head upon resisting nails. He successfully established a solid foundation for a nation that is presently the 11th largest economy on this planet.

On April 28, 1789, the Royal Navy HMS (Her Majesty's Ship) *Bounty* experienced a mutiny, led by Acting Lieutenant Christian and his followers against their captain, Lieutenant Bligh. Apparently the captain was very tough in dealing with his men, particularly Christian. Once succeeded, the rebels let Captain Bligh and his 18 loyalists adrift on a dinghy. For the men, drifting on a small vessel with a limited food supply was effectively a death sentence on the vast waters of the South Pacific. It was essentially the same as a condemned man being pushed off the gang plank with the tip of drawn sword down to the open ocean. But, the story (history) continued with Captain Bligh and his followers somehow not only having survived but also prodding the Admiralty to dispatch the HMS *Pandora* to apprehend the mutineers one year later. Some of the mutineers were captured, but not Christian. On the way back to England, with captured rebels on board, the *Pandora* ran aground on the Great Barrier Reef and lost 31 crew and four prisoners from the *Bounty*. Since then, historians have considered Bligh an overbearing captain and Christian a tragic victim of circumstances. Here, the mutiny occurred not because the captain was too lenient, but too stringent. One could say that the nail received too much force from the hammer head, and the nail was broken to pieces. (10/09/18)

Startled by a turtle and now by a caldron lid.
자라 보고 놀란 가슴, 솥뚜껑 보고도 놀란다.

[138]

Before electricity and natural gas became the main energy sources, up until about 60 years ago, or just after the Korean War, most Korean households would fix their meals with coal or burning wood. The kitchens were invariably adjacent to, but separated by a wall, from the living room. The most unique feature of the kitchen was the presence of a wood stove attached to the wall. The furnace was made of mud brick or fire-resistant cement. It usually had two or three big holes on the bench that accommodated different sizes of cast-iron caldrons, or *sot* (솥). The Korean *sot* has a heavy lid, again made of cast-iron, heavy enough not to let steam escape, even with boiling water inside: a pressure cooker, you may say. They are also much shallower than the ones you see in this country. A common feature is that both are heated underneath by open fire. Heat from coal or wood is primarily used for cooking, but also channeled through an elaborate network beneath the living room floor. This tunnel-like network is graded in such a way that the back of the living room, leading to a chimney, is slightly higher than the spot closest to the furnace, or the hottest spot in the living room. This system is referred to as *on-dol-bang* or 온돌방. These letters literally mean "warm-stone-room."

Now let us go back to the proverb, which is concerned with the lid of a *sot*. Just like any other objects made of cast-iron, the circular lid is heavy, black in color, and usually bears a decorative ring on the upper surface. In the middle, there protrudes a handle. The proverb says that a person startled by a turtle is also startled by the lid of a *sot*, or 솥뚜껑. They, a turtle and the lid of a *sot*, are hardly similar in appearance: a turtle is green or brown, and alive; while a lid is rather black and dead like a nail. One is moving, albeit slowly, on legs; and the other is completely immobile with a handle sticking out of the middle. How do these dissimilar objects remind us of each other and startle a person? At first glance it sounds absurd, but that may be the whole point.

Let's say that early in the morning, one summer day, I am walking along a small trail absent mindedly. All of a sudden, I come across a box turtle slowly crossing the path that I am on. I am now startled not so much by fear, but by the presence of an unexpected object at that brief moment. My feeble mind causes rapid throbbing of my heart. From this experience, I could become frightened by anything remotely similar to the small turtle. Several months ago, I saw a video clip on national TV news showing a lady in a bath robe on her driveway to get the morning newspaper. Just as she stooped down to pick up what appeared to be a twig beside the newspaper, the twig became a live snake, either a rattler or a diamondback! She shrieked and pulled her arm back, in an extreme state of horror. Just imagine what she will think, throughout her life, whenever she encounters a twig.

Such an association of a bad memory with a given encounter is common and most of us have suffered similar experiences. We often find people avoiding height, darkness, open water like the sea, flying, etc., not to mention certain foods (not necessarily because of allergies). We all experience that a certain smell, sound, including music and strange noises; or even scenery, triggers a given memory. Many new Korean pop songs I learned since I left Korea, are particularly memorable: The song, "Night mist (밤안개)" immediately put me back to my student life in Vancouver. It must have been 1968, when the Korean National Basketball Team visited Canada, for a series of exhibition games. Players at the reception after the game sang the song and I was so mesmerized with the melody, I decided to learn it right there and then. "Oh, my friend (친구여)" is associated with a trip to mainland China, in 1998. At the first hotel we stayed at in Beijing, a girl played the melody on piano in the lobby welcoming Korean tourists. Who could forget where they were when the "9/11 attack" took place in 2001? (I was in a lab, running an experiment). Then, only a few weeks ago, I heard the host of a music program on the radio, mumbling about color association. "Color association?" (10/10/18)

Like kites tangled on a jujube tree….
대추 나무에 연 걸리 듯….

[139]

Both kites and jujube, also known as Chinese date, were quite popular in Korea when I grew up there. Here in this country, kites are seen mainly on the beach. The so-called sport or stunt-kites that both kids and adults are enjoying nowadays are pretty high-tech stuff: made for quick change in direction and speed, they appear to require a high level of dexterity and hand coordination. Lying on the beach, I can watch them in awe for a long time. The kite I used to fly when I was a little boy was not like the modern version. We made them out of rice paper, thin bamboo strips, and the paste of steamed rice for glue: a simple square thing of about 1´ by 1.5´, with a circle cut out in the middle. The top bamboo rod was slightly bent with thread and two more bamboo rods span diagonally across the kite. A tail was attached to each of the two corners at the bottom. Finally, thread from the four corners was tied to one line in the center, providing a desirable angle.

During autumn and winter, we had wind favorable for kite flying. When the air was barely moving, one had to run to lift the kite while the other guy hoisted it. More often than not, the kite would plunge to the ground, but once in a while it would catch wind and go up. A real disappointing occasion was when the kite became tangled on the bare branches of a deciduous tree. I did not grow up on a wide open field or with a beach nearby. If the kite landed on a tree and was within reach, we of course retrieved it. If not, we had to give it up with resignation and sagged shoulders. It was particularly frustrating to lose a brand new kite on a virgin flight. Early in the spring, we used to see many abandoned kites in the trees, all beaten-up by the winter weather. "Pathetic" would be a good word to describe them. I cannot explain why, but the above proverb particularly cites a jujube tree, which was not a common tree in Korea.

As written, the proverb is not a clause, but a phrase that can be used in describing a given desolate scene in a metaphoric comparison. It may be equivalent to English expressions such as "left high and dry" or "few and far between." The book of Korean proverbs for children, from which I selected this phrase, interprets the above as meaning "debts scattered here and there." Of the various debts we, as a nation, are facing at present, the most troublesome must be the debts associated with the student loans. Presented below is a direct quote from Wikipedia.

> Student loans are a form of financial aid used to help students access higher education. Student loan debt in the United States has been growing rapidly since 2006, rising to nearly $1.4 trillion by late 2016, roughly 7.5% GDP (Gross Domestic Product). Approximately 43 million have student loans, with an average balance of $30,000. In 2017, average student loan debt reached $39, 400, an increase of 6% compared to 2016. Americans owe more than $1.48 trillion (44 million borrowers) which is roughly $620 billion more than the overall credit card debt in the country. Loans usually must be repaid, in contrast to other forms of financial aid such as scholarships, which never have to be repaid, and grants, which rarely have to be repaid. Research indicates the increased usage of student loans has been a significant factor in college cost increases.

As of August 31, we still have as many as 500 children separated from their parents, who had illegally entered this country, primarily from Latin America. Just like the kites on a date tree, they were once loved and are still dearly missed by someone with a broken heart. Obviously, the current Trump Administration does not seem to have any clue what-so-ever, on these two issues: student loans and immigration. If they cannot handle them, they should let others solve the problem. Then at least I would consider them honest admitting their own inability. (10/11/18)

Parents can take care of their ten children, but not vice versa.
한 부모는 열 자식을 거느려도 열 자식은 한 부모를 못 돌본다.

[140]

Parents would rear their own ten children with utmost devotion but, according to the above proverb, the children cannot, or will not, take care of their own parents. It is right on the money when I look back on how my parents raised us and how I paid them back in return. The ten children referred to is a bit of an exaggeration, but the point is that the sheer number doesn't matter. Even if you had more than a dozen kids, they may not be able to look after you, when you become old: just as you were not with your parents. Here is a story involving me and my mother, somewhat relevant to the above proverb.

JR was my best friend, hands down, when we were in high school. My siblings and particularly my mother were very fond of him. Likewise, his family treated me as if I were one of their children. This was in spite of a significant difference in our family backgrounds. He was from a well-to-do family, with his father being one of the most powerful congressmen, while my parents were just average citizens, who worked hard for mere survival. Our respective mothers looked alike in appearance, always wearing clean and well ironed *hanbok* (한복), the traditional Korean dress. Both raised at least eight children, me being the last in the family and JR buried in the middle. At school, neither JR nor I were what you might call outstanding students, but we were not terribly bad, either. I would say just about average. JR may recollect differently, but I was a better student, in terms of academic standing as well as studiousness. It did not matter though, because both of us failed the college entrance examination in 1961. As it turned out later, it was at that point in time where our lives began to drift away from each other.

In 1967, I left Korea and my mother passed away in the fall of 1972. One of my sisters, who lived in Phoenix, Arizona at that time, received a X-Mas card from an old friend in Korea. After a few seasonal greetings, one line in the letter struck my sister like a bolt of lightening. It read, "Sorrow not as we will all go there eventually. I am sure she is now in the heaven." My sister immediately knew our mother had passed away earlier, but we didn't know. After I left Korea, once in a while JR visited my family, my mother to be exact. He must have witnessed his own mother aging slowly, and was curious about how my mother was doing. My mother must have seen me in JR, whenever he visited her. In due time, however, his visits dwindled to almost none.

One morning, JR realized that he had not seen my mother for quite a while, and decided to visit with her. When he arrived at the place we used to live, a stranger opened the door, saying that the Chos had moved to a new home some time ago. JR wasn't the most persistent guy I'd known, but later, he wrote me and stated that at that moment, something urged him to move on. It was from *Hyoja-dong* (효자동) to *Segeum-jung* (세금정), a distance too far for walk, but only a few stops by bus. Doggedly, he went to the address given to him by the new occupant of our old home. It was not like looking for a direction on Google Maps. I could almost see him mumbling some complaints along the way. Somehow, he managed to get to the new place and noticed a funeral procession was taking place. Immediately, one of my brothers asked JR to serve as a pallbearer in my place.

My mother had apparently instructed everyone in the family not to tell that she was dying to my sister and me. True to the Korean spirit of sacrifice, she did not wish to interfere with our studies. The truth may well be that she realized we could not afford the trip back and forth. I was a graduate student, living on a fellowship. All said and done, I was glad and grateful that JR was there in my place. Later, I heard from other pallbearers that the coffin of my mother was a lot lighter when JR lifted one corner of the casket. JR wrote me a long letter soon after the funeral, but my immediate older brother asked him not to send it to me right then. Months later his letter finally arrived, and I learned about what I am writing now. So, how did I repay my mother? (10/12/18)

One feels a splinter under a fingernail, but not a troubled heart.
손톱 밑에 가시 드는 줄은 알아도, 염통 곪는 줄은 모른다.

[141]

There are many different ways one can torture a person, say, during an "illegal" interrogation. One simple and "convenient" method is to tie down the victim's hand, firmly on a flat surface, and push in a sharp, needle-like object such as toothpick just beneath a fingernail. Apparently, it is one of the most sensitive parts in our body to pain. In contrast, we are not always aware of slowly deteriorating cardiovascular system until a stroke or heart attack occurs. So, the above proverb says that we know a lot about pending trivial matters and argue with a raised jugular vein, when we should actually address a more serious, and disastrous event sneaking up on our own bodies.

Single-cell organisms like bacteria do not need a circulatory system because both metabolic needs and the removal of cellular wastes can be attained within a short distance. That is, spontaneous transport processes such as diffusion are sufficient enough to satisfy such needs. When organisms are big as in mammals, the rapid exchange of oxygen and carbon dioxide as well as nutrients and waste is so critical for survival, they evolved with a two-pump, dual circulatory system. In humans, blood that has just left the lungs delivers oxygen throughout the body. It is pumped by the left side of the heart. The blood, which has passed through various organs, such as the kidneys and liver, comes back to the lungs via the right side of the heart. If you have lived for 75 years, both left and right pumps would have propelled approximately 106 million gallons of blood without any pause. This volume can fill a lake 0.6 mile long, 130 ft wide, and 33 ft deep (or 1 km x 40 m x 10 m)!

In essence, the circulatory cardiovascular system consists of three parts: the pump or heart, the circulating liquid or blood, and the closed tubes or blood vessels. A malfunction of any tiny piece of these parts can cause a significant impact on life, if not outright death. Heart attacks occur when the heart muscle is damaged, deep vain thrombosis (DVT) originates from the blood, and hemorrhages as well as atherosclerosis occur in the blood vessels. Together, these cardiovascular diseases are the major cause of death in this country, which is followed by cancer. When the above proverb was in use, preventive diagnostic tools or medical interventions could not have been available and any heart problems must have been a death sentence. Most alarming is the fact that many cardiovascular diseases occur without warning in advance: for instance, about half of all DVT cases have no symptoms at all. Even when we feel a slightly dull chest pain, we are most likely less keen about it than a sharp pain in the fingertip when a sliver gets under the fingernail.

The proverb is mocking short-sighted people who only see their immediate surroundings: not even ten yards beyond; think only about today, neither tomorrow nor future generations; yell all the time, me-me-me and not-not-them; and look for a quick profit, rather than a long-term payback; etc. All of us can cite such people in our lives right now. We don't need to go far to find one either. Just last week, the U.N. released a landmark report on man-made global warming and its predictable impact on future human civilization. A majority of Americans indeed understand and believe that climate change is real. However, we have yet to prioritize the emerging problems associated with global warming. This is in spite of two recent Category-4 hurricanes, Florence and Michael, which have resulted in over 50 devastating human deaths and property damage in the billions of dollars. This seeming public apathy may originate from President Trump as well as some of the U.S. Congressmen. Nowadays, most naysayers have hidden themselves in the corner of the cupboard, trying to avoid any public discussions as best they can. Shame on them all! In the midst of it all, the President tweeted a few days ago, calling the porn star, Stormy Danielle, "Horse Face." Obviously, his one-night dalliance with her was a sliver under the fingernail. In return, Stormy Danielle described Trump "tiny." I am just curious which part of Trump's body she was referring to. (10/18/18)

A mad dog can kill a tiger.
미친개가 호랑이 잡는다.

[142]

An excited, altered state of mind can often lead a person, or a dog in this proverb, to achieve something extraordinary. I suppose it is possible for a dog, cornered by a tiger, to fight bravely till the end. During this furious battle, he could kill the tiger by pure luck. An alternative outcome is being killed and devoured by the tiger. Here, fighting back is almost an instinct for survival, rather than a deliberate analysis of the situation at hand. Heroic deeds of soldiers, on a battle field, must be a similar case, not that I am trying to equate brave soldiers to a mad dog. These individuals are usually recognized in due time and properly appreciated by the Medal of Honor for their valor and sacrifice. It is the highest military honor offered by the United States government. Individual bravery is seldom recorded in history books: rather, they become a legend or subject of story books or films.

According to the so-called Transition State Theory, for a chemical reaction to occur, the molecules involved should acquire a certain amount of energy from a source such as heat, to reach an activated state that proceeds to the product. Sometimes, the activated transition state falls back to the initial state instead of heading to product. The moral courage we all maintain is counter-balanced by anticipated physical pain or even death. Overcoming and tilting the balance toward a brave action would be similar to acquiring a sufficient amount of energy for a chemical reaction to go through the transition state. Although there are numerous attempts to define bravery, it is not clear how one obtains the required "energy." Some scholars and philosophers insist that bravery is an act of dispelling fear. As such, it is a matter of endurance and not so much of aggression. The topic becomes more complicated when we introduce religious faith as the source of courage. In short, it would be difficult to generalize what triggers a foot soldier on a nasty battle field to behave so courageously. Some save the lives of numerous comrades when the odds are against him.

In contrast to heroic act of individuals, a group of people can be instigated to committing to an extraordinary act. The coach of an amateur sport team, for instance, can lead a group of mediocre players to a national championship. *The Boys in the Boat* by Daniel James Brown describes how the eight-oar crew team from the University of Washington beat not only the elite teams of the East Coast but also the almighty Great Britain team and ultimately the German team who were rowing for their own Adolf Hitler in the 1936 Berlin Olympics! These college kids were not from wealthy, well-established families: they were the sons of "nobodies" living at the margin of poverty in the State of Washington. The story is based on an interview by Brown of Joe Rants at his dying bed. Rants, one of a few survivors of the crew, was then a teenager without family or any future prospects to speak of.

We do not know exactly what makes such instances possible, where the outcome is certainly greater than just the total sum of individual contributions. One may call it synergy. We often refer to it as the "chemistry" of a team, without really trying to understand what is meant by the chemistry behind these "miracles?" Believing in each other in so-called herd mentality can also results in a tragic disaster. On November 18, 1978, over 900 followers of Reverend Jim Jones died in what appeared to be a mass suicide, in a remote settlement, infamously named Jonestown, Guyana. It is a small country on the northern mainland of South America. People just blindly followed what Jones preached. His hypnotic power was obviously persuasive enough for them to die "for paradise," after swallowing a red liquid tainted with cyanide. Brainwashing a whole nation with mesmerizing speeches and re-educating on social norms is indeed nothing new: just witness what Adolf Hitler in the 1930s and Kim Jong-un at the present time were able to do. See also Entry #61, "I can't find my sword in somebody else's scabbard." Here, Jones, Hitler, and Kim were all mad dogs, but why and how did people let those wicked leaders dictate their own fate? (10/30/18)

Everybody sheds dusts when brushed up.
털어서 먼지 안 나는 사람 없다.

[143]

Interpretation of this proverb is rather straightforward: it plainly says that nobody is perfect. It is concerned with humility, a concept that Koreans regard very highly. It used to be anyway. A corollary is that you ought to be generous towards people who are less than perfect in relation to your own high standards. This egalitarian philosophy has been introduced in so many proverbs thus far that I will not revisit each entry here. A derivative of the above proverb refers to clothes, rather than a person, which makes it more logical: "There are no clothes that will not shed dusts when shaken."

A ray of light that peeps through a gap of drapes displays sparkling dust suspended in a room, a phenomenon commonly (but erroneously) called the Tyndall Effect. We usually do not see the spectacles, but we become surprised to realize how dusty the room is when we can see them clearly from a certain angle. Dust particles are small enough to float in air seemingly forever. My wife has to drive east in the morning and comes home driving west. This is the worst combination for driving to and from work. She also complains about the dust on the dashboard and windshield inside the car. I declare the car is now dust-free, after cleaning the car interior very thoroughly. But it is a lie, of course. A sterile room in the pharmaceutical industry or semiconductor factory is not dust-free, even with all those HEPA (High-Efficiency Particulate Air) filters, positive room pressure, and special garments for employees.

Now, on humility: regardless of cultural and religious backdrop, denying self-promotion and self-righteousness is considered a virtue. This does not mean that we "think less of ourselves," but rather we "think of ourselves less." If one maintains a low profile for his or her talents and accomplishments just to gain the adulation from others, it is "false humility." Humble people recognize and pay due respect to others, whose ability surpass their own ability. Why is humility a virtue? Of the many answers advanced, which certainly includes various religious perspectives, the one I like most is that humility helps us define our own limitations in ability. This is in agreement with the old Greek maxim, "know thyself." How, then, was the concept of humility born? Could it be possibly because we are lonesome nobodies in this vast universe? Once we remind ourselves of this undeniable truth as often as we can, everything especially self-promoting seems like a silly vanity.

Not everyone is "qualified" to be a humble person. A person, who cannot offer anything to anybody either materialistically or empathically, cannot be humble, since there is nothing for that person to self-promote or to be self-righteous about. By definition, the concept of humbleness and humility makes it necessary for a person to have something to offer. How can a person at the bottom of social ladder go down further to become humble? How can a person who is lack of empathy offer words of comfort to others? There appears to exist a relationship between humbleness and social status: the better socially established a person is, the more profound his or her humility becomes. In a sense, this may explain why it is difficult for those with means and success to become truly level-headed, down-to-earth, open-minded, or egalitarian.

A son of a British aristocrat family, Henry Cavendish (1731 - 1810) was a great experimentalist as well as a theoretician in physical chemistry. He was famous for his discovery of hydrogen gas. In spite of his great achievements in science, Cavendish published no books and only a few papers. He could be one of the humblest scientists we have ever known: compare him with contemporary research scientists, especially in the field of medical sciences, where "publish or perish" is their daily mantra. Their professional success is often accompanied with an alias, "slave driver" of his or her students. I would not go that far and call Howard Hughes a humble man. Although he was one of the richest men in the world during his time (1905 - 1976), he maintained a reclusive life style later on, hiding in an obscure hotel in Las Vegas. For him, eccentric is a better word than humble. As a footnote, an antonym of humility may well be Donald Trump. No, he won't shed any dusts under any circumstance. (11/01/18)

Buy and slaughter a cow on credit.
외상이면 소도 잡아 먹는다.

[144]

For ordinary Korean folks at the time this proverb was in use, purchasing and slaughtering a cow for its meat and body parts would be an almost insurmountable task in logistics alone: right off the bat, where would I find the money to buy the cow, how and who would slaughter it, do I know how to process a freshly killed animal, what do I do with the leftovers as there is no way to consume the whole cow myself, what should I do with the parts nobody wants like the intestine and its content, etc. However, according to the above proverb, these issues become a moot point, so long as someone gives me sufficient credit to buy the cow. That is to say, if I don't have to pay for it right now, I would be more than willing to buy the cow and process it. Borrowing money or using credit to buy a cow is not as good as "free," but still better than paying for it out of my own pocket right at this moment. See also Entry # 136, "People will even swallow TSP, if it is free."

We do not need to look far for a situation where the above proverb is relevant. It is our current national debt, which currently runs at about U$ 21 trillion. According to the "Debt to Penny" clock, it was exactly U$21,676,608,763,810.66 when this sentence was written at 12:45 PM, on November 6, 2018. It is too large a number to really visualize. If we divide this number by the total U.S. population, including children, or 325 million, we obtain a personal debt of $66,700, or in Korean currency W75,000,000 (i.e., 7천5백만원). That is, each man, woman, and child (!) who lives in this country, carries a debt of more than double the U.S. per capita income of approximately $33,000. See the "National Debt 101" at https://www.thebalance.com/what-is-the-national-debt-4031393 for more information. One "honest," and most straightforward ways to reduce the national debt, and ultimately maintain a balanced federal budget, would be to spend less and collect more taxes. Exactly the opposite is happening now: revenue has shrunk from tax cuts for the rich, and spending has increased for the national security budget such as that for the Department of Defense.

An affinity to living with credit or in debt must be reflecting the prevailing self-centered wisdom of contemporary life. The mentality involved cries out: "don't rock the boat, don't try to fix till broken, hide the unpleasant stuff under the rug, what empathy? build the wall not bridges, steal if you can, sue them all if possible, study tax law for loopholes, cheat but don't get caught; just focus now, not tomorrow, or next month, or year; me-me-me," etc. My parents fled Seoul during the Korean War to the southernmost city of Busan. It must have been 1952. The corner dime store, where my mother used to buy groceries and odd supplies, maintained a ledger for each household in the neighborhood. I often ran errands to the store. The owner would go through my shopping list and I would bring the items back home, which was a small rented, crowded room above a post office. The store owner simply jotted down how much we spent, on what day. In appropriate intervals, my mother paid off the accumulated debt. This was the extent of our life in credit. It is still hard to believe that the store owner trusted our family, essentially refugees from Seoul.

Speaking of faith and trust, here is another story. In 1976, I lived in Kalamazoo, Michigan. My home — I was single at that time — was in a quiet neighborhood, tucked away from a nearby college. Close to home, there was a hill. Almost at the top of the hill, the passenger side of the road was walled in stone for a good-size residential home. On the wall, there was an indented space, for what appeared to be for some sort of sculpture or even a cross. In the fall, there used to be a basket full of freshly baked bread in the space. On the way back home from work, people stopped at the top of the hill to pick up a loaf of bread and paid whatever price was posted. No one was around.

My friends, who are savvy with finance, consider my wife and me too naive, as we do not owe anything to anyone: no mortgage, no credit card debt, no car payment, no nothing. However silly it may sound, we like the situation. We are neither poor enough nor ambitious enough to buy a cow on credit and butcher it ourselves. (11/06/18)

Thread follows the needle.
바늘 가는데 실 간다.

[145]

Neither thread nor needle alone can perform the function of sewing. First, a thread must go through the eye of a needle before one can start sewing. Their relationship is like that of "lips and teeth." Without lips teeth get cold, and without teeth the lips cannot maintain the shape of the mouth. Yet, we usually keep needles and threads in separate boxes or drawers: a set of needles of different sizes in a small but sturdy envelope, and threads of different colors and materials in a drawer. The separation is desirable considering the needle has a sharp tip that can hurt our fingers if handled improperly, while a spool of yarn or thread is perhaps one of the safest things one keeps at home. Besides, the two parts can provide a number of combinations for various sewing conditions.

An absolute requirement of two parts for a successful existence cannot be clearer than the pair of husband and wife. After describing how the Lord God created man and woman, Genesis (2:24) says: "That is why a man will leave his father and mother and clings to his wife, and the two of them become one body." Without the union of opposing sexes, humans would cease to exist. As to the husband-wife relationship, this is what the Bible has to say. "As the church is subordinate to Christ, so wives should be subordinate to their husbands in everything" (Ephesian 5:24). This, and other clauses in Chapter 5, became a sour point several years ago, among the modern-day feminists. I would not blame them for their irritation, since the literal reading sounds quite outdated, to say the least. On the other hand, if we read the verse in the overall context of the chapter, it is not terribly offending. The relationship was addressed in comparison with our interaction with the Lord. Furthermore, there were plenty of other "conditions" or "directives" given to husbands and married couples. "Be subordinate to one another out of reverence for Christ" (Eph 5:21) and

"Husbands, love your wives, even as Christ loved the church and handed himself over her" (Eph 5:25). Perhaps we should not overreact with unwarranted sensitivity.

    A toddler chasing the heels of their mother or father is as natural as thread follows the needle. This summer, on July 24 to be exact, *the New York Times* carried a picture of a female duck, a common merganser, which was followed by 76 (!) ducklings on a lake, about 150 miles northwest of Duluth, Minnesota. Wherever "Mama" went, they followed in a long line. All 76 of them. "It's an extraordinary sighting," said Richard O. Prum, an ornithologist at Yale University. Speaking of thread following the needle, none can be more impressive than this gathering. Apparently some birds, including common mergansers and ostriches, raise their babies in a 'day-care center system." Here, mother ducks must have left their ducklings in the care of one female, probably an older female who had experience in raising babies. But still··· 76 of them? "Everybody is really just amazed," said Mr. Cizek, the amateur photographer who took the picture. "Everybody keeps saying, 'Mom of the Year.' " Well said.

    All said, the above proverb is undoubtedly concerned with a leader and followers. Purely based on probability, most of us at a given time would belong to the category of follower: student rather than teacher, soldier rather than general, sailor rather than captain, player rather than coach, employee rather than Chief Executive Officer, voter rather than a candidate, church parishioner rather than reverend, consumer rather than producer, the suppressed citizen rather than dictator, etc.

    Owing to the competitive nature of humans, however, all of us wish to become a leader rather than a follower. Theories are abundant on leadership and practical workshops are popular among youths, as if there was a certain set of traits one could learn and acquire to become an extraordinary leader. Such important leadership traits as intelligence and physical appearance come with one's birth: and hence "Great leaders are born, not made." What are the important attributes of becoming a good follower? Per Harry S. Truman: "It is amazing what you (as a follower) can accomplish if you do not care who gets the credit (as a leader)." (11/09/18)

Quitting is worse than never starting.
가다가 중지하면 아니 간 만 못하다.

[146]

Once you take out a sword from its scabbard, you are supposed to do something with it. Don't just put it back: if nothing else, stab it into any defenseless object like a spoiled squash. This is another famous Korean proverb we used to hear all the time, while growing up. 칼을 뺐으면 썩은 호박이라도 찔러라. Once you start something, for Pete's sake, finish the job! It is an order of high purpose.

One of the most unsightly scenes one can come across in the countryside is high-rise buildings abandoned years ago, right in the middle of construction. They are now surrounded by tall grasses and weeds growing with the total freedom of the wilderness. If the construction site is close to a big city, trash can pile up here and there, along with rats, snakes, owls, and what-not. Old newspapers and plastic bags finally settle between the tall grasses, after floating aimlessly for a while in the wind. They are like pieces of lunch meat lodged between molars. The skeletons of empty structures are a scary silhouette under a full moon, or when reflected by distant city lights, beyond a river. They can be as scary as head stones in a cemetery. In most of these cases, the screeching halt of development can be traced to poor planning such as inflated sales projections or an insufficient investment fund.

"Bridge to nowhere" refers to not only unfinished bridges but also the pork barrel spending of federal money, which a local congressman brought in with pure political muscle. In these instances, big projects are usually terminated prematurely because they lack any merit. An empty airport lobby, serving no one in particular but a few lazy fliers, is as pathetic a scene as one would ever encounter. Recently, the construction of the so-called "Friendship Bridge," between China and North Korea, was abruptly stopped after over $300 million had been spent. They said it was because the relationship between the two countries became sour, subsequent to several nuclear tests and missile launches by the North Koreans in early 2016. It greatly embarrassed Beijing on the stage of international theater. Right now, one end of the unfinished bridge, high above the Yalu River, appears to be a hot spot as the backdrop for tourists taking pictures. These abandoned cement and steel structures, which seem to defy the height of the sky with their humongous dimensions alone, have now become desolate monuments, verifying the above proverb. If you quit digging a well, you will never have water. Half-baked potatoes do not taste any good at all. It cannot be remedied later either. Unfinished books, music, and art will never get exposed to the public, and they, in effect, do not exist. Practicing coitus interruptus may allow one to avoid pregnancy, but it is not as satisfactory as the real one.

As it is written, the proverb is actually speaking of a journey: if you stop before you reach the destination, it would be worse than not starting at all. *Baekdudaegan* Trail (백두대간) on the Korean Peninsula is approximately 860 miles (1,400 km) long, starting at *Jiri-san* (지리산) and ending at *Baekdu-san* (백두산), the tallest mountain in North Korea at 9,000 ft or 2,740 m. In September of 2013, I went for a 106-mile (170-km) backpacking trip, from *Sam-cheok* (삼척) to *Seorak-san* (설악산) National Park. I meant to trek the section in 12 days. I failed just one day after and had to come back to Seoul. It was an embarrassing venture for me and a laughing stock to others. To this day, I still regret that I had to quit.

Poor planning and an old body were to blame. The western part of the Korean Peninsula slowly elevates toward the ridge of the Tae-baek Mountain Range (태백산맥) in the east, from which point the altitude drops precipitously to the East Sea. Had I been smart and less cocky, I would have taken the western approach. Instead, I went over the mountain range on a bus and tried to climb up the trail from the East Sea. It was the toughest climb I had ever taken. Somehow, I managed to arrive at *Daet-jae Hostel* (댓재민박), the destination of Day 1. Mr. Noh, the proprietor of the inn, was watching me, with a great deal of concern, as I walked unsteadily toward him. He was alarmed not so much because I was about to collapse to a certain death, but because he saw a "dead man walking" toward him. (11/12/18)

Old tigers go home to die.
호랑이도 죽을 때는 제 집을 찾는다.

[147]

I don't know about tigers, but the salmon run begins and ends at their birthplace. Salmon eggs are laid and hatched in freshwater streams. Juvenile salmon spend much of their life in natal rivers for as long as a few years. Toward the end of this period, their body chemistry changes so they can survive in the ocean with a high salt concentration. Their life up to this point would be analogous to our life, up to college graduation. Young people, entering society to earn a living in earnest, should be equivalent to salmon going out to sea, where they gain most of their body mass as adults. After three to five years in the ocean, fully mature salmon return to the rivers to spawn. In this salmon run, it is understood that they come back with an amazing precision, to the same river even to the very spawning gravel ground where they hatched. After spawning, the salmon die and a new life cycle starts all over again.

Let us put aside the physical meaning of a home for a minute, and try to define a home. This is certainly a subjective task and I will speak for myself only. If home is where I wish to "bury my bones" or "scatter my ashes," my home is definitely Korea. This is in spite of the fact that I have lived here in the U.S. for 51 years, while I had lived in Korea for only 24 years. This immediate conclusion has less to do with a preference based on which country I dislike than what I am attracted to like a nail to a magnet. For reasons not clear to me, memories of earlier life bring about a stronger association with my own demise. These memories again have nothing to do with the living conditions under which I grew up. In fact, if a comfortable life defines where my home is, it must be where I live now. Why do we, as salmons do, go back to our birth place as we age?

The 92-year-old Vietnamese monk, Thich Nhat Hanh, "who taught the world mindfulness," used to say that we could all be a Buddha "by finding happiness in the simple things, like in mindfully peeling an orange or sipping tea. You know that at times you're like that. So enjoy being." He went back "home" last month from Paris, where he had lived most of his spiritual life in a kind of exile from Vietnam. According to his disciples in Vietnam, the return to his homeland to end his life, or "awaiting liberation from the cyclical nature of existence," is teaching them the meaning of "roots." Roots? Could it be anything to do with sentiment as well as being homesick?

Life in Foreign Land (타향살이)

How many years by now?	The willow tree at home	Strange land can be home
Count with my fingers.	Must be green again this spring,	Once lived long
My youth's gone	But it was many moons ago	And acquainted with.
So have decades	That I played songs	But all goings and comings
Since I left home.	With the willow flute.	Still do not make it home.

This was the type of song I used to look down upon with contempt and with a frown on my face because it was not sophisticated enough for the highly educated, and cultured young man I was. We sang only when we were totally drunk with bad-quality rice wine, *mag-geol-li* (막걸리) or soju. Even then, we sang the song, not because we liked it but because its simple rhythm in three-beat accommodated well our banging of tables with chopsticks. How could we sing, say, a piece from an Italian opera, with *mag-geol-li* (막걸리)? Our fervent drinking climaxed as the night curfew was about to start. There was a time when I had to spend a night in a police station, and my parents insisted in the following morning they did not know me. And there were numerous times I pawned my watch to have a drink. Several days, I had to survive without the watch before my payday arrived from the students I privately tutored. These are the roots for my home. (10/20/18)

Looking for tofu in a soybean field.
콩밭에 가서 두부 찾는다.

[148]

Tofu, or bean curd, is typically prepared by adding calcium ion (Ca^{++}) to once boiled soymilk, to coagulate proteins from the soybean. Magnesium (Mg^{++}) salts can also be used. Their counter ions can be a sulfate (SO_4^{2-}) or chloride (Cl^-), and the gelation step can be carried out in a mold so that one can make various shapes. Tofu is a good source of calcium and protein. It is low in calories and doesn't carry any discernable taste or flavor, but has a unique texture. It can thus be used in a variety of dishes, ranging from soup to a stir-fried dish. My favorite is the Chinese dish *mapo tofu*, which can be poured over a bowl of steamed rice and broccoli. A cup of warm sake would be optional. In short, tofu is good stuff. Although tofu is from soybean, a field of beans is certainly not the place for anyone to ask for tofu. It is like looking for ground beef at a cattle ranch, or "Seeking hot water under cold ice." In a direct interpretation, we can say that everything has to go through necessary steps, in a timely manner, before we can have it.

Looking for something at a wrong place at a wrong time is quite a common occurrence, often leading to a tragic consequence. "On August 5, 1949, a crew of 15 of the United States Forest Service's elite airborne firefighters, the Smokejumpers, stepped into the sky, above a remote forest fire, in the Montana wilderness. Less than an hour after their jump, all but three of these men were dead, or mortally burned. Haunted by these deaths for forty years, Norman Maclean puts back together the scattered pieces of the Mann Gulch tragedy." (from the back cover of *Young Men and Fire,* by Norman Maclean, which won the 1992 National Book Critics Circle Award). At the time of this writing, on November 14, 2018, there are three major infernos taking place in California, with a death toll approaching 50. There is no doubt it is the deadliest wildfire in California history.

In the case of the Mann Gulch fire, Maclean's painstaking investigation established that the dead firefighters were the victims of a major assumption that the wind would be south-bound, or upstream of the Missouri River. Instead, the wind was blowing exactly the opposite direction.

We go to a local grocery store rather than a cattle farm for hamburger meat. The NRA (National Rifle Association) convention may not be the best place to campaign for gun control. If one wishes to denounce President Trump, he or she would go to a gathering sponsored by Democrats. If you want your children to marry a Korean descendant, you would encourage them to attend a Korean church, or social gatherings sponsored by a Korean community. Meetings of a lady's book club are hardly a place to recruit an accomplice for robbing a bank. Inland is not a good place to look for fresh seafood. In terms of timing, we should fix a barn before the horse escapes and repair an old bridge before it collapses. As they say, the game isn't over till it's over, and thus withhold your celebration until the game is really over: Remember "It ain't over till the fat lady sings"? If there is one matter you ought to attend sooner and more often than later is visiting your parents while they are still alive. When you are ready to take care of your parents, most likely they have been dead for a while. See also Entry #66, "I have few invites, but many places to visit."

Looking for a spouse is perhaps one of the most significant events one goes through in his or her life. How and where to meet your future wife or husband is not as straightforward as looking at a bike at a bike shop, beef at a grocery store, a wedding band at a jewelry shop, etc. Unlike other situations, where we have a certain level of control over options and thus can develop a thorough plan beforehand, collecting physical data on potential mate is one thing, but jumping into marriage is a completely different matter with unknown levels of risks. Will this marriage be a happy and enduring one? There are unmeasurable qualities involved, which we call affection, love, respect, and trust. Absolute faith goes both ways and there is little else one can muster in a successful marriage. (11/14/18)

My cousin buys land, I have a bellyache (second version).
사촌이 땅을 사면 배가 아프다.

[149]

This proverb was already introduced earlier in Entry #111. Here, in this second version, I'd like to further address the words "envy" and "jealousy" quoting proverbs I found from other cultures. In my dictionary, "envy" is less evil than "jealousy", but both of them are looked down upon as undesirable human emotions. Here are several proverbs I have gathered via the internet. I have modified some of them for easier presentation.

Envy

- and hatred follow honor and state.
- goes beyond avarice.
- is between neighbors.
- corrupts man as rust corrupts iron.
- withers another's joy.
- of enemies is better than the pity of friends.
- always pursues the fortunate and meritorious.
- and covetousness are never satisfied.
- beats itself.
- does not enter an empty house.
- is blind and is only clever in depreciating the virtues of others.
- is its own torture.
- is the mean man's gratitude.
- is productive of hatred, and pity borders on contempt.

- is the sorrow of fools.
- is the worst disease.
- like fire soars upward.
- makes sorrow.
- never has a holiday.
- brings about suffering.
- admits inferiority.
- hurts others something, but himself more.
- makes man grows lean at the success of his neighbors.
- makes man's face grows sharp and his eyes big.
- dies with man, but envy itself never.
- inflicts the greatest mischief to others if you do well.
- makes a man unwise.

Jealousy
- in man causes wife's departure.
- in woman sets a whole house in a flame.
- in husband is brought by a lewd bachelor.
- is found in a neighbor's eye.
- is the evil daughter of a good family.
- is the greatest evil.
- shuts one door and opens two.
- of the wife is the path to divorce
- is in everyone however noble or humble one may be. (11/15/18)

The arm holding a shot of sake bends only one way.
잔 잡은 팔이 밖으로 휘지 못한다.

[150]

When I was much younger and thus much more "creative," one wintry autumn evening, I introduced warm sake to a whole bunch of American friends at a party in my place. This was in a small town in Michigan. I told them we would use only one small porcelain cup, which goes around the table, serving only one person at a time. The person who empties the cup would serve the friend sitting next to him. I showed them how to properly pour the warm sake for the other people; using both hands, from a small jar also made in porcelain. This was a matter of etiquette, I said. I also showed them how to hold the cup when their turn comes up for receiving sake; placing the cup forward with two hands to show respect to the person who offers you the drink; right hand holding the cup while the left hand supporting the other hand from beneath. Most of the procedures were what I invented on the spot. As I said, I was quite creative then and they didn't know anything about the ritual involved in drinking warm sake anyway.

At any rate, up to this point, everything was going quite "honky-dory," as everyone quickly imitated my demonstration. The difficult part began when I told them that they have to say something philosophically profound, like an aged proverb, before they swallowed the drink in one gulp. They protested when I told them they could not have the drink, if they did not have anything to say. Upon urging, I gave them a few examples; "A big tree faces more wind," or "An empty wheelbarrow makes more noise." Having grown up in an old country, I had hundreds of such words of wisdom. Although some declared, "Yeah, I know that one," when the roving cup actually arrived, their tongues got tied and couldn't say anything intelligent for a while. The only noise coming out of their mouths was "um, um…." After several statements of nonsense around the table, which were invariably mocked by others, one finally blurted out, more out of frustration, "Michigan will beat the hell out of Ohio State in no time at all!" and everyone said in unison, "Yeah, yeah, I hear you." They sure knew about the football. From then on, the quality of the party quickly went downhill.

The above proverb says that the hand holding a shot of sake would bend only toward the lips, implying that no one would readily give up what is being offered without serious assessment first. Can you just ignore the ten-dollar bill rolling about in the wind on the street? Can you give up a front seat at a concert, or an air kiss thrown to you by a lady sitting yonder at a bar? (11/20/18)

No son is good enough for the long-term care of parents.
긴 병에 효자 없다.

[151]

It has been a long-held Korean tradition that grown children, normally the oldest son, take care of aged parents, often living together. This custom seems to be rapidly fading away in the contemporary Korea. I am not simply referring to the traditional family get-togethers during the holiday seasons, like Korean Thanksgiving day, *choo-suk* (추석), or on the birthday of parents. The above proverb is more concerned with caring for sick parents, and points out that even the most devoted and dutiful son can take care of parents with a chronic illness, only so much. The son must have not only his own family to raise and a job to attend but also his bed-ridden parents to visit. How could the son not? After all, his parents have reared him and all his siblings to what they have become now. Their love and best efforts for raising the family should amount to something, right?

The time and financial resources of the married son are funneled to several different, seemingly independent, directions. Every day appears to be a testing time for him: shall he attend the ball game his son is playing, see a music recital his daughter is part of, visit an ailing father at the hospital, "hit the town" with buddies, which has been put off several times already, or take his wife out alone for a quiet dinner? It is a matter of prioritizing and, for most married men, taking care of his family must be at the top of the list. Early this year, Paul Ryan, the 54th Speaker of the United States House of Representatives, since 2015, announced his retirement. He was only 48 years old. "If I am here for one more term, my kids will only ever have known me as a weekend dad. I can't let that happen." More often than not, I have disagreed with his political philosophy, but I have to respect his view on the family, and by extension, his wisdom of life.

Looking after rapidly aging parents may not be high on a son's daily to-do list, but it is and will be in his mind all the time till his parents depart this world. When they are no longer with him, it becomes a regret that he had failed to do more for his parents. On the parents' part, it is tempting to resent son's seeming lack of attention to their wellbeing. The old parents may realize belatedly that they should have taken better care of their own parents when they were young: see Entry #41, "Clean upstream begets clean water downstream." At this point in time, the parents may not be able to bring the subject up to their children, since they had not listened to what their own parents had told them when they were a newly married.

The world population will increase to about 10 billion by 2050, from the current 8 billion, with the elderly population increasing from 10 to 22 percent. According to a UN's projection, it is the oldest cohort, among the old people, whose numbers will increase most rapidly. Collectively, the welfare of the ageing generation is an important societal issue throughout the world. They will raise economic, medical, and housing issues, including possible ill-treatment by the younger generations. Institutional provisions, be it national or local, sound all nice and dandy; however, they are just numerical analysis, providing statistics for a PowerPoint presentation at some conference. It does not address dilemmas at the level of individual families. What can you do if your parents are chronically sick, and you have to provide them with health care and mental support with only limited time and financial resources?

As we grew up, we were taught and constantly reminded that we were expected to take good care of our parents as they approached their final days. We would keep hearing, from our own parents, that so-and-so is such a devoted son, from whom we were to learn something. I don't remember my parents having ever outright saying so, but there were always strong hints. However one may look at the issue, there is no simple solution for the younger generations. The novel, *Like Water for Chocolate,* by Laura Esquivel (1989) follows the story of a young girl named Tita, who does not or cannot marry her lover, Pedro. It was because of the family tradition that the youngest daughter could not marry until the remaining parent died. Could this be a new norm? (11/22/18)

Ordering to plant soybean here, red bean there.
콩 심어라 팥 심어라 한다.

[152]

Both soybean and red bean (adzuki bean) are species of legume (콩류) and grow under similar conditions. However, their consumption by Koreans differs significantly from each other. Soybeans are primarily consumed as food, while red beans are famous for their sweet paste, which serves as a filling in various cakes and desserts. The word for each is just one-character long, *kong* (콩) and *paat* (팥), for soybean and red bean, respectively. Both words sound pleasing and somewhat entertaining. When spoken together, it is always *kong* followed by *paat* but never the other way around, *paat-kong*. When naked they look alike, not only in shape but also in size.

Before delving into the above proverb in earnest, let us visualize a scene on a farm. The landlord, with limited knowledge in agriculture and horticulture, is ordering his men, most of whom are experienced farmers, what to plant, on which plot, and exactly when. Some of his directives are out of touch, as he is not as well acquainted as his farmhands in terms of weather, soil, water, pests, etc. Yet, the farmers follow his order, as he is their undisputed boss. In the harvest time, any failure would be the fault of sharecroppers, while any successful outcome would be the result of his brilliant ideas. The above proverb depicts such a boss who tries micromanaging, often without the technical knowledge needed. He keeps on barking, "OK, plant soybean here and red bean over there. No, I changed my mind. Let's keep this piece of land empty for the sake of aesthetics and …"

Some years ago, I came across a series of philosophical debates on why and how the American auto industry lost its global hegemony to Japan. One argument I remember was that the decline of the American auto industry coincided with the time when MBA-majored wizards in finance began to take over the CEO positions from the engineers. In recent decades,

I have also noticed that many big industries, no matter what they manufacture and sell, are now run by folks from finance. These experts in finance do not seem to care much about what they are selling, but are interested only in the performance of stocks. Firms managing venture capital do not, or cannot have, in-house experts in all possible areas of investment. Instead, they hire per diem consultants on an as-needed basis. Once a deal is made and the expert consultants are all long gone, the venture capital firms demand "what, when, and where to plant" to technically well versed professionals such as engineers and scientists. This one-way directive from money men is in contrast to the "desirable" tension we used to have between management and research scientists. The following story may highlight what I am alluding to.

Wallace Hume Carothers (1896 - 1937) is considered the inventor of nylon. He was a group leader, in an organic chemistry lab at DuPont. When he was hired in 1927 from Harvard, there were no practical strings attached to his position. He was to run basic research, not really aiming at developing any products that promised a great deal of monetary payback. In early 1930, another chemist, Elmer Bolton, became his immediate boss and wanted practically significant results from the basic research carried out in Carothers' lab, nicknamed "Purity Hall." Carothers knew what was possible, and more importantly, what was the limit of technological know-how available to them. The constant pressure upon his shoulders to come up with money-making products had been creating an "interfacial tension" between management (i.e. Bolton) and the basic scientists (i.e., Crothers group). Historians in science later attributed the success of Carothers' lab to this very tension, which might have been an adversarial factor at that time. It must have been a tug of war, or give-and-take, rather than one-way directives from venture capitalists. This must have been possible as Bolton was also a chemist, not a money-man.

Micromanagement, driven by paranoid obsession, must be avoided at all cost, especially when done by someone not technically qualified. Instead, one should delegate authority to subordinates along with responsibility. They said Dwight Eisenhower, the 34th President of this nation, played more rounds of golf than any other president, and yet his tenure was the only time this nation was free of any major wars. What does that tell you? (11/24/18)

Easier to see *jeong* (love) leaving than arriving.
드는 정은 몰라도 나는 정은 안다.

[153]

The word, *jeong* (정), is one of those Korean nouns that deals with an abstract concept and thus defies a simple, direct translation. It describes positive feeling, emotion, sentiment, love, affection, compassion, etc. The context in which the word is used would dictate translation, more or less in alignment with nuance. If one wishes to be a bit more specific, another word can be added as a descriptive adjective: *ae-jeong* (애정), *in-jeong* (인정), and *dong-jeong* (동정), meaning passionate love, human nature, and sympathy, respectively. This proverb says that affection, or *jeong*, develops slowly and in stealth, often without us being aware of its maturation, but we know immediately when the love becomes sour. See also Entry #127, "A bad wife is better than a good son."

Let us deal with the easy part of the proverb first: that is, a break-up in a relationship. Any tell-tale, subtle but significant, sign can speak volumes about the dire state of a relationship. Even without any outright verbal declaration of an end, one can feel what is coming. Examples may include; undue silence, avoiding direct eye contact, ignoring one's presence, unfulfilled promises however trivial they may be, a display of apathy, or slow response in conversation, apparent lies, and so forth and so on. Any nagging with inquisitive accusations would only exacerbate the already-bad situation. It would be spilt milk. A mutually amicable breakup is impossible in most instances. Although one party involved would suffer more upset for a while, it is better to let the relationship rest in peace, at least for better memories later. For the third party, it is easier to give such advice. Here is the famous poem, *Azalea Flowers* (진달래 꽃), by Kim Sowal (김소월) (1902 - 1934).

Will let you go in peace
When you no longer wish to see me.
Will sprinkle aplenty over your path
Azalea flowers from Yak-san of Yung-byun.
Walk on them quietly
One step at a time lightly.
But I will never shed tears
When you no longer wish to see me.

The primary changes one goes through during puberty are not only the gain in height and weight, but more importantly, the development of ovaries in girls and the testes in boys. Changes in hormonal physiology stimulate libido, transforming us to be prepared for reproduction. Puberty is really when we notice the presence of the opposite sex more clearly for the first time in our lives. During this period of time, love and sex are all parts of a confusing mystery: a mystery that no educational program can really help us solve. Puberty is the time we somehow define the purpose of the opposite sex and acquire the first taste of love, most often a forlorn one.

A happy ending comes by only grudgingly, in most cases of first love. Of the tens of friends I had during our puberty period, I can think of only one guy who eventually married his first love. Even in this case, my friend had drifted from her for a while, before going back to her. He must have finally realized he had loved her more than anybody else. That realization was slow in coming to both of them but resulted in a happy marriage. They have raised two children, who are by now, married with their own families. It is often said that the first love is the toughest one to get over and yet its memory always makes us smile. This may well be because the first love develops with many agonizing hours of heartache and longing, in a slow but intense maturation in both mind and body. (11/29/18)

One thief outsmarts ten sentries.
지키는 사람 열이 훔치는 사람 하나를 못 당한다.

[154]

Just like any other proverb, this one also speaks of a simple truth. It is true basically because the thief's job, compared with that of law enforcement, is of higher intensity often determining life or death, and wealth or prison time. If there are 10 policemen monitoring and maintaining peace in a given territory of say, 1,000 inhabitants, their responsibilities would inevitably be diluted and shared between all 10 men. Additionally, their job would be primarily preventive and hence there is no simple way to tell which one of the 1,000 residents would be subject to a burglary, not to mention when. The accountability for failed prevention of a disaster is difficult to establish at the individual level.

On October 1, 2017, one Stephen Paddock opened fire from a room on the 32nd floor of a hotel-casino on the Las Vegas Strip, killing as many as 58 people who were attending an outdoor country music festival. Police are still struggling for establishing his motive. In such a random killing, how can the law-enforcer prevent the tragedy? In this particular instance, the assailant was also killed by the police and thus we lost any opportunity to interrogate him, leaving everything a mystery. Likewise, we can see how difficult it would have been in 2001 to stop the September 11 attack by the Islamic terrorist group al-Qaeda. The U.S. intelligence community had known that Osama bin Laden and al-Qaeda had vigorously opposed U.S. foreign policies for many preceding years, but preventing their specific operation on that particular day would be like finding a needle in a hay stack.

To some extent, the harsh punishment of criminals can serve as a preventive measure: however, it would be difficult to assess its efficiency. Osama bin Laden was finally killed in Pakistan by the U.S. Navy SEAL team, almost ten years after the actual 9/11 attack. Even historians will have a hard time to evaluate how much influence the killing of Osama bin

Laden has on future attacks by similar extremists. It may not be a relevant question, as the main objective of the retaliation must have been that we, as Americans, are willingly to go to any length to re-establish justice on this planet, especially when dealing with American security. Another problem in the crime-and-punishment equation is how one deals with the horrific events committed by mentally deranged people. Here, punishment of the instigator would be meaningless and victims were simply a casualty of "fate."

If punishment cannot discourage future criminal acts, what other options do we have? Gun violence in Japan, Korea, and China is very rare. In Korea, the number of gun-related deaths hovers around 30 a year. According to the Gun Violence Archive, a US-based survey group that collects information on gun violence, that figure was 15,612 in the United States in 2017. On average, 42 people were killed each day. Compare that to the total of 44 gun-related deaths in Japan, over the past eight years. Our society owes potential assailants, who are mentally unstable, adequate medical facilities and preventive measures. Even for this particular category of people, gun control would certainly help reduce the risk of gun violence. Maybe it is warranted to revisit the Second Amendment of the United States Constitution. It was adopted in 1791, over 200 years ago, as part of the Bill of Rights. As to domestic violence, there appears to be little a third party can do for prevention. Once again, having a gun around the house would not help prevent a serious outcome arising from a domestic dispute.

In the case of an international skirmish or a full-blown war, there should be numerous forewarnings. They can be from intelligence agents or from the observations of the population involved. I even argue that children's play can be a tell-tale sign of what is coming, however innocent they may appear. See Entry #40, "A kid's fight becomes an adult's fight." On December 7, 1941, the Imperial Japanese Navy Air Service attacked Pearl Harbor without any warning, or a declaration of war. It was thus a bona fide war crime, and directly led America into entering the Second World War. The above proverb also seems to support such an occasion also. (12/03/18)

The butcher looks down on ordinary people.
저는 잘난 백정으로 알고 남은 헌 정승으로 안다.

[155]

During the Joseon Dynasty of Korea (1392 - 1897), one's social status was more or less predetermined by family pedigree. I suspect that many societies on this planet, during that period of time, must have maintained similar caste systems, as they didn't know any better. Of course, the aristocratic ruling class never wanted to change what had served them well for many generations. They might have mumbled, "Why rock the boat?" In Joseon, at the top of the four-tiered pyramid, was the so-called *yang-ban* (양반) class. See more in Entry #37, "No need to envy others; you take care of yourself." They were the descendants of the *yang-ban* family, usually working in an important government position: often working inside the king's palace subsequent to passing a nation-wide test called the *gwa-go* (과거). They were scholars of Confucianism. The second tier consisted of medical professionals with good standing, government bureaucrats, and diplomats. They were subordinates to the *yang-ban*; however, the enjoyed a certain level of perks. Sons of the *yang-ban* father and his second or third wife could apply for gwa-go, but their promotions were limited by a ceiling.

The majority of the Koreans belonged to the third class, called *sang-min* (상민). Here, the farmer outnumbered fisherman, blacksmith, businessman, and others with some responsibility in government, such as foot-soldiers. In general, they had limited education, little opportunity for betterment in life, obligations to government directives, including taxes, and usually relied on the judgments of local landlords, or *yang-ban*, whenever disputes occurred among them. Compared with today's standard of living, they certainly suffered hardship in almost every aspect of their daily lives.

At the bottom of the totem pole was the *cheon-min* (천민), or the class of servants. They were the ones who lived at the margin of social acceptability, although their jobs were essential for the rest of society. Belonging to this category were people involved in the entertainment business such as clowns, tightrope walkers, comedian, lady fortune-tellers known as *moo-dang* (무당), geisha at a tavern or fancy restaurant, and so and so forth. In less than a century, entertainers have leaped in social status, from the bottom to the top, as we all see how K-pops have become the idols of the younger Korean generation. One of the *cheon-min* class, the subject of the above proverb, was the butcher and slaughterer, or *baik-jeong* (백정). An elder female in most households could take care of small animals such as chickens, but cows were slaughtered by professional *baik-jeong*. Once again, it was a job we all needed and yet they were treated poorly. This may well have been because handling the bloody business involving flesh and killing animals was something no noble man would aspire for.

So, the proverb goes on saying that this butcher, with such a lowly social status, thinks and behaves as if he is some kind of hot shot, looking down on all other people around him. He treats others, according to the direct translation, as if they were all old, and hence useless bureaucrats, from some obscure local government. His assertive self-esteem may have come from the realization that he was one of the most indispensable professionals. His arrogant behavior may simply reflect his personality of self-importance and possibly self-indulgence. Finally, he is keenly aware that others do not know how to use a knife as well as he does. He epitomizes those people who, without knowing on which rung they stand on the social ladder, butt into any and every issue presented before *sang-min*.

The 1956 epic film drama, *Giant*, develops a story of how a young man of humble origins (played by James Dean) becomes filthy rich after he strikes oil on a small patch of land, on a huge Texas ranch owned by Mr. Benedict (by Rock Hudson). James Dean had been infatuated with the young wife of Rock Hudson (Elizabeth Taylor). With the sudden, newfound wealth, he also dates the much younger daughter of Hudson and Taylor. The above proverb depicts the plot of *Giant* quite well, through the life of the character played by James Dean. (12/08/18)

A tiger appears at the fun party in a valley.
재미나는 골에 범 난다.

[156]

I interpret the above proverb in a most liberal manner, so my version may sound far different from others. The direct translation could be: "A tiger will show up in the valley of fun." The appearance of a tiger means that bad things can happen. The tiger, an animal that Koreans considered most ferocious, would not only ruin a party but also devour the drunken and rowdy people at the party. Why "valley, or *gol* (골)?" I cannot tell for sure but it sounds reasonable that both party-goers and tigers roam around a valley. Where else they encounter each other? Although people can have fun at a party without alcoholic beverage, I am assuming that the party referred to here is with people enjoying drinks.

It is said that drinking alcohol usually follows three distinct stages. In the first stage, "man drinks drink". This is a warm-up phase, or a starting point. Everyone has a different style of drinking, especially in terms of speed, with or without a full stomach, straight from the bottle or diluted as a cocktail, not to mention favorites like scotch versus beer, etc. The outcome is the same though. It is the blood level of ethyl alcohol, or ethanol, that counts. See more in Entry #96, "Drinking can be medicinal with proper consumption, but ·····." It is followed by a stage of "drink drinks drink". At this stage, people really enjoy themselves and each other's company. They become uninhibited, boisterous, merry, generous in promise, easily but genuinely laughing, and bantering with patting on each other's shoulders; in short, everything moves along in quite an agreeable manner. Ideally, people should stop at this stage and go home, still in a good mood and shape. But, we seldom stop short when having fun, and move onto the third and final phase. In this last stage, "drink drinks man". Drink becomes the master. This is when and where all hell breaks loose and anything unexpected can really happen. There can be quarrels, fist fights, or more serious consequences like outright murder, and even sexual assault. That is to say, the tiger finally appears.

Anything that gives us pleasure or alleviates physical pain is a potential cause of addiction. Sometimes, they are associated with our instinctive desires such as food, sex, or even work. They can also be purely recreational, such as smoking, gambling, drugs, alcohol, etc. Either way, an addict succumbs to instant gratification while paying dearly with long-term deleterious effects, such as liver cirrhosis from chronic alcoholism. When one tries to quit the addiction, the accompanying withdrawal symptoms retaliate mercilessly. People experience headaches when they skip a daily dose of coffee. When people try to quit smoking, they suffer from such symptoms as restlessness and frustration. In some serious instances of opioid addiction, a tragedy like suicide can strike the person who has been struggling. Appearance of a tiger, in the above proverb, may well describe such a tragic end.

Nothing, regardless of whether it is good or bad, lasts forever on this planet. Time will eventually settle all matters. That much we all agree, while the above proverb deals with how and why it all ends. It says a party in a valley, with too much fun, is inevitably visited by an uninvited tiger. One of the greatest empires of all time, the Roman Empire, had enjoyed prosperity for centuries, often in a most hedonistic manner as depicted by wall paintings that survived the volcanic eruption of Mount Vesuvius in AD 79. The Tang dynasty of China (AD 618 - 907) was a golden era of Chinese civilization. Their influence upon Korean culture is felt even nowadays. The period was famous for leisure activity, and lavish feasts, especially for those in the upper classes. It was during this time drinking wine was ingrained into the Chinese culture. In the end, its demise was accelerated by revolts by warlords, and factional strives among government officials along with eunuchs of the palace yielding enormous power.

Excess of anything seems to bring the "tiger" at the end. As history attests to again and again, any decadent society falls miserably at the end, just like a fun party gone too far. Why am I now feeling that this country, or for that matter the current Korea, has begun the descending path to the end? (12/11/18)

Use krill for baiting carp.
새우 미끼로 잉어를 낚는다.

[157]

"Buy low sell high" is a mantra in business, especially in stock trading. Essentially, everyone wants a maximum return out of a minimal investment. Had you purchased 10 shares of Apple Incorporated during their initial public offering in December, 1980, it would have cost you a total of $220. Since then, the stock split four times and the current price is hovering around $180. This would make your initial investment worth about $100,000 now. According to an inflation calculator, the $220 you invested in 1980 is valued at $673 today. Although it has taken almost 40 years, it is an excellent return. If you are not excessively greedy, you should be happy with this outcome. The increase in value amounts to approximately 150-fold. Not bad at all.

A krill is one of the smallest, and thus possibly the cheapest, aquatic animals on Earth. If you used a krill as bait and caught a carp, or better yet, an expensive koi fish, you have done very well. Heck, you could become fisherman of the year. Koi, about three feet on average, were derived from carp, and can live for 100 to 200 years. Keeping koi in a home pond is an expensive, world-wide hobby, especially in Japan. Because of their longevity, owners change from one generation to another. They can be purchased in pet shops, but high-quality ones are usually from special dealers. On average, one will cost between $1,000 and $2,000. Some can be as expensive as $5,000. So, as an advice in business, the above proverb is indeed a wise one: try to invest as little as you can, for a maximum payback. The gain you realize is absolutely yours to keep, after you pay taxes, that is. If you can, repeat the feat again and again. You will become a wealthy man in no time. Unless what you have done is illegal, no one will accuse you of any wrongdoing. All is fair and square. Everybody should be happy with the outcome.

However, the proverb seems to beg for another line of interpretation. It is quite often said that a good thing will not come about without sincere effort on your part. They even say, "easy come, easy go," implying that anything you achieved with little investment will not last long. It can, instead, ruin your life. Until one Jack Whittaker won the Powerball in 2002, he had been just a small-time construction contractor in a town called Hurricane, West Virginia. The lottery jackpot was worthy of $314 million, and he netted $113 million after taxes. He said he would live as if nothing had changed and turned to God for guidance. His initial magnanimity, such as generous donations to local churches and helping needy neighbors, was soon replaced with frequent visits to strip joints and gambling parlors, in the company of comely women, often in a stupor from heavy drinking. He used to dote heavily on his granddaughter, Brandi. Soon, Brandi carried a large sum of cash and ran around in a fancy sport car, with some questionable friends. She was eventually found dead with a drug overdose at the tender age of 18. Jack's wife of more than 40 years, now estranged, changed the lock of their home. The Jack Whittaker Foundation ceased to exist just one year later, and so was all of his charity work. Several weeks after Brandi's funeral, he still did not blame the Powerball for his family's downfall.

Entry # 5, "Would a pagoda of labor crumble soon?" emphasized the diligent and honest work ethic as a prerequisite to long-lasting success on a solid foundation. However one may look at it, there is no other shortcut. Respect the law of probability before you waste your money in buying lottery tickets. Squelch the daydream of what you could do with the millions of dollars from the lottery. Go out to the real world and work hard with your own blood, sweat and tears, for what you are after. How ridiculous would it look if one tries to catch a big koi fish with this tiny krill as bait? If one displays such a nonsensical attempt, people would say in mockery that this man behaves like he's "fishing for carp using a krill as bait." He will become a big-time laughing-stock. Even if he wins a lottery, there will not be any admiration for his effort (if buying a ticket at a nearby dime store can be called effort). Much envy and jealousy will follow him until he makes a mistake. His misfortune will be met with contempt on one hand and celebrations from his acquaintances on the other hand. (12/16/18)

Are siblings treasure or foe?
형제는 잘 두면 보배, 못 두면 원수.

[158]

My parents raised a total of eight children, four of each gender, and me at the bottom of the pecking order. I learned that one of my older sisters passed away before I was born and thus I don't have any memory of her. Soon, my parents adopted our long-time housemaid so that the total number remained the same. As I was the last one in the family, my oldest sister married before I was born, and her first child is of my age. As we grew up, mother used to tell us that we were all brothers and sisters, but it would stay that way only if everybody was equally successful (or equally unsuccessful). Her "lecture" was primarily for my older siblings, but I overheard it quite often. Each time, I was not sure what she meant, but gradually I saw the true element and wisdom behind her observation.

Here, I would like to present three cases relevant to the above proverb, all real stories from this current world. First is the case where siblings truly serve as a treasure to one another. Most of these stories are heartwarming. The second case would be somewhat the opposite where they cannot quarrel more often and nastier enough. When they meet as grownups, they maintain a required level of civility for a while, but soon underlying tension rears its ugly head, palpable to everyone around. Unfortunately, this case may be more common than one would assume. Finally, the third case is where siblings conspire in criminal acts with synergy. It is rare and hard to believe, but it can happen.

One of my favorite professional golfers, Jordan Spieth, was the world number one golfer at the age of 22, and since then has received well-deserved fame. His sister Elli, who is seven years younger, appears to be autistic. Apparently, Ellie has been the star and center of the Spieth family and everyone in the family thinks that "no matter what's going on, it's all about her. At least Ellie thinks that," according to their mother. Ellie's life has been described as "a happy dance interrupted by cloudbursts." Her big brother, Jordan, kept referring to her as "the best thing that ever happened to and the most special part of our family." When Jordan was praised for his affection-filled relationship with Ellie, he replied, "You might as well praise a man for not robbing a bank." He said he could not comprehend how his life would turn out without Ellie in it. They are precious treasures to each other.

Examples are aplenty of siblings that do not get along well. Just look around your own family and relatives. As one becomes quite rich and famous, while the other siblings aren't, there tends to be some level of resentment, often publicly displayed. It can be just a bellyache, as we saw in Entry #111, "My cousin buys land, I have bellyache." Why one cannot celebrate together the success of another sibling is difficult to understand, but it seems quite common. The stories we hear or read are in the realm of gossip and unpleasant to repeat. Why would one want to see the underside of a family? The Green Bay Packers' quarterback, Aaron Rodgers, seemed to have some nasty rift with his brother Jordan Rodgers. I do not know what caused the falling-out between the two celebrities, but I do not want to know. Just as Meghan Markle was about to marry Prince Harry and become Duchess of Sussex, her own sister, Samantha Markle, lashed out with a nasty claim that Meghan did not care for her or her father. It was and still is an embarrassing display of ugly sibling relationships. Here, both the Rodgers and the Markles showed what the above proverb is warning: siblings can be bitter enemies to each other.

The Menendez brothers, Lyle born in 1968 and Erik in 1970, were raised by wealthy parents in Beverly Hills, California. On the evening of August 20, 1989, they killed their parents with a shotgun fired at point-blank range, apparently out of greed. During the trial in 1993, which was televised live, the brothers claimed that they were sexually abused by their father. In the end, the Menendez brothers each received life sentences without parole. Here, the brothers served as pure evil to each other.

As to my own siblings, all but two have departed this world. As I look back, we all had average lives and were quite even in success and failure. We might not have been treasure with one another and thus we must belong to a fourth category. (12/18/18)

All is well in fine clothes.
못 입어 잘난 놈 없고, 잘 입어 못난 놈 없다.

[159]

"Nobody looks good in poor clothes, everyone looks great in fine clothes," is what the above proverb is saying. Nice clothes may not make an ugly man look handsome all of a sudden, but poor clothes can certainly make a person in good standing look awful. As far as I can remember, while I was growing up in Korea, we were very keen about what we wore every day. This was troublesome for people with a so-so income. As luck or curse would have it, unlike here with only two seasons, four distinct seasons, each exactly three months long, are bestowed upon the Korean peninsula. It costs a lot of money to have clothes in concert with each season, year after year following the current fashion. Women tend to pay more attention to their appearance, and they would spend a significant portion of their income on clothes and accessories such as shoes and handbags. This trend among women in Korea, at least while I was living there, might have reflected the lack of anything else they could display in promoting themselves. Nowadays, I understand, it also involves cosmetic surgery.

In the animal kingdom, males generally develop more elaborate sexual ornaments than females. Scientists attribute this finding to the fact that semen is "cheaper" to produce than eggs and that competition among males for mating is much steeper than among females. In humans, ladies dress up, while men tend to downplay or show more subtleties in clothes. If we consider clothing and cosmetics nothing but an ornament for luring opposite sex, why are women different from females in other animal species? Since when has this custom prevailed? After all, the male-to-female ratio is close to unity anyway, so statistically speaking, there should not be any real make-or-break competition. The following speculation may explain the situation.

A bachelorette donned in fancy dress and expensive jewelry would undoubtedly discourage poor, or ugly bachelors, from approaching her with any romantic intention? "How dare you ask me for a date? I am the oldest daughter of so-and-so chaebol family!" Some cold glances would complete the job of fending off any unwanted proposals. Here, the lady holds the upper hand. She may think she can pick and choose whom she wants to date and eventually marry, so long as neither party really hates the other. Most likely, the man would be a handsome and wealthy man. After marriage, they would enjoy as much prosperity as their parents did. Their offspring, when they grow up, will be just like their parents, albeit in a new social setting. In due time, these children will marry with another wealthy family, and so on. In a nutshell, this must be why people demonstrate their own prowess in social status and wealth, along with a set of fancy dresses. You may call this explanation my version of Fisherian Runaway.

So, what constitutes "fine" clothes? Some generalizations can be made for the answer. First and foremost, the cloth must fit well to your body. Color and cut should also serve you well. In my opinion, heavy people should wear more roomy clothes, perhaps one size bigger. It may be a psychological craving for a petite body, but there are too many heavy ladies wearing tight pants. Note that tightly fit clothing seems to emphasize the body size. Secondly, one should be careful in trying to be cute or fun. It can easily backfire, especially if you don't have confidence in what you are wearing. For men, the fit across the shoulder is a major factor in the fit of a jacket. A man should wear the clothes, not the other way around, meaning it is his way of wearing that impresses people, not necessarily the price. Needless to say, what you are wearing should always be clean and pressed.

For a perfect fit, you have to have your clothes custom-tailored, ideally in fine fabric. It would cost a fortune to acquire proper shoes, ties, watches, etc. for men; and jewelry, purses, shoes, and of course dresses, for women. This is how people would assess your worth, when you meet a person for the first time. Finally, but most importantly, we have to feel comfortable with what we are wearing. Indeed, fine clothes to me are the clothes people feel comfortable in wearing. See also Entry #32, "New clothes are okay, but old friends are better." (12/20/18)

Plant an acorn to build a pavilion.
솔 심어 정자 짓는다.

[160]

After pollination, female pine cones mature in two to three years. They open up to release seeds usually in dry weather so that their winged seeds can travel a far distance. Once germinated on the forest floor, they begin to grow in earnest. Pine trees can grow as tall as 150 feet (45 m) and survive 100 to 1,000 years. The felled trees are sawed into timber, which in turn is used in building a gazebo, if not a huge pavilion. From planting seeds to building a gazebo is a long path of many years. This proverb says that one can plant pine seeds so that later he can harvest the tree to build a gazebo. The original version speaks of planting cones, not seeds, but it will not change the message to be conveyed. I also changed "pine cone" to "acorn," as I thought oak is perhaps a more desirable wood than pine for building a structure. This proverb simply says that a certain project or job can take a long time to complete.

Time is a measure used in recording events, determining the intervals between them, or calculating rates of changing quantities. It is the fourth dimension, after length, area, and volume. See also Entry #88, "No warrior can stop aging." A clock defines a temporal point within a day, while a calendar is used for those points longer than a day. The base unit of time is the second, which is defined, in the International System of Units, as a certain number of oscillations of a caesium atom, 9,192,631,770 to be exact. In a solar calendar, the time required for the earth to rotate around the sun defines one year. Our ancestors used to follow the lunar calendar. Here, one month was defined as the period needed for the moon to completely go around the earth. Although officially banned in 1896, by then King Go-jeong of the Joseon Dynasty, such festive events as Korean Thanksgiving Day (추석) and New Year's Day (새해), have still been observed on the lunar calendar.

If I recall, the birthdays of my parents were also celebrated according to the lunar calendar. Because we could see the size and shape of the moon every night (as long as there were no clouds, that is), one could easily guess the calendar date. The sundial can tell us the time of day, but not the date of the month. I suppose discussing pros versus cons involved in lunar versus solar calendar are all pointless nowadays, as one can just look at their mobile phone. Since there is no constant difference in days between the solar and lunar calendars, it is not as simple as one may assume to use both calendars. Fortunately, Korean calendars usually show the dates of both systems.

Just like anything else in our practical world, time is also a relative concept. Our life span of, say 80 years, is significantly longer than that of mayflies, but can be much shorter than that of old trees. A millisecond is a huge quantity in terms of distance of traveling light, but practically nothing at all for a slow moving turtle on the land. We thought that the Korean War, from 1950 to 1953, was lasting forever while we were right in the middle of the war itself. Now, we have a war in Afghanistan that has been going on and on, for 17 years, and still counting.

In what instances would the above proverb be relevant? A young couple has just had their first baby. They may immediately fantasize that the baby will grow up to become a physician, a lawyer, or extremely wealthy so that he or she can take care of them when they are old. It will take a while for the parents to see the outcome of their fantasies, but not as much time as building a pavilion from pine seeds. The planet earth exists as a very small and tiny speckle at this indistinct corner of the universe. And yet, we fight tooth and nail for whatever excuse we can find; like justice, religion, freedom, peace, etc. Expecting a war-free planet may take much longer than the time involved in acorn-to-pavilion, or perhaps it will never happen. The construction of the Roman Catholic Church in Barcelona, Spain, Basilica and the Expiatory Church of the Holy Family, began in 1882, almost 186 years ago. It was famously designed by Antoni Gaudi (1852 - 1926) but is still being constructed. We do not know when the basilica will be completed But it may depend on funding as it is completely based on donation and entrance fees to the unfinished structure. (01/02/19)

Looking for one particular Kim in Seoul.
서울 가서 김서방 찾기

[161]

Seoul is a crowded and noisy metropolitan city with heavy traffic and all. Kim is one of the most popular family names in Korea, which is followed by Lee, Choi, Park, etc. The above expression is concerned with finding a certain Mr. Kim in Seoul without any further information except that the person who is looking for this particular Kim would recognize him, if they accidentally come across each other on a street. He may not even know Kim's first name. Why this man is looking for this particular Kim is beside the point. So, finding this man in Seoul likens to "looking for a needle in a hay stack." An interesting word in the above phrase is *seo-bang* (서방). Its direct translation could be "mister," perhaps originating from a "young husband" in an established family. When spoken, it can be "sir" or even "master." Taken together with the last name, it becomes *Kim seo-bang* (김서방), or Mr. Kim. The word is also used in jest, carrying a nuance of rascal, charlatan, black sheep, bum, and so on and so forth. It's not the most flattering designation of a young man, but it is not terribly depreciating either. If your last name is Allen, a Korean friend of yours may call you "Allen *seo-bang*," with a wink in the eye.

What could be the occasion that deserves the above expression? A police detective arriving at a murder scene for the first time would be clueless of the crime. He could well be the person looking for a Kim *seo-bang* on a busy street in Seoul. His first task will be collecting as much background information of the victim as he can get. If the victim is a pretty young girl as in many TV dramas, the detective would be looking into her social network, including her current as well as past boyfriends. Building a most likely case would be next. It is the natural deduction in logic. He will build "a case" based on what is known to be true. Any seemingly trivial, single deviation from the facts, would rule out his most plausible supposition, however appealing and plausible it might be to him. Discarding a particular suspicion can be rather painful, but he must. It is thus natural for the detective to go over the evidence against his suspicion, again and again to establish that the evidence is indeed flawless.

In a new scientific research project, one of the most important steps is when the investigator develops a hypothesis. It is a critical step because once a narrowly-defined, well-stated hypothesis is developed, designing experiments becomes an easy task. In reality, scientists do not develop a hypothesis that cannot be tested experimentally. There is always a facilitated exchange of ideas between developing a hypothesis and designing experiment. Just like a gumshoe, a scientist should discard his hypothesis if he finds a report in the literature that disputes his own thinking. He may try that particular experiment himself to make sure the negative experimental evidence is indeed correct and sound. He may even call up the authors of the report, to go over how tight their experiment was. It is hardly a fishing expedition like a man embarking on a journey to Seoul to find one Kim.

What is most maddening and frustrating in our society right now is the pathetic health care system. It is expensive and ineffective. It is not that the politicians are clueless; in fact, they seem to have too many plans. Instead of "finding one Kim in Seoul," the U.S. Congress and the Whitehouse should adopt a top-down approach, starting with a guiding principle of universal coverage and applying the principles of reverse engineering, or "hierarchical reductionism," to ask ourselves what the next level down would be. This modus operandi should lead us eventually to the universal coverage without any undue, external influence such as the one from insurance industry.

One day, many years ago, I was quoting the old expression of finding a needle in a haystack in my weekly lab meeting. One PhD student blurted out, "Oh, it would be easy to find the needle. All we need is a powerful magnet!" I didn't appreciate this smart comment from this smart aleck back then, but now we are so desperate to find a solution to the current dilemma on health care, I am more than willing to invite a powerful magnet, alias "political will" from all parties involved. (01/05/19)

Hunger is the best appetizer.
시장이 반찬이다.

[162]

What could be a better appetizer than an empty stomach? And so it goes. In the same token, people with full stomachs tend to complain about the food offered to them. During the historic event, known as *imjin-oeran* 임진왜란 (1592 - 1598), the Joseon Dynasty of Korea was invaded by a Japanese insurgent. It was a pretty nasty battle that lasted several years and left many legendary war stories. King Seon-Jo (선조) had to flee from Han-yang (한양), the capital at that time, which was later renamed as Seoul. While the King and his entourage were in the countryside, the meals were prepared with whatever they could find locally. One time, the King was served a platter of broiled, small freshwater, hornpout catfish. The original name of this fish was *meggy* (메기). It was so delicious, the King directed his men to call it silverfish (은어). It was quite an honor for the fish, which the King didn't even know existed, to be bestowed upon with such a flattering new name. Years later, after *imjin-oeran* was over, the King remembered how delicious the meal of broiled silverfish was and thus ordered his chef to present the same dish. Now, in his palace and among many other exotic dishes, the fish wasn't as tasty as he once remembered. Disappointed, the King then told his chef and everyone else, to go back to calling it *meggy* or *doru-meggy* (도루메기). Here, *doru* stands for "going back to." To this day, the fish name remains *doru-meggy* (도루메기) although the taste remains the same.

The people who seem to have everything, including time and money to spend, are easily distracted and become indignant by what appears to be minor or trivial inconveniences. To them, every job, or meal they request, takes too long to be ready, and is seldom satisfactory to their standard. The same dish, prepared exactly the same way, does not taste any good any more. The whining and tantrums are endless, and make the people on the receiving end miserable to no end, especially when their complaints are baseless. In many Korean fables, the servant-turned-master often retaliates against his former master in justifiable vengeance. As a child reader, I was quite satisfied with this turn of the story, firmly believing that the bad former master well deserved such condemnation. That was justice in my world then. My rallying behind the weak still remains the same when I watch sport competitions. Now, I see why the team I root for always loses. But, the most important lesson I learned from those stories was that you can somehow overcome the adversities and become a legitimate "master" in the happy ending.

In a nut shell, we were learning that any hardship we went through, when we were young, was a blessing in the long run. It helps one build character with resilience and endurance. When my parents said something along this line of logic, it sounded like an excuse for the poor conditions in which we lived. As I look back now, their stories were not just an excuse or justification on their part. Like the legendary Japanese sword makers, banging red-hot metal on an anvil all day long, I was well disciplined as a child, and grew up as strong as the Japanese sword. To be fair, it was not really their design to give us well-planned hardship: we were simply poor, but we somehow survived alright in the end.

My mother was a seamstress and a very good one if I may say so. During the Korean War, her work was the major source of income in our family. She would buy in the black market, at very reasonable prices, the children's clothes donated by American families, which were sent to Korean children deprived by the War. After removing stitches and she ironed them to maximize the size of the fabric, and re-tailored them to fit Korean children. She then brought them back to the market retail stores. As the last child in the family, for many hours I sat across from her, watching her running an old Singer sewing machine. I often held the original clothes from the U.S. at the seam, so that she could go through it with a sharp razor blade to open up the fabric. Her stories, always in a casual and non-charlatan voice, not only diminished the hardship that I recognize now but also made me and all seven siblings grow up strong without much whining. (01/14/19)

When a hen crows, the whole household collapses.
암탉이 울면 집안이 망한다.

[163]

It is the rooster, not the hen, who crows. A standard interpretation of this proverb would be: "If a woman makes noise, as if she were the head of the family, the household would collapse under a universal condemnation of denouncement." In this day and age, this is certainly an outdated and outrageous assertion. That being said, two tracks of thought come to my mind for the theme of this essay. First, we should not judge the past with contemporary rules and criteria. Secondly, as I sit back and regurgitate the message hidden herein, I have to admit that there is some element of wisdom to learn from this proverb beyond the apparent gender-based bias.

A bronze statue of a Confederate soldier holding a gun used to stand in a small park, just off Franklin Street in downtown Chapel Hill, North Carolina. I had lived there for almost 30 years with many fond memories. The statue was erected in 1913 with funds raised largely by the United Daughters of the Confederacy. Since 1954, the statue has been known as "Silent Sam." The monument was to honor the students of the University of North Carolina who participated in the American Civil War (1861 - 1865), "in answer to the call of their country," but never came back home alive. A part of the dedication speech, by then Governor Locke Craig, reads as follows:

> *This statue is a monument to their chivalry and devotion. It is an epic poem in bronze·····.. The soul of the beholder will determine the revelation of its meaning. It will remind you and those who come after you of the boys who left these peaceful classic shades for the hardships of armies at the front, for the fierce carnage of titanic battles, for suffering, and for death. We unveil and*

dedicate this monument today, as a covenant that we, too, will do our task with fidelity and courage.

On August 20, 2018, just a few months after we moved to the West, we learned, via national TV news, that the statue was toppled by protesters. To them, "Silent Sam" had been an epitome of racial slavery, anti-black racism, and white supremacy that persisted in the state as well as the country. A similar accusation had also prevailed earlier in protesting the Charlottesville statues of Robert E. Lee and Stonewall Jackson. In the midst of what appeared to be nothing but a hysterical outcry, what we will eventually lose forever is the physical reminders of what this country used to be. In 1861, when the University kids volunteered for the War, they were heroes. Now that a long time passed from their defeat, they became a symbol of the public enemy. Does time define patriotism?

Throughout history, women were treated as if they were secondary citizens. See, for example, Entry #146, "Thread follows the needle." Why do we have boy sopranos in Anglican churches? The Hindu temples in India ban women from entering. Roman Catholic churches have no female priests. When was women's suffrage was granted? Why gender-based bias in pay? Wherever one may look, there seems to be discriminations against woman. Why? Was it something to do with Eve in the "original sin?" If so, why has the same attitude been prevailing in non-Christian cultures, as illustrated by the above Korean proverb?

In any organization there exists a tectonic structure, one of whom is a spokesperson. They represent the organization, with a consistent message to be delivered to the public. In last week's National Football League playoff game, the Chicago Bears lost to the Philadelphia Eagles, by just one point. The Bears could have won the game, had their kicker been successful with a field goal in the final few seconds. The kicker was then going around telling everyone within an earshot, how sad and disappointed he was. It is the coach's job to wrap up the losing season in a press conference, not an individual player's. The kicker was "the hen that crowed," here. I doubt, very much, he will be back on the team next season. (01/16/19)

Liquor brings jaundice, wealth brings a corrupt mind.
술은 얼굴을 누르게 하고, 황금은 마음을 검게 한다.

[164]

The red blood cell, or erythrocyte in biology jargon, circulates in the blood stream for about 120 days. The membrane of senescent cells become rigid and spouts out hemoglobin as it breaks open. This iron-carrying protein eventually degrades to bilirubin and other products. Bilirubin, when existing at high levels in the blood stream, results in a yellowish or greenish pigmentation in the skin: this is jaundice. When the function of the liver to metabolize and excrete bilirubin is compromised, as often to be the case with people with alcoholic liver disease, jaundice appears. The term "alcoholic liver disease" includes fatty liver, alcoholic hepatitis, and chronic hepatitis with liver fibrosis, or cirrhosis. Here, the main culprit is, of course, the overconsumption of alcoholic beverages on a regular basis. Our Korean ancestors, albeit ill-equipped with current medical knowledge, were able to associate a yellow face with excessive alcohol consumption. The first half, of the above proverb, deals with this physiological phenomenon, the cause of which can be diagnosed with ease.

Tangent to the above, the blood concentration of hemoglobin, from dead red cells, is relatively constant in the blood. Glycated hemoglobin, known as A1C, is formed upon biochemical reaction of hemoglobin with glucose. As glucose levels increase, as in the case of diabetic patients, the A1C level increases proportionally. This is the physiological basis of using A1C as a measure of average glucose level, for the preceding three to four months. Remember that the red cell survives about four months.

The second part of the proverb says, "Gold makes our mind dark." By "gold," it means money. "Dark" may not be the best word in the context, so I replaced it with "corrupt." This part is concerned with the intangible mental attitude towards money. We have come across such negative connotation of money quite often: see, for instance, Entry #7, "Seas can be filled, but not greed." As to money, there are two aspects to discuss: making and spending. See, for instance, Entry #112, "Brag about spending, not making money." Money is nice to have since "a golden key will open most locks." The process of making money, however, often entails corruption. Any harsh environment, with cut-throat competition for survival, may bring about a maligned justification of means for garnering wealth. One marginally acceptable practice may beget another, which is slightly worse on moral and ethical scales. If a man can make a living this way, why can't I? Such negative feedback will gradually lower the standard of what are acceptable ways of making money.

An ideal job would not only provide an income for maintaining a comfortable family life, but also allow plenty of personal time for self-reflection of one's own life. How a person balances these two seemingly opposing factors, time-consuming process of making money and desire for free time for meditation, would depend on the individual. Medical professionals such as physicians and pharmacists command good salaries, as well as respect from society, but at what cost? Training to become a professional and practicing after schooling seems to consume every moment of their lives. How many hours did physicians sleep when they were interns and residents? How long is the lunch break for a pharmacist? Is the more than six-figure salary worthy of your time?

We especially admire those professionals who sacrifice their valuable time and monetary compensation for the original purpose of their profession. "Doctors without Borders" comes to my mind. Based on a true store, the 2016 French film *The Innocents*, introduces a young female medical student, who works with doctors at the French Red Cross in Russian-occupied Poland, just after World War II. She comes across a group of nuns who were repeatedly raped by Russian soldiers and began to give birth in their convent nearly simultaneously. Her humanitarian efforts, to deliver the babies within the rigid Catholic tradition firmly held by Mother Superior, were extraordinarily heroic, and well rewarded in a happy, if not completely satisfactory, ending. I doubt that money could corrupt those folks, since the purpose of their lives was well aligned with their profession. They are the happy people. (01/19/19)

Encountering a foe on a log bridge.
원수는 외나무 다리에서 만난다.

[165]

Not a long time ago, just a few weeks after we moved to this town, my wife and I went to a huge oriental supermarket. Our cart was overflowing with stuff and there was a long queue at the cash register. I noticed, just behind us, a Japanese lady with only a few items in her hand, so we let her go first, a gesture anyone under such a situation would do. While she was going through her purse for payment, I whispered to my wife in Korean, "How come this old lady didn't even say thank-you." The lady immediately turned around and told us in no uncertain terms, "I did!" I had to apologize hurriedly for my mistake. My wife, the one who is always proper and without undue errors, later scolded me with a dirty look, "Be careful from now on! Not only was she not Japanese, but you also spoke too loud." It was a double whammy alright, from two women within a few-minute span. Pushing the cart full of groceries to an adjacent food mart, I ordered a few simple Korean dishes. This "Japanese-turned-Korean" lady was working at this joint. She greeted us with an inscrutable smile. When my wife picked up our orders, she said, "I am sure the lady spat on your dish." A triple whammy: It was not my day.

This sort of somewhat awkward encounter of negative nuance is depicted by the above proverb. Just yesterday, I saw a cartoon in a weekly magazine, showing a couple on a suspension bridge, hung high above a deep gorge. On the opposite side of this foot bridge, another couple was approaching. The lady whispers to her husband, "Oh, God, it's Alvin and Meg: pretend we don't notice them." How could you not notice them approaching you on a five-foot wide suspension bridge?

When you come across a person whom you really do not care to see, the greeting and follow-up chat seem to last a very long time, while you want to get out of the situation as quickly as you can. Often saying, "Listen, I've got to run. I have to⋯" Such particular occasions are registered in your memory. That may be the reason why you feel that you keep seeing them so often. It is no doubt an inconvenient and irritating encounter. Later, you may describe the occasion to friends by saying, "Guess who I saw at the grocery store the other day? ⋯. She seems to have gained a lot of weight but ⋯." This is always a nice way to start gossip.

Log rolling is one of the most interesting, at least to me, lumberjack sporting events. Here, two men, standing on a log floating on water, face each other several feet away, and try to get the other guy to fall into the water by rolling the log with their feet. You either follow the rapidly rolling log with your feet, while maintaining your balance, or try to reverse the rotation abruptly so that your opponent falls into the water. There are only two outcomes: either you or the other man will fall into the water and get wet. It is a matter of "live" or "die." If you meet an enemy in your life on a narrow bridge, say, the man who sexually assaulted your younger sister, you will fight till the end for the sake of justice and the honor of your family. If you do not like such a chance event as meeting your enemy on a log bridge, you can always arrange a duel with either swords or pistols.

What happens if and when, you alone meet your enemy on a narrow bridge well above a deep gorge. Three possibilities exist. One is fighting till the end. A second possibility is that one of you turns around and flees the scene or takes a plunge into the deep water of the gorge. The third possible scenario would be reconciliation. Since no one else is around, neither of you will have anyone to appeal your case to. Since both parties involved clearly understand what the cause of enmity is, both know who is really at fault. And that man, the defender, has everything to lose, since the other man, the plaintiff, has a good reason to fight. Justice is on his side and he has all the incentive he needs. Even if he dies, he will be remembered as a hero. The bad guy may flee from the encounter especially if he is the weaker of the two. In the final analysis, this is the man who will ask for forgiveness and mercy. So, it can be concluded that a chance encounter with an enemy on a log bridge can be a good thing, albeit often awkward. Such thing needs to happen more often in our lives. (01/21/19)

The head of a rooster is preferred to the tail of a dragon.
용 꼬리 보다 닭 머리가 낫다.

[166]

The head and the throat of a rooster are decorated with an impressive array of what is collectively known as caruncles in a brilliant red color and unique shape. Together with slender but muscular shoulders, caruncles make a chicken a magnificent rooster. And just listen to its loud crow at the dawn of a new morning with its head held high, as if he defies the depth of the sky and owns the whole world. Now let us imagine a legendary creature, the dragon. In Western cultures, a dragon is presented as a monster to be defeated by a fearless nobleman, who rescues a beautiful princess from its clutches. In Eastern cultures, dragons enjoy a much more positive reputation: they are the symbol of the Emperor in old China and are a truly awesome creature. Its head is most fearsome, with fire-breathing nostrils and mouth. However, their main body is serpent-like, albeit with legs and often with wings, and the end fades to a meager thin tail. So, the above proverb asks which you would prefer becoming, the head of a small rooster or the tail of an almighty dragon? It says, "the head," hands down, like "Better be the head of a dog than the tail of a lion," or "Better be first in a village than second at Rome." Why is it then that everyone says the head of a small animal is better than the tail of an awesome creature?

My professional career of 40 years consisted of two parts: 17 years at a large American corporation as a research scientist and 23 years in a research-strong academia. Unlike the current employment systems prevailing in American corporates, in the 1970s and 80s we still had a very good package of health insurance and pension system. Additionally, the pay scale was largely based on one's merit, not to mention annual bonuses. Working for a big pharmaceutical firm was thus all about comfortable living and a secure retirement in the future. On paper there was little to complain about, especially for a person without a family to support: that was me. Its downside was a seemingly slow contribution of my research efforts to the overall direction of the company. I was anxious to see that my efforts did indeed make a significant dent in the progress of a given developmental project. More often than not, a given project was abruptly abandoned for reasons other than scientific or technical feasibility. Unless you are part of the management, such decisions were beyond your jurisdiction. I did not complain, since the company had to make profit and I had faith in the management.

One of the interns I had in the lab, a chemistry-majoring senior from a local college, entered a dentistry program at a state university after he obtained his Bachelor's degree. Four years later, after he passed the board exam, he opened his own practice and in due time became one of the most successful dentists in town. I was his first patient and have been monitoring his life closely. Everyday he made every decision himself. He opened a bar as well as a restaurant. He sold them with sizeable profits. He was a football player at the college and has now become a head coach of a varsity rugby team, just for the sake of fun. He bought some land in Utah as he enjoys skiing, and his family is now living on a lake because they all enjoy water-skiing. They also bought a small farm and are raising horses because they all enjoy horseback riding and their daughters show horses. Self-employment with financial means offers such an interesting life with many options.

In the mean time I left the industry job for a position at a state university and stayed there for 23 years. The job consisted of teaching, research, and service. Service is the least difficult to carry out. As a "good citizen" you just participate in various committees. Although I was a course coordinator of classes, in both professional and graduate programs and hence carried much responsibility, they were all team-taught courses. The school provided teaching assistants and adequate support staff but more importantly, I enjoyed teaching. Research was a different beast. It is the professor's responsibility to bring in grants. With "your" big grants, you maintain a big lab and various research projects. From this perspective, the position in academia is very much like the self-employed. As I see it now, the transition from the industry to academia was from the tail of a dragon to the head of a rooster. (01/22/19)

Flapping wings under a blanket.
이불 속에서 활개 친다.

[167]

A few boastful gestures from animal and man may include: the flapping wings of an eagle against a strong wind on a high treetop; the roar of a lion with formidable muscle and penetrating stares; or a barrel-chested man with swaggering gait. These are all reflections of self-confidence, to a point of cockiness, shown to others. They are all handy-dandy when other people accept them as such. But, in the real world, there are people who behave as if they are really somebody to be reckoned with, only under certain circumstances. A man who is a tyrant to his family could shrink in a heartbeat to a docile coward when someone yells at him. There are lowly managers, who are unduly stringent to their subordinates, but do not or cannot have any eye-to-eye contact with their own bosses.

We see the spineless cabinet members surrounding the current president, almost every day on TV. If what they say and how they behave are truly what they believe in, their brains must be examined to confirm their bean-size. They are indeed true believers of something horrible and terrible. In my mind, they are as bad and idiotic as their boss. If, on the other hand, what they say and how they behave are just empty words to appease their boss, they are simply too cowardly to say what they truly believe. They are cheaters, in a truest sense, as they lie to themselves. Either way, they are pathetic. They should hide themselves in a dark and protected place, like the corner of a "cupboard" or under a blanket where they can be self-righteous and quite vocal. Better yet, they should just sleep quietly under the blanket: no flapping wings on national TV, please.

Immigrants to this country, who did not speaker English, invariably suffer from communication problems from day one and everyday day for the rest of their lives. Many years later, as their English skills improve, their understanding of the new "home" brings about much new joy and hope. And yet, they are keenly aware that the English they speak still carries accents from their mother tongue and that their knowledge of culture and history of this new country is not as good as their own children, who are born and educated here. The feeling of inadequacy from these handicaps hardly finds an outlet for its catharsis. For Korean immigrants who used to be "somebody" back in Korea, this situation is particularly frustrating. Becoming "nobody" can be maddening, especially if their current job here is not what their past education or social status deems warranted. Imagine an immigrant, with a much sought-after university degree back in Korea, now running a motel, dry cleaner, corner grocery store, restaurant, liquor store, etc. Every night, they may ask themselves how their life turned into what it is now.

The major social network among Korean immigrants in this country is via churches. There are so many churches, Protestant as well as Roman Catholic, that you would think that three Koreans must have started four churches. It serves two purposes: praying in peace and socializing afterward. Typically, there will be a special Sunday brunch after service, say, commemorating the Korean independence day. In a separate recreation room, usually in the church basement, every household is to come with a favorite dish or two, spreading them out over a long, cloth-covered table. This is the same ritual as what American churches do, say, on the Fourth of July. Volunteers, wearing disposal plastic gloves, scoop out steamed rice onto a disposal plate along with kimchi and various condiments. Lively conversation is in contrast to the previously solemn prayer service in the nave.

More often than not, this is the place where those feelings of inadequacy turn into "bragging" of their expertise almost on any topic. Now they can blurt out their opinions and feelings in the language they can really commend. Their "know-it-all" in this setting is not so different from "flapping wings under a blanket." Inevitably, there will be many different opinions on any given topic. Even different factions are born, based on the different opinions on how to run their church. A group of people of like mind then spins off to form a new church, not far from their original location. It may explain why we have so many Korean churches in the U.S. (01/23/19)

Earth hardens after rain.
비온 뒤에 땅이 굳어진다.

[168]

Chemistry-wise, the red color of clay soil is from water-insoluble iron oxide, the same substance found in common rust. When dispersed in a large volume of water, the clay produces a very fine, or colloidal, suspension with an extremely slow sedimentation rate. This is the main soil in Southeastern States such as the Carolinas, Georgia, Alabama, and Mississippi. When wet clay swells, but shrinks when dry. On a rainy day the ground of clay forms and maintains muddy puddles with a slippery surface. Your shoes slip and slide underfoot. As the sun comes out the ground becomes firm, and eventually shows cracks as we see in dried lake bottoms or water-drained rice fields. When fired in a kiln, as one makes pottery or bricks, permanent changes occur. These naturally occurring phenomena involving soil, rain, and drought, are the subject of the proverb.

One easy way to digest this old saying is by considering rain as the adverse events one may go through in his or her life. "Hardening earth" could be a happy outcome, as we have seen in Entries #25, "Strong plants in strong winds," and #81, "Big trees face more wind." Mental suffering renders us acutely aware of happiness, the poverty we have gone through defines wealth in a new perspective, and the hardships we experienced during war makes us desire peace. Additionally, a suppressed population continuously longs for freedom, the sick wish for being healthy again, a well-disciplined team usually wins a sports competition, the continuous hammering of hot-iron makes the final sword stronger, and rainy days make us pray for sunny days. If the reflection of adversity is a necessary requirement, as in "Failure is a mother of success," another Korean proverb goes so far as to say that "A dragon is born in a small stream." This is to mean that a successful man can come from a poor family, telling any youth that they can become whatever they want, so long as they put in the necessary effort. "Rain," in this context, is thus "paying your dues" for a successful and happy ending.

Helen Keller's story may well illustrate the case. At 19 months old, Helen Keller (1880 - 1968) became deaf and blind and yet she overcame many obstacles, and lived a most fulfilling life "at sea in a dense fog." With her teacher, Anne Sullivan, she had become an internationally renowned author, social activist, lecturer, and has remained one of the most inspiring people on this planet. She, for instance, campaigned for women's suffrage and labor rights. Her autobiography, *The Story of My Life,* was a best seller, and was also adapted to film: *The Miracle Worker.* Her birthday is still commemorated and several museums are dedicated in her honor.

A parallel story can be developed at a community level as well as a national level. The French Revolution of the late 18th century is arguably one of the most significant events in modern history. It abolished a monarchy and established a new republic with liberal democracies. We cannot visualize such a revolution by a happy population. The original pacifist constitution of Japan, which was somewhat modified in recent years, was from the devastating consequences of World War II. In Korea, democracy has been slow in coming, often with violence. It has been a continuum of "growing pains." Just to name a few, we've gone through freedom from Japanese occupation in 1945, the Korean War in 1950, the 4 · 19 Revolution led by student and labor groups in 1960, the 5 · 16 Military Coup in 1961, the 5 · 18 Kwangju Massacre in 1980; and most recently, the impeachment of President Park Geun-Hye in 2017. Through them all, Koreans have somehow managed to come out stronger and healthier.

Some people are not elastic or resilient enough to bounce back from an adversity. It can instead result in an irreversible change to a damaged state. A man rejected by a woman may commit suicide, or become misogynistic for the rest of his life. A boy, who was sexually molested, may later become a sexual predator himself. Opposite to Helen Keller would be physically handicapped people who have prematurely given up any hope and their futures too. They are the fire-cured clay. (01/26/19)

A tree with deep roots survives drought.
뿌리 깊은 나무는 가뭄 안 탄다.

[169]

There are two major functions of the roots of a tree. First, without roots the tree topples. That is, roots allow the tree to anchor firmly into the ground. Secondly, roots gather water as well as nutrients from the soil for the tree to survive. Roots are so important that an embryonic root is the first development during germination. The size and shape of a root depends, of course, on the environment and plant type. In dry land such as Arizona, roots tend to be very deep, sometimes as deep as 200 feet (60 m), although many exist close to the soil surface where nutrients and aeration are more favorable for growth. All things being equal though, trees that have neglected to develop deep roots, because of generous surroundings, will have a more difficult time when an unexpected dry spell persists. That is essentially what the above proverb is telling us.

An obvious interpretation of this proverb would be that a person who is always prepared, and thus ready for the worst situation possible, can survive much better than lazy freeloaders when a hard time comes. In one of Aesop's fables, a cold and hungry grasshopper begs for food from an ant, during the winter time. In the summer, the ant worked very hard to prepare for the winter, while the grasshopper was enjoying an easy life. In the end, the ant never showed any mercy or compassion, and left the grasshopper to his own devices. Needless to say, the story presents a moral lesson on the virtue of hard work and planning for the future. Here, the merit of preparedness is clearly illustrated by the reference to the miserable state the grasshopper was facing in the harsh winter.

In many instances, however, we do not know exactly how our preparation would save us from a disaster because a tragic accident seldom happens in a predictable manner. Only when a disaster strikes us, do we start to regret that we should have done this or that. It is like missing the sun only during a long, rainy, monsoon season. By its own nature, all successful maintenance work functions as such. This may sound like a sentence from *Catch 22* by Joseph Heller: "What did not happen did not happen, we will never know what we would never know." In an analogy, predicting and proving experimentally, a negative outcome in scientific research, can serve only for the purpose of eliminating, but seldom establishing, a certain hypothesis. This is because the absence of something on a given occasion can cover a wide range of possible reasons. The opposite of A > B is A < B, but what about the chance of A being equal to B?

There has been an ongoing discussion as to what type of educational and training background, given comparable work experiences, is desired for a person who will become the head of a research and development division of a corporation. As an example, in the auto industry, would a PhD in engineering be better suited than a person with an advanced degree in some sort of business administration? A similar question in academia would be, "Which is easier, for a biology-major to learn more about basic science such as chemistry, or for a physic-major to understand biology?" Based on my own experience, the answer is always the latter. Just like a thermodynamic law, knowledge is accumulated on a sound foundation of basic science, then disseminated to other fields of "applied" science. This conclusion may explain the popularity of Master of Business Administration (MBA) programs for scientists who are groomed for a company's executive.

In reality, those scientists with a shaky foundation tend to look around some alternative positions, including opportunities in management. If they are not well rooted in one area of basic science, how can we assure ourselves that they will be a good manager? As implied above, it is far easier for a scientist to learn administration, than a man with MBA degree to learn, say, chemistry or engineering. In recent years, wizards from the financial industry with venture capitals, start to effectively run tech startups without much knowledge on what the company attempts to develop. They are the ones who do not have deep roots and are trying to survive in a drought. This may explain the high failure rate of startups in recent years. (01/31/19)

A woman's curse brings June frost.
여자가 한을 품으면, 오뉴월에도 서리가 내린다.

[170]

Here, the key Korean word is *haan* (한). It defies a simple translation. My Korean-English dictionary defines the noun as grudge, rancor, spite, hatred, regret, lamentation, etc. To me, it often represents a desperate and long-lasting emotion of resentment, impotence, and sadness. It all depends on the context. If you happen to have insulted, offended, slighted, or upset a woman, and the recipient of your assault is fully aware that your wrongdoing was intentional, you had better watch out, as her revenge can be swift as well as severe. Her *haan* may not directly result in physical harm to you, although it is quite feasible if and when she acts in hysteria. More often, she is physically weaker than a man but could be more cunning or clever. She will curse under her breath for the rest of her life. Her sole reason for existence could well be based on the wish for your demise. Her sense of happiness will be inversely proportional to yours: she will be ecstatic when you fail, awful when you succeed. Her mental power is so chilly, it may bring about a frost in May and June, 오뉴월 (*o-new-wal*).

In what I understand as traditional New Orleans voodoo practice, the victimized woman may stick needles repeatedly into a voodoo doll, really an effigy made of rags, in the hope of inflicting maximum pain on the cursed, while muttering nasty spells. Her concentrated sixth sense may be transmitted through a magical, ethereal medium, to the accused, causing a physical pain. You'll never know what hit you. I suppose she can hire a professional practitioner, a "mambo," or female priest, for a formal ritual. If I were her, I would do it myself for fully releasing my *haan*. As a side note, a mambo would be equivalent to 무당, or *moo-dang*, in a traditional Korean superstition: see Entry #36. "An unlucky man breaks his nose even when falling backward."

Both a mambo and *moo-dang* are female. So is the subject of the above proverb. This begs the question as to why women appear more often in such a context with a somewhat negative connotation. Earlier, I alluded to it possibly being that women are physically weaker and perhaps less bold than men. But we cannot and should not generalize that way. Recall the incident that happened during the summer of 1993, in Virginia. One Lorena Bobbitt cut off her husband's penis with a knife, while John Bobbitt was sleeping after an unwanted sex, "rape" according to her claim. The root of their problem stemmed from what she told the arresting police: "He always have [sic] orgasm and he doesn't wait for me ever to have orgasm. He's selfish." I received the following note from one of our secretaries in our department, when I was working for a pharmaceutical firm many years ago. Apparently someone belittled their work. She wrote: secretaries "lift buildings and walk under them, kick locomotives off the tracks, catch speeding bullets in teeth and eat them, freeze water with single glance. THEY ARE GOD."

The crux of the above proverb is that one should not have an enemy, or commit any wrongful act on others, in his lifetime. Avoid such situations at all cost, if manageable. Enemies are a perpetual spy. Their curse can be quite devastating. True or not, examine these cases: the so-called Kennedy curse involves; the assassination of John F. Kennedy (1963), that of Senator Robert Kennedy (1968), the Chappaquiddick incident involving Ted Kennedy (1969), and the untimely death of John F. Kennedy Jr. in a plane crash (1999). In the World Series, the Curse of the Bambino reined the Boston Red Sox for 86 years, and the Curse of the Billy Goat deprived the Chicago Cubs of the World Series for 71 years. The 112-carat Hope Diamond was passed to King Louis XVI of France, where it was worn by Princess de Lamballie and Marie Antoinette. Both were beheaded, along with the King during the French Revolution.

The literature of adages on wisdom involving feud is definitely favorable for the victim side. Would it ever be possible to have a life without any enemies? Living a life with hatred cannot be a peaceful life. The British poet and writer, Hannah More (1745 - 1833) goes so far as to say, "If I wished to punish an enemy, I would make him hate somebody." On the other hand, the ancient Latin writer, Publilius Syrus (85 - 43 BC), who was famous for his witty remarks, said "It is a miserable lot to be without an enemy." (02/06/19)

When dirt poor, burglary looks appealing.
가난하면 마음에 도둑이 든다.

[171]

When one is very hungry without any money, he or she may try to find a way to steal the loaf of bread displayed in a bakery window or cast an envious look at those inside a restaurant. As the winter comes along, a homeless man starts to look for a shelter as well as warm clothes. When you are in physical pain, you would like to see a physician, but then you realize you do not have any medical insurance. As the head of a family, you wish you could send your children to school with their stomachs full. These desires are as natural as looking for water when you are thirsty and so essential that they appear to be a human right given to everyone when they were born. So, the above proverb says that to a poor man, without any means for a meal, burglary appears as if it is the only viable option.

According to the ancient Chinese philosopher Mencius, or 맹자 (372 - 289 BC), we are all born with goodness in each of us. This is somewhat different from the Christian view of "Original Sin," which we are born with, as heralded by Saint Augustine (354 - 430). If we follow Mencius, people become corrupt as they fall to external temptations, blaming nurture. Even if one is born innocent, lives a most honest life, and works as diligently as he knows how, there still exists a distinct possibility that "fate" will have him or her live a poor life. In movies like *Forrest Gump* or in stories like Aesop's fables, innocent people can enjoy a happy life, but these are exceptions we find in fiction. The reality is that there are many desperate people out in this world, for no fault of their own, continuously struggling. How can we then condemn their thoughts of stealing a loaf of bread or warm clothes?

I am not exactly the most vocal champion of the poor, always vaguely believing that our taxes would be wisely allocated for such social issues as poverty by our ever-compassionate president and congress. However, as I begin to pay attention to how our government uses our tax money, I often find that their guiding principle is so devoid of humanity that I become dumbfounded. A few cases on this point are presented here. Why does anyone object the Affordable Care Act (ACA), aiming for health coverage of as many Americans as possible? How can one justify the family separation at the Mexican-American border? Why do we spend over $900 million dollars to buy a single B-2 Bomber? And a $5 billion for a part of the idiotic wall along the southern border? In November last year, the citizens of Utah voted for the expansion of Medicaid benefits under ACA, for additional tens of thousands of vulnerable people. Against this voter's will, however, the Republican state legislature modified it to a new bill that allows fewer people to benefit. The governor signed it off in the blink of an eye. There was some monetary justification from the Republican plan, but this was like stealing money from the poor. A Korean expression of such a miserly act is "Go ahead. Take out and eat the liver of a flea!" How could they be so cruel? Speaking of *The Merchant of Venice*⋯.

Four of us used to get together at 5:30 AM to prepare breakfast for the hungry folks every other Friday. Being in the South, the main entry was grits, my specialty. To 40 gallons of boiling water, I would add a dozen Styrofoam cups of grits, one at a time, while continuously stirring. Without stirring, the whole thing gets lumpy that one cannot easily break up later. In this critical step, I would ask a helper who had a long-neck, stainless-steel ladle. We all wore heavy-duty gloves, lest our hands got burnt. If available, I put in a generous amount of butter. On average, we fed about 50 men. I did this volunteer work for more than a decade, and got to know the "clients" quite well. They were not necessarily homeless; in fact, most of them had jobs: hospital orderly, road crew, construction worker, building custodian, yard worker, etc. I always celebrated myself, when a familiar face did not show up, as I assumed he had moved on to a better life. Afterward, as I was driving to work, I often felt frustration as well as anger with the disparity of living conditions that I witnessed. Admittedly, at some unconscious level, I must also have felt gratitude as I did not have to contemplate stealing bread. (02/12/19)

Neither a flamingo nor a phoenix.
학도 아니고 봉도 아니다.

[172]

If you keep changing plans while your project is still under way, you may end up with something no one, including yourself, can recognize. If you ask for directions from every yo-yo on the street and follow all of their directions, you will be completely lost. You could have been much better off, had you stayed at one place and waited for a policeman or a mail delivery man. If you try too hard to please everybody, you may soon be surrounded by a maddening crowd. They will ask you to make up your mind, once and for all, demanding you choose one side or another. In art, music, and literature, if you mimic other's work, you will be severely frowned upon. People will accuse you of plagiarism, big time. Of course you get inspired by masterpieces of the past, but you will need to thoroughly digest them first, before processing them as your own. Finally, you are to keep only one faith at a given time, whatever it might be: "Blessed is the man who trusts in the Lord, whose hope is the Lord." (Jeremiah 17: 7).

The sort of wishy-washy behaviors, which the above paragraph discourages, will result in an outcome that is neither this nor that. Let's say you are drawing a flamingo but with the legendary phoenix in mind. The final picture will show neither *haak* (학; flamingo) nor *bong* (봉; phoenix). This is the crux of the above proverb.

The building that the Korean National Assembly is currently using was completed in 1975, six years after groundbreaking. It all had happened several years since I had left the country. Thus, I am not familiar with how it was conceived and built. But one thing is clear: it is one of the strangest and ugliest, if I may add, buildings I have ever come across in my long life. I am glad I live far away from that darn thing so that I don't have to see it as often as Korean citizens do. This square structure, made in what appears to be plain grey concrete, actually granite, and surrounded by 24 tall columns, each 33 m or 107 feet tall. Together, they appear to be supporting a rather non-descriptive flat roof. The columns were to mimic those in the main pavilion on a pond in Gyungbok Palace, Seoul. The building walls, with many small windows, recede from these pillars. One side has a front entrance door, as if it were an afterthought. All said, however mundane and characterless the building may look, it is still tolerable to most people, including myself especially when I am in a good mood, as it seems to function adequately as an assembly hall.

But, wait! Out of nowhere, they put a huge dome on the roof: it is more than one third the length of the building, 64 m, or 210 feet, in diameter at the bottom, to be exact, and it is as tall as half the building. It is so big, the aerial picture I saw makes me feel like the whole structure could collapse at any moment because of its weight. As far as I can tell, it looks like a humongous cyst or benign tumor, growing with no obvious function, but just to irritate onlookers. Although Bundestag in Berlin also has a similar dome on the roof, it does not look as odd as the one on this Korean Parliament Building.

A blueprint for a new assembly hall was in place as early as 1960. However, the military coup in 1961 cancelled the plan once and for all. It took the Third Republic of Korea more than a decade to come up with the current building. Rumor has it that the dome was added later, by the government powers-that-be, most likely then President, J.H. Park. These ill-advised politicians pressured the architects involved to add the dome. As far as they were concerned, the blue print must have been like a drawing in the sand. The ultimate outcome was that the building is now neither this nor that, or "neither flamingo nor phoenix." As it turns out, I am not the only one who complains about the aesthetics of the building. Many citizens, who have any artistic opinion, have criticized the appearance of the building. In addition, people who work there do not like the functional aspects of the interior either. Whenever parliamentary members bring forth the subject of remodeling and ask for necessary funding, most citizens have offered rather cynical comments, a typical one being, "What's the point of facelift? The folks inside the building are the ones we have to replace." (02/19/19)

Listen to the elder, rice cake will come to you.
어른 말을 들으면 자다가도 떡이 생긴다.

[173]

There are several letters in English words that Koreans cannot pronounce easily: for example, the Pf in *Pfizer* comes to my mind. In general, *f, h, p,* and their combinations, can give puzzling times to a novice in English. To the surprise of English speakers, distinguishing between *l* and *r* is not straightforward either. Then of course there is *th*, which often sounds like *s, t,* or even *d* to Korean ears. It is not that we have a pronunciation inability embedded in our DNA: just look at those second-generation Korean youths. It is because we do not have alphabets or characters that produce a given sound such as the *pf* in Pfizer. Somebody in the Ministry of Education should look into this problem, at least in pronouncing those English words frequently used among Koreans, and invent a few new alphabets.

Conversely, I have noticed that Americans have a hard time making certain sounds commonly found in the Korean language. Many Korean consonants, such as ㅂ (b), ㅈ (j or z), ㄷ (d), ㄱ (g), and ㅅ (s) can be doubled up to designate "hard" sounds: for example, ㅆ sounds similar to s in sun, and ㅃ in *bag*. However, English speakers will find it difficult to pronounce other double consonants such as ㄸ in 떡 (cake). It is patently not *d* as in *dog*. Koreans, kindly offer a new set of English characters for these hard sounds: for instance, *ss* for sun, and *dd* for 떡. What then is *ddeok*, or rice cake (떡), and what does it have to do with listening to the elder?

A variety of cakes are broadly called *ddeok*, or 떡. A typical cake in this country would be made with some kind of flour, plus sugar, milk, egg, butter, etc. In contrast, traditional Korean rice cakes may contain chestnut, red bean, date, persimmon, peach, etc., and be fixed with oil, if needed. Rice cakes are an excellent treat, or reward, for good deeds done by children, neighbors, friends, and even strangers. Rice cakes are in demand for many occasions, including weddings, birthday celebrations, sacrificial rites, and social gatherings. They are so highly desired that we used to say there was another stomach specifically for the *ddeok*. The above proverb is telling young people that there will be *ddeok* when they wake up from a sleep, if they had just listened to the advice from an elder like their parents or teachers. Speaking of reward, nothing can be better for young Koreans than a piece of rice cake.

Why are listening to older people and following their advice important enough that you get free rice cake? You are not required to do anything. In fact, the proverb says you could go back to sleep after listening to them, and you would still get the cake. When we are infants, it is a matter of survival to have parental protection and guidance. As we go through puberty, blind obedience begins to lose its grip. Although we would have liked to agree with our parents as much as we could, by then, we also developed our own opinions on many subject matters. From there on, listening to others gradually becomes more difficult. We develop a tendency to talk back to them, with our own thoughts.

"Listening to elders" implies "following their advice," which is the difficult part for most young listeners. Here, a person has two choices. Talk back and argue in the hope that you can win over the elders so that you no longer have to listen to their "nagging." Although you may feel good about the hard-earned victory, it will leave the advisor in a sour mood: your father may even disown you in the heat of an argument. You may shout "Okay" to him and storm out of the room and never look back. The second choice is to just pretend you agree with the advisor, but do whatever you think is right, without letting the advisor know what you are actually doing: a sort of cheating. In the 1971 musical film, *Fiddler on the Roof,* the father of five daughters got himself trapped in an argument between daughters, and sided with one. Another daughter developed a counter argument, and the father agreed with her as well. The third one insisted that he make up his mind, one way or another. The father then said, "Yes, you are absolutely right." It's hard to imagine a 65-year old woman arguing with her 90-year old mother. The younger old lady would keep saying, "Yes, mother, you are absolutely right." (02/21/19)

My ax injures my foot.
믿는 도끼에 발등 찍힌다.

[174]

Imagine this scenario: I have been using this ax for many years without any incidents. Then, one day this beloved and trusted ax betrays me and hits my own foot. The physical pain and medical treatment of the injury is one thing, but the feeling of betrayal is another matter to deal with. It is similar to the old saying, "In trust is treason." We all have experienced some level of sadness or disappointment, when our trust betrays us in broad daylight. It can be a minor event, like losing a bet on a horse race to the most devastating feeling of loss when a husband discovers the infidelity of his wife. In between, we have the following. A friend spills the beans on you in spite of an earlier promise not to. The price of the stock you just purchased keeps sliding downward. You don't see the question in the exam that your teacher promised to include. The picture of a dish on a menu has nothing to do with its taste. A movie is not as good as the book. You lose a friend after he fails to return the money you lent him. A man loses his job at the company he had been working at for years with the utmost loyalty. What would you feel if your own dog of many years bites you out of the blue?

One day in my youth, friends and I were very much surprised to learn that a young lady, walking in front of us, was the daughter of a prominent politician we all supported. We thought she was gorgeous. Most of us drooled and uttered "really?" We hurriedly walked faster and passed her to see what she looked like from the side and front. We all ended up crying in disappointment, "Oh, no!"

The man whom the nation elected to president has quickly lost the public trust through his constant lies. Your car mechanic claims to have just found another serious problem with your car. Insurance companies, who deal with seniors, attempt to take advantage of the Medicare program. Physicians are ordering unnecessary tests. The list of disappointment and betrayal can go on for a while.

The Education of Little Tree by Forrest Carter is one of the most favorite books I've ever read. Published in 1977, the book was widely reviewed and universally acclaimed: "… a memorable reading experience… poignant, happy, warm, and filled with love and respect for the Indian way of life." It is the (true) story of a Cherokee Indian boy named *Little Tree*, who grew up during the 1930s with his grandparents, from whom he learned almost everything in his life. The book provides a fresh and alternative perspective for the materialistic world we live in now. I liked the book so much, I bought several copies for my friends. In 1991, the book was chosen as book-of-the-year, by the American Booksellers Association and was the best seller in *the New York Times*. Then, the book was quickly proven to be a literary hoax, done by Asa Earl Carter, a KKK member from Alabama. He was a rabid segregationist and the author of George Wallace's infamous war cry, "Segregation today! Segregation tomorrow! Segregation forever!"

Betrayal does not always end up with disappointment. One spring day in 2000, I wrote the following as part of a letter to a newspaper in the small town of Laurinburg, North Carolina. Like many other people at that time, we believed in the error-free GPS-guided map. It betrayed me and my wife.

At the national collegiate equestrian competition at St. Andrews College my wife and I were to meet a family of our old friend from Michigan. Their daughter Katie was competing and we haven't seen them for a few years. We drove down south from Chapel Hill. As we were close to Laurinburg, the GPS led us to an open field with lots of cows but not a single horse. Only two cars had passed while we were sitting there for several minutes pondering if we would after all miss Katie's performance. A truck stopped asking us if all is OK. We were certainly not okay then and there. Upon hearing our misfortune, this middle aged couple drove several miles out of their way, I am sure, all the way to the St. Andrew College. You do have wonderful people in this town. (02/23/19)

Oil droplets on water.
물 위에 뜬 기름과 같다.

[175]

This phrase presents an analogy of a simple natural phenomenon to human interactions. The expression can be best used as in "It was like an oil droplet floating on the water." There are many liquids that are completely miscible with water at all proportions: ethanol and acetone would be good examples. We also have liquids that are only partially miscible with water. Some triglycerides belong to this category. In this case, one can think of mutual solubility: how much water is dissolved in the liquid and how much of the liquid is in the water. If the liquid it is hydrophobic, then we can say that both the liquid and water like themselves more than the other.

In human terms, it is very natural for a group of people, say Koreans, to like themselves because they share almost identical cultural heritage, language, political history, religion, etc. "Birds of a feather flock together," so to speak, and there is nothing wrong with that. Indeed, we find various expatriates form their own communities in major cities of this country, like the Korean Culture Center and Korean Town in Las Vegas. A dangerous time is when this cohesiveness is translated directly to exclude others. The worse scenario is the despicable attempt to employ xenophobia to unify a population, or nation. We all know what Adolf Hitler did with the Jewish people in the early 1940s. The current U.S. President, Donald Trump, appears to adopt such a strategy to advance his own political gain. He declares, without any hint of shame, that everybody else is bad except the Americans. By Americans, he implies white Americans. He justifies a wall on the southern border so we can keep Latin Americans away. Most pathetic is the fact that a significant number of Americans have bought into this scam that is essentially based on hatred and separation, rather than love and accommodation.

Surface tension arises at the interface between two immiscible liquids: in the case of the above proverb, it would be the contact surface of an oil droplet facing the water underneath. It is the net result of the fact that each liquid attracts its own, while "disliking" the adjacent foreign liquid and thus trying to minimize the area of exposure to each other. Both sides of two groups of people may indeed feel "apprehension" or "tension," when they meet for the first time. What are the natural examples of this phenomenon? An object made of materials denser than water can still float on water, so long as the water surface is calm and the surface of the object is rather non-wettable. Bottom sides of our nose are always a good source of body oil. If you rub a paper clip on your nose and gently place it on top of water, it will stay floating. Likewise, the repulsive forces derived from surface tension also allow some insects to walk on water. Give due credit to the hydrophobic surface of their feet. Of course, if the subject is very heavy, it will sink. After all, it is the difference in density that will ultimately determine if an object will float or sink. Since water is most dense at 4° C or 39° F, the above experiment is best run at this cold temperature.

Detergents are a class of compounds that structurally consist of a hydrophilic head and lipophilic tail. That is, they are amphiphilic. These molecules align themselves at the oil-water interface, with the tail embedded in the oil phase and the head buried in the water, thereby reducing the surface tension. Introverts, like myself, suffer from anxiety whenever they are invited to a big party with many people they have not met before. My wife and I would often prefer being alone, at an ill-lighted corner of the room, nursing stale beer all night. We are like oil droplets on water. If no one disturbs us, we will probably remain isolated from the rest of the party and can "survive" the night. Then, a friend comes along and drags me out to the main crowd. These mutual friends are the surfactant. Once the tension is reduced, we find ourselves enjoying the party quite well.

Tension between nations is best reduced by diplomacy based on a genuine understanding of cultural differences: it is neither military force nor forced religious invasion. It is called sunshine diplomacy via cultural exchange. It is the surfactant working among the nations. (02/25/19)

Rest when you fall.
넘어진 김에 쉬어 간다.

[176]

When you get tripped up from something on the ground and fall down after backpacking all day in a rugged terrain, you might have been simply tired and you did not know it. Maybe it is then a good time to take a break and rejuvenate yourself for the next leg of hiking. Now that you are on the ground, you may as well have some snacks and take a nap. This is what the above proverb is saying. When you stumble on a busy street in broad daylight, you are probably upset as much from your own silly misstep as embarrassed by others passing by. To demonstrate your vitality, you may quickly bounce back up to start renewed, vigorously walking, if not running. If you are an old man like me, you may faint and fall down again from postural hypotension. Why do I bother how others perceive me anyway?

When you face an adversity, try to use the occasion for your advantage instead of lamenting your misfortune. The two-letter Chinese word for crisis, *wee-gey* (위기), is composed of two seemingly contradicting meanings: danger and opportunity. A wise man would know how to turn the misfortune into an opportunity for gain. There is always a positive aspect of a tragedy, if you look into it very hard. As they say, "every cloud has a silver lining," and it is you who ought to find it. In the end, this is what distinguishes wise and resilient men from the weak. I believe that this is the essential message of the above proverb, somewhat analogous to: "Failure is the mother of success."

When your child spills milk, yelling is what we do automatically, especially when we are in a hurry or in a bad mood. But can't you consider it an opportunity to clean the floor, a project you have been postponing for a while? When the market is down, isn't it the best time to buy stocks? If the price hits the bottom, it can only go up, right? While preparing a meal, you added sugar rather than salt, owing to some distractions. As it turned out, the dish didn't taste bad at all. Your football team is trailing their opponent in the first half. During the halftime break, you devise a new game plan to have a comeback win. Strategic retreat on the battle field is common for winning the war. Legend has it that Socrates would not have become a great philosopher if he didn't have his 'bad' wife. Many words starting with "re" implies improvement from a prior dormant, possibly adverse state: retool, recreate, refresh, realign, reclaim, rejuvenate, regurgitate, renew, reunite, etc.

The imperialism of the 20th century backed by military power climaxed with the end of the World War II in August, 1945, when Japan surrendered. Earlier, in February, the future of Korea had already been discussed among Franklin D. Roosevelt, Winston Churchill, and Joseph Stalin, at the Yalta Conference. It was essentially the U.S. that proposed the Korean peninsula be divided into two territories with a clean cut along the 38th parallel. The Soviet and U.S. would occupy the North and South Korea Peninsula, respectively. As we look back at this particular point in history, there was no rhyme or reason to divide one set of people into two. In the south, the Republic of Korea was born in August, 1948, while the north was run by a dictator, the grand father of Kim Jung-un. The Korean War began in 1950, in an effort by North Korea for forceful reunification. During the War, North Korea owed much their war effort to China, while South Korea to the U.S.

Since then, every effort for peaceful re-unification by Koreans has been consistently met with "disapprovals" from China or the U.S. We, the Korean people, have been merely "lapdogs" of these powerful nations, always trying to read the political minds of our "masters." "Pathetic" would be a good word to describe the current political dilemma we have been facing. This is a world where nobody trusts anyone, a dog-eat-dog world. At this very moment, Kim Jung-un and Trump are meeting in Hanoi to stabilize the Peninsula. Its outcome will ultimately affect the effort of South Korean President Moon's push for reunification. We have been down for more than 70 years since the birth of the Republic. We have rested long enough. It is time to get up and dispel all influences from outsiders, including the U.S., China, Russia, and Japan. (02/27/19)

Get the land, then build the house.
터를 잡아야 집을 짓는다.

[177]

Prior to building a house of your own, you will need to have a piece of land first. It is, once again, an obvious statement. Even a child would fully understand and wholeheartedly agree, but still this conveys the importance of proper order in embarking a business or a project. There are many Korean proverbs of such nature. For example, see Entry #31, "Dig one well at a time;" #39, "Stone masons also learn how to blink their eyes first;" #46, "Would the first spoonful of rice satiate?" #47, "Have you ever seen hair without skin?" and #57, "There is always a first step in a long trekking."

In almost anything you do, there is always a proper way to do it. The Korean word for this concept is *hyung-sik* (형식), which can mean: convention, method, form(ality), mode, etc. If you do not practice *hyung-sik* appropriately in a given circumstance, you will be frowned upon or become a public laughing stock.

Here are some *hyung-sik* that I grew up with in Korea. You are to wear a watch only on your left wrist. There is only one proper way to use chopsticks. Up to high school, all students have an almost identical haircut and wear school uniforms. Calisthenics, or any form of physical exercise, has a strict order to follow. There is a certain way of drinking or smoking in front of older people. Clothes are seasonal: you cannot wear shorts on a cold day even if you want to, lest others will think you are weird. In school, the curriculum is not something you can pick and choose: it is God-given. No, home school is not allowed in Korea. You never sleep with your head directed toward the north. You never cut your nails in the morning hours. You never whistle during the night time. Women never, ever, wear men's pants: all women's pants have a slit on the side. Sex is something you talk about only among your friends. Once formed, you are not to change your political alliance. There is a set of gifts you are to offer on given holidays, like dried persimmon during Korean Thanksgiving.

All those procedures in ceremonies, religious or otherwise, at any public gathering are something else all together. Any deviation will entail punishment as well as long-lasting reprimand. If you think that the Japanese tea ceremony is elaborate, witness a Korean formal family gathering for remembering deceased parents and ancestors. The offertory can range from a simple cake and fruits, to a pig's head holding paper money in his mouth, but more importantly, you will have to know in what order to display them on a table. Likewise, you have to master a set of salutations. Some of these *hyung-sik* must be of etiquette or superstition, in origin. No matter, we just follow them without questioning, as they are firmly embedded in our behavior and mind. I suppose such idiosyncrasies must exist in every culture at any point in history, but one cannot identify each oddity as such unless the person is a third party. It would be a matter of curiosity to foreigners, who are visiting Korea for the first time.

Why are we, Koreans, such conformists? A conspiracy theorist may suggest it was all about controlling the next generation of citizens under the name of tradition. I do not have any alternative explanations. This is consistent with my recollection of how passive our education was even at the college level: memorize by heart, not with a questioning brain. Korean kids excel in math on a global level, but yet we do not produce any great pioneering scholars, say, theoretical physicist. What is missing in all these stories is an entropy-driven spontaneity.

Religiously adhering to *hyung-sik* is greatly revered in martial arts. Only a great deal of physical as well as mental practice and training with much *hyung-sik*, can render one to become a Kung Fu grand master. Ordinary, people assume these masters would beat anybody in a fight. In 2017, a social media video went viral, which showed an unknown mixed martial art practitioner, named Xu, knocking down Kung Fu master Wei, in 20 seconds into their match. Here, Wei was summarily defeated by someone who amounts to a good street fighter. (see http://time.com/5448811/mma-kung-fu-xu-xiaodong/). (03/02/2018)

Fish evaded are always bigger than the fish caught.
놓친 고기가 더 크다.

[178]

In my teens, I did fish with this one particular friend of mine, quite often during the summer recess. We usually explored small ponds on the outskirts of Seoul, after getting off the terminal station of street trolleys and walking aimlessly for a while around the rice paddies. We really didn't know where to go, but eventually we would use our intuition and sit down at a pond we found appealing. Our equipment consisted of a hook, sinker, float or buoy, line, and a bamboo rod. Bait was invariably earthworms we, ourselves, dug out of the wet ground. The float was a thin wood piece, about five inches long. It was painted white, but had thin lines across it in different colors. Once we cast the line, all we had to do was watch the float for any movement that might have indicated that a fish was nibbling the bait. On windy days, one could be misled into believing that a fish was biting when it was just a trick of the breeze. Being overanxious would make you do that. When the buoy went down abruptly, it was time to yank the line up quickly, quick enough not to let the fish get away, but not too quick or the fish wouldn't have time to swallow the bait and hook. Timing was everything in this rather patience-testing endeavor. Over-eagerness was the culprit of my dismal track record as an angler.

Once in a long while, one of us would catch a fish. Such was the occasion to wake both of us up with a sudden excitement, from the numbing trance of watching the buoy. It was the eureka moment and the very reason we got addicted to the business of waiting, waiting, and more waiting. Another occasion of higher, but rather disappointing excitement was of course when we lost a fish that we almost caught, sometimes in the air or sometimes just below the water surface. Either way, the silvery underside of a fish reflected day light, while tumbling down back into the pond. It could have been an illusion, but we always swore to each other, that it was a very big fish; "Man, oh man, that was a big one!" On the way back home, I thought about the possibility that the lost fish might not have been that large, but I never admitted it aloud. Such self-reflection renders each angler to accept another fishermen's story with certain skepticism. Since no one asked for proof of our story, we never questioned other's fish stories either. Thus, the legacy of the fisherman's story continues.

Throughout our lives, some things that we could not get, for one reason or another, looms bigger or more significant than what we eventually received. One time, I was "forced" to go out with my wife for clothes shopping. She eventually found a two-piece, rather formal business suit, but procrastinated for a long time, in front of a mirror looking this way and that way. In the end, she decided not to buy it. She thought it was a bit too expensive, and the cut was a bit too revealing for her age. This was in spite of my encouragement, saying something like, "It would be perfect to wear for your presentation at a conference. You really look like a professional, nice color, etc." And even "you look slender." Truth be told, it was part of my ploy to get out of shopping as quickly as possible. At home, all night, she sorely missed the opportunity to purchase the suit. The following morning, she went back to the store, but it was gone. Her disappointment likened to the misery over the lost fish, if not more.

History is full of "what-ifs." At a personal level, one may ask, "What would have happened to my life, had I married the girl I first loved?" What if I had majored in business administration or even become a Buddhist monk? Could I have become a billionaire or a great philosopher? What could have happened to me, had I been much better looking and a few inches taller in my youth? What would I have missed then? What would Korea have become if there had not been a partition on the Korean Peninsula along the 38th parallel north just after the Second World War? In the 7th century, the Silla Dynasty unified the Korean Peninsula after it subjugated Baekje in the West, and Goguryeo in the North. In doing so, Silla lost, to the Tang Dynasty of China, most of the vast Manchurian territory that Goguryeo used to control. This must have been the biggest fish we ever lost in our history: much, much bigger "fish" than the one my friend lost. (03/07/19)

Save a penny, or pun(푼), to lose a fortune?
한 푼 아끼다가 백 냥 잃는다.

[179]

There is a famous axiom we all know by heart: "A penny saved is a penny gained." Then here is another one, from a significantly different perspective: "Trying to save a penny unwisely can lead one to a disaster." The key word here would be "unwisely." If saving is from "cutting corners" or shoddy work, we will pay dearly later on for the short-term gain we may realize now. One of the Korean coins used during late Joseon Dynasty (1392-1897) was the *pun* (푼). It was of the least value and was worth just one hundredth of a *yang* (양) or *nyang* (냥). A literal interpretation of the proverb may be that a fool who tries to save one *pun* could ultimately lose 100 yang. That's exactly 10,000 times more in value, all because he was a short-sighted miser. It is like "To lose the ship for a half penny worth of tar," or "To spoil the girder for a piece of roof tile ("기와 한장 아끼다가 대들보 썩힌다").

Witness the following two accidents that happened in Korea. On October 21, 1994, during the morning rush hour, *Seongsu Daegyo*, one of the major bridges spanning over the Han River in Seoul, collapsed, resulting in 32 deaths and 17 casualties. The bridge, opened in 1979 after two years of construction, was 1.2 km (0.72 mi) long and accommodated four lanes. The accident forced two city mayors to resign in tandem, and triggered a nation-wide inspection of infrastructure. The cave-in was attributed to fraudulent construction and negligent maintenance.

Less than a year later, on June 29, 1995, one of the fancy department stores in Seoul, Sampoong Department Store, collapsed completely in just 20 seconds. Over 500 people were killed and about one thousand were injured. It was one of the biggest man-made disasters since the Republic was born. The building had four floors underground and five stories above the ground. It was completed in 1989, but later expanded in bits and pieces without much scrutiny and tests for safety. The causes of the accident listed a poor blue print, construction, and of course maintenance. Several hours earlier on the same day of the collapse, employees of the store noticed some significant cracks on the wall, but the management apparently decided to fix them while the store was still open.

As introduced earlier in Entry #30, "Salt beside the pot won't change the taste of its contents," a faulty ignition switch, which costs only a few dollars to fix, forced General Motors to pay a hefty penalty of one billion U.S. dollars to the federal government for more than 120 innocent deaths by the summer of 2015. I doubt very much that the mistake was intentionally for saving a few bucks per car, but still, the incident seems to be relevant here. Nonetheless, saving money along with neglect becomes the cause of the unfortunate cases presented above.

Saving for the future, as in retirement, is always encouraged for insuring a comfortable life later on. You surely do not want to be like the grasshopper when the winter comes in Aesop's fable. Likewise, preventive health care yields a big dividend later in life. In many instances, it doesn't even cost a penny. You may not even have to go to the gym. Light exercise every day, proper diet, regular life schedule, and avoiding anything excessive, shouldn't cost any money, but will challenge one's will power. Some zealots save every penny coming their way, just for the sake of saving. We often hear about some millionaires who still travel on a cramped seat in economy class and practice every measure of frugality every day of their life. It is said that Sam Walton (1918 - 1992), the founder of retailers Walmart and Sam's Club, practiced utmost austerity, even when he was considered one of the richest men in this country. That may well be the reason they became rich, as in "A penny saved is a penny gained." I wonder though, why they save every penny if not to spend on a more comfortable life. Have they forgotten about the big picture? Are they hurriedly living from one moment to another without "stopping to smell the roses?" I'd think most of us would be in-between these two extreme cases, saving some here but also spending some over there. (03/12/19)

Straight words from a tilted mouth.
입은 비뚤어져도 말은 바로 해라.

[180]

When you examine your own face carefully in a mirror, you will soon realize that your face is far from being in perfect symmetry: one eye may be slightly bigger than the other, your nose may not run down straight, but curved, and your closed lips may be somewhat tilted. And yet, they all function properly. They can see, hear, and speak. "Three wise monkeys" avoid evils in a passive stand, but the above Korean proverb urges you to speak the truth all the time, even if your mouth may be a bit slanted. Perfectly shaped mouths do not guarantee a truth will come out of them. We don't have to look very far for an example of a perfectly formed mouth uttering nonsense all the time: our current President Trump. Being a pathological liar, he seems to make other liars look like saints. Yes, it is that bad. This proverb is particularly timely, considering how rampant lies and fake news have become in this society. There are so many of them nowadays, we seem to spend more time in determining if a given story is reliable or not, rather than examining its significance.

Wherever you look, there appears to be an unprecedented level of intentional deceptions prevailing in our society: a teacher who is conspiring to give better grades to students for whatever purpose he may have, a dentist who is strongly recommends an unnecessary procedure, a pharmacist diluting a drug product to result in weakened potency, a physician who over-prescribes opioid medicine, fraudulent tele-marketers, insurance schemers, lying Catholic pedophile priests, corrupt policemen conspiring with drug dealers, secret transactions between a judge and a criminal, a billing department of a clinic on some obscure corner of town, etc. These are crimes committed by "educated" people, unlike a car repairman exaggerating the problem of your car.

In November 2017, a homeless drug addict used his last $20 to buy gas for a young lady in panic. Her car just ran out of gas on I-95 around Philadelphia. An outpouring of donations to the *GoFundMe* website, ultimately reached up to $400,000. The story presented humanity in a most positive angle, at a most desperate point in time in this dystopian world. The woman who received the tankful of gas said of the donation: "It has changed my entire outlook about people; my outlook about people has skyrocketed." Along with this upbeat pleasantry, she presented a financial plan for the homeless good Samaritan. Oh, well, as it turned out, it was all a ruse. They had planned the incident in advance to steal money from ordinary people who have been begging for any emotionally up-lifting stories. We are now betrayed and lost in this murky water, trying to grab any floating straw. Now that we've all become paranoid, whom and what shall we believe?

I graduated from one of the best high schools in Korea. Admission to the program was quite competitive, and entailed an open exam-based competition. There were, however, many students who were admitted, via donation from their parents to the school. No one, including myself, expressed any qualm about it. It was then (1950s) and there (Korea). But, just yesterday, we learned that as many as 50 well-to-do folks, including a few Hollywood actors, bribed the admission officials in some prestigious colleges so that their children could get accepted. Is this how they raise their children? Don't they love their own children? If this is their love for children, the very definition of the word has changed to something many of us do not recognize. A reader of *The New York Times* submitted the following comment. Regardless of the shape of this writer's lips, this is a truthful statement.

It's obviously a scandal when rich people are accused of breaking the law to get their kids into top schools. But the bigger outrage should be that a legal version of purchasing an advantage happens every college application season and that there's an entire industry supporting it. (03/13/19)

Fists are closer than the law.
법은 멀고 주먹은 가깝다.

[181]

As this young kid, driving a sport car, suddenly cuts into your lane at a high speed, almost causing a collision, you are entitled to a great deal of irritation and yelling, perhaps with your middle finger raised. Your anger is well justified. At the next red light, you walk over to the car and say something related to manners, etiquette, respect, courtesy, etc. The lecture leads to an unpleasant confrontation on this busy intersection, at the busiest part of town. As push comes to shove, fists begin to fly, well before a cop shows up. Your old karate chop still works, and the kid gets floored. This is essentially what the above proverb is saying. Taking care of an urgent business with emotion is a lot easier than with logic.

You may feel good, knowing that your karate chop is still working and that your nemesis is on the ground, albeit he is much younger than you are, and that justice, after all, prevailed. And yet, you get embarrassed by the inability of controlling your emotions. Hasn't this hot temper of yours given you big trouble in the past? How many times have you heard the same warning from your mother? To be fair, you are not the only one who explodes into road rage at the spur of the moment. Such scenes used to be quite common when I grew up in Seoul. If I may generalize, Koreans are people of short temper, especially those Koreans from the North, where the rugged, mountainous terrain dominates the landscape. Koreans who grow up in the flat land of the Southwest are more relaxed and seem to move about in careful deliberation, or seeming mindfulness. They also speak slowly: there is a joke that by the time the folks from Chung-Cheong Province complete a sentence, the sun has already set.

Just like individual personalities, every nation on this planet seems to have their own characteristics. Italians and Latinos are considered passionate people, just like Koreans. We Koreans run first as fast as we can and later ask why we have run, while the Chinese examine a situation while strolling with their hands at their back. The Japanese, living on an island, tend to be clever and decide what to do depending on circumstance, not so much out of principle but through their own beliefs. These are all gross generalization based on my own experience with these nationalities.

Even for a given person, the personality seems to change with age: "becoming mellow," as they say. I can certainly attest to such change in me. At this stage of my life, anger and accompanying hatred, are all too much consuming of my energy. They are simply not worth my time in the ever shortening days of my life. Even if it occurs, such undesirable emotion dissipates its steam in no time at all, almost out of "laziness" or "tiresomeness." I simply do not see any point of it all. Let it go is my attitude on many daily emotions, especially irksome ones.

As I was writing the first paragraph, the following story came to mind from my long-faded memory. Then I dug out details from the Internet. On February 8, 1994, one of the greatest actors of our time, Jack Nicholson, then at the age of 56, used a golf club to smash the windshield of a Mercedes-Benz at a red light in North Hollywood. Misdemeanor charges of assault and vandalism were filed against Nicholson, but soon dropped after the actor and the victim reached an undisclosed settlement, which included a reported $500,000 check from Nicholson. He later said, it was "a shameful incident in my life." According to Nicholson, he went "out of my mind" after being cut off and snatched one of his golf clubs from the trunk of his car. Although the press variously reported that the club he used must have been a 3- or 5-iron, Nicholson, who was a beginner back then, cleared up the hearsay in a 2007 interview with *Golf Digest*. "I was on my way to the course, and in the midst of this madness I somehow knew what I was doing," he said, "because I reached into my trunk and specifically selected a club I never used on the course: my 2-iron." Yeah, even I know about 2-iron.

He still had the presence of mind to sacrifice the long iron, but somehow let his fists, alias 2-iron, take care of his frustrations. No other stories could have summed up the above Korean proverb better than Nicholson's story. (03/27/19)

Having kimchi juice before the rice cake is served.
김치국부터 마신다.

[182]

Two main staples in daily Korean meals are undoubtedly steamed rice and kimchi. The latter, kimchi (김치), is basically salted vegetables such as cabbage and radish fermented with various seasonings including; chili powder, scallions, garlic, ginger, and sometimes picked krill or other small fish. Because kimchi contains garlic and sea food like krill and is fermented for a period of time, its unique, pungent smell is quite notorious among those who know anything about Korea. For those American friends who are visiting us, but have never encountered kimchi, I always take it out of refrigerator and open the bottle under the exhaust fan above my cooking range. Only after the odor escapes sufficiently, will I serve it. When they serve kimchi at a restaurant, by the time it arrives at your table, the odor has dissipated already. It is a dish whose taste you will acquire for the first time with the tongue rather than through the nose. Once one gets "addicted," however, people usually look forward to having kimchi at a Korean restaurant. People, who were first exposed to the smell, can hate it; just like those who do not care much about some stinky cheeses. Indeed, one can classify foreigners into two groups: people who like kimchi and people who hate kimchi. You seldom find one in-between.

Napa cabbage is first soaked in a generous amount of salt for a few days. Because of the high salt concentration, the water flows out of the cabbage, rendering the cabbage to shrink and produce much liquid. The phenomenon is similar to crenation of a red blood cell in a hypertonic solution. To this, various condiments are added, like crushed red pepper as well as pepper slices, minced garlic, and green onion. During the fermentation process, the red peppers turn the liquid oxblood red. This, we call kimchi juice or 김치국. When served cold, this spicy juice, somewhat sour in taste, wakes you up from any state of stupor. It hits your taste buds on the tongue and the throat, like something people have never been exposed to.

It opens your sinus like fresh mint: it is good stuff, hands down. Traditionally, this juice was often taken in the company of other offerings such as rice cake. So, this proverb describes a situation where one drinks kimchi juice first, then anticipating rice cake being offered, which may never materialize. In essence, it is analogous to: "Don't count your chickens before they are hatched."

We are all familiar with this expression: "Hope for the best, expect the worst." Hoping for the best is just basic human nature when we are waiting for the outcome of an ongoing event. Winning the jackpot in a super lottery has a chance of one in millions, but people still buy the ticket knowing that somebody will win and hoping that it can be him or her. Who am I to discourage them from their hopes? After all, aren't we to encourage people to maintain a positive outlook for their future? A pessimist would never take risk and venture into an uncertain future. The world would be too dull to inhabit if everyone took a conservative, risk-free stand in life.

The second part, "expecting the worst, is where we fail quite often. We tend to stop short with an impossible dream, like winning a lottery, but without "expecting the worst." "Taking kimchi juice too prematurely" may entail; love in vain, stock losing its value, a tanked housing market, homilies from a new priest, a new girlfriend of the eldest son, a diagnosis of illness, a jury verdict, water on uneven beaches, and more of the same. Over-indulging parents might have already developed a scenario for their son, who has just written an entrance exam to a university and is now waiting for the results of pass or fail. Parents believe that their son will surely enter the college. They have prayed with their hearts out, day and night. They also enrolled the son in a remedial course, specifically designed for the entrance exam. For these efforts, they have forgone their vacation plans abroad and neglected other siblings! Any negative thoughts of their son failing the examination are unconsciously suppressed and expelled to an obscure corner of their minds. Then, the unexpected arrives. It must be one of the most devastating incidents their family has ever experienced together. Here, the parents surely took the kimchi juice a bit too early. We offer them sincere words of solace instead of rice cake. (03/30/19)

Praying for another rainy day during monsoon season.
백일 장마에도 하루만 더 왔으면 한다.

[183]

In Korea, we have rain almost every day during the summer months, mainly July and August. It's just awful: clothes get all soaked and stuck to your skin and seem to be perpetually wet due to either sweat or drizzling rain. Wherever you go, you struggle with humidity and the odor of wet clothes. We couldn't wait another day for the famous Korean blue sky of autumn with its cool and dry air. Then, who in the world would hope for another rainy day at the end of monsoon season? But some people might, like an umbrella manufacturer or the salesmen of raincoats. This proverb goes beyond just these people: it is concerned with people who maintain some questionable standard in running their businesses.

Let's assume that you are the Chief Executive Officer (CEO) of a drug company and that you've just learned from your scientists that they discovered a way to completely eradicate a life-threatening disease. You've also learned, almost simultaneously, that there is a treatment modality that necessitates daily use of a medicine that your company can also develop. Of course, you decide to pursue the former approach without any hesitation. From a business perspective, however, being able to sell the medicine, for the rest of a patient's life, is also quite appealing. Here, your moral judgment prevails.

You are CEO of a cosmetic company and your people present two options for restoring hair growth. The first option is a one-step solution that takes care of baldness once and for all. The second option is a kind of medical intervention that requires constant use of a cream that your company can develop. Here, you may seriously consider selling the cream rather than fixing the bald head in one treatment. The imperfect solution makes a perfect business decision for you, as money will come in from each bald man till they recognize the vanity of it all.

As a new resident in this town, I was looking for a dentist. At the first get-to-know visit to a dentist who was highly regarded among the Korean community, he showed me a picture of my mouth he took (with his mobile phone!) to point out a thin brownish line on the top surface of each of two molars. He warned me that they could crack and chip off at any time and recommended immediate crowning. It was a wrong diagnosis: those two teeth are just fine, even more than a year later. On the other side of my mouth, I was losing an implant. He recommended a denture instead of a new implant. I noted that his office handles dentures but not implants. Another dentist, at another later time, recommended extracting the two molars because there was an infection and the teeth were somewhat mobile. It was a false alarm again. The antibiotic, amoxicillin, and diligent mouth washes with a water-pick fixed the problem. To this day, I still do not know if these episodes reflect their incompetence or their somewhat non-professional goal of, for the lack of better words, making money. Some auto repairmen of a long gone era used to fix one thing but break another, for extra business. For them, these practices were just another rainy day at the end of monsoon season.

By 2014, Purdue Pharma agreed to pay more than $600 million in criminal and civil penalties for its unethical marketing of the highly addictive opioid painkiller, OxyContin. Every day, the addiction to opioids kills more than 130 people in the U.S. As the crises worsened, the family who owned Purdue Pharma for two generations, came up with a "brilliant" new business idea. They decided to market treatments for the very problem their company had helped to create: that is, addiction to opioids. Details of the effort, named Project Tango, came to light in lawsuits filed by the attorneys general of Massachusetts and New York. "Pain treatment and addiction are naturally linked," one Project Tango document said. It depicted a big blue funnel. The fat end was labeled "pain treatment," while the narrow end was labeled "opioid addiction treatment." They called the project Tango because "it takes two to tango," one is disease and the other is medicine. This type of dubious business is alluded to by the above proverb. (04/02/19)

Acupuncture onto a pumpkin.
호박에 침주기

[184]

In acupuncture, thin needles of about an inch and a half are inserted into various parts of the body. Depending on diagnosis, the practitioner determines where the needles are to be inserted. Once inserted, needles can be spun, flicked, or moved up and down. They can be stimulated by hand, for various sensations. At present, this ancient Chinese practice is neither completely understood nor supported by modern medical knowledge. And yet, its popularity, spanning over several thousands of years, tells us something. I, for one, used to receive acupuncture treatment for a terrible hypersensitivity towards tree pollen and many other allergens, including nickel, a metal commonly found in many devices like the frames of eye glasses. I could not tell if it was working or not, but enjoyed the accompanying 30-minute nap with about 20 needles sticking out of my body. In the end I quit, because the treatment cost was not covered by medical insurance and we moved to a different part of this country.

As one can imagine, learning acupuncture must require years of practice, possibly under the tutelage of a master. However, inserting the needle into a pumpkin or squash hardly needs such skillset. Why a pumpkin? I cannot answer that, but it is as dead an object as anything else for inserting an acupuncture needle into. Then, what would be the metaphor for giving acupuncture on a pumpkin? The above phrase may simply describe an easy job that anyone can handle. The job was so easy one can say later, "It was like administering acupuncture on pumpkin."

What appears to be an easy job often turns out to be with full of surprises. Listen to this old Chinese parable. There was some leftover liquor after a sacrificial rite. The head of the event then decided to give it to those servants who had helped him to run the rite.

Unfortunately, the leftover was too small in quantity for everybody and hence the master suggested a competition, the winner of which will take all of the leftover drink. Everybody agreed. The competition was drawing a snake and whoever finished the drawing first would be the rightful owner of the drink. One man quickly drew a perfect snake, and looked around to realize he completed the competition way before others. Instead of asking for his prize, he decided to add feet on his snake, probably out of "boredom" or attempt to demonstrate his "cleverness." So, he lost his drink.

Making a seemingly difficult job look much easier could be another interpretation of the above phrase. A mother luring her child to jump onto a swimming pool, with wide open arms and a bright smile, may say a few words of encouragement like, "Look, I am here to catch you. The water is not deep here at all." Likewise, imagine the virgin flight of chicks from their nest, high up in a tree, under the watchful eyes of their mother who is flying gracefully above them in a most assuring way. Or making a job look like "a piece of cake" can be deceptive in purpose. A conman would keep saying, "Look, all you have to do is sign your name right here, then the money will be yours." All we have to do, according to this scammer, is indeed a very simple task, like giving away his or her social security number or tapping a key on one's laptop. They are indeed "inserting an acupuncture needle into pumpkin."

The world we live in now is so full of swindlers that we are under a constant paranoid state of mind. When was the last time you truly believed in something "free?" What do you find in your mailbox every day? All phones in this household are on the so-called Do-Not-Call Registry, but I still get unsolicited phone calls. What do these mails and phone calls want? Why are gated communities so popular? How do you believe in strangers on the street? How do we know what we see on TV is truthful? They show factual scenes, but who decides the camera angle and who determines the priority among the topics to be covered? Why do people hate each other so much? Is this world, dystopian at its apotheosis, an alternate world based on quantum mechanics? Indeed, "the acupuncture needle going into a pumpkin" suggests us to be mindful when an easy job comes along. (04/05/19)

Begging for mercy can melt steel.
비는 데는 무쇠도 녹는다.

[185]

Unless you have a wooden heart, you are inclined to forgive or at least offer a lenient punishment to someone who is sincerely begging you for mercy. How can you just walk away from this poor guy? He is trying to save his own life for something he has done, probably not knowing any better. So the above proverb is saying that a sincere begging for forgiveness is so powerful that it can melt even steel, or an iron heart. The Bible seems to go one step further with unconditional forgiveness: "Judge not, and you shall not be judged. Condemn not, and you shall not be condemned. Forgive, and you shall be forgiven." (Luke 6:37). In the Gospel of Matthew (18:21-22), Peter asked Jesus how often he must forgive his brother who sinned against him. "As many as seven times?" Jesus answered, "I say to you, not seven times but seventy-seven times."

Who am I to judge and condemn others when I am also a sinner? After all, there are no clothes that will not shed lint when shaken. See Entry #78, "Three shoemakers can outsmart Einstein." The other extreme case of forgiveness would be death by public decapitation (!) on a guillotine. In Korean history, the cruelest death penalty might have been dismemberment of a guilty person by four horses pulling a torso away simultaneously. This punishment must be equivalent to stoning in Islamic countries, but death comes much more quickly.

The pettiness of President Trump has been firmly established by now and well illustrated by the following event. In March, 2018, the U.S. Attorney General, Jeff Sessions, fired the Deputy Director of the FBI, Andrew McCabe, just 26 hours short of full retirement. The move was to cost McCabe his federal pension after more than 20 years of service. It is not my concern whether McCabe's dismissal was political in nature or not.

The important point was that many American citizens, certainly including myself, believed that the timing of his dismissal was not just coincident with the alleged crime, but part of a ploy to deprive him of his retirement pension in full.

Trump had been taunting McCabe repeatedly, once reminding McCabe of "racing the clock" in his retirement. When McCabe was fired, Trump immediately celebrated on Twitter because McCabe lost his pension. Later, people learned that McCabe was to lose only some portion of his pension. I doubt that Trump was intelligent enough to realize his victory celebration was premature.

In *Les Miserables,* Victor Hugo's (1802 - 1885) masterpiece, we meet the protagonist of the novel, Jean Valjean, who is sent to prison for stealing a loaf of bread. He did so to feed his sister's seven starving children. After repeated attempts of unsuccessful escape, he is released having served 19 years of incarceration. As an ex-convict, he lives a miserable life: homeless, angry, frustrated, and bitter. Luckily, a local Catholic bishop offers him shelter but he steals and runs off with the bishop's silverware. When arrested, the bishop tells the police that the stolen items were actually given to Valjean. The bishop further says that Jean Valjean forgot to take two silver candlesticks given to him. After the police leave them, the bishop tells Valjean that he should use the money from the candlesticks to make an honest man of himself. This is the turning point in Jean Valjean's tortuous life to redemption.

On May 13, 1981, as Pope John Paul II was entering St. Peter's Square in the Vatican City, he was shot four times by a Turk named Mehmet Ali Ağca. The Pope suffered severe blood loss. The assassin was immediately arrested and later sentenced to life in prison by an Italian court. Following the shooting, Pope John Paul II asked people to "pray for my brother, whom I have sincerely forgiven." In 1983, he and Ağca met and spoke privately at a prison. The Pope also kept in touch with Ağca's family over the years, meeting his mother in 1987 and his brother a decade later. He was pardoned by the Italian president, at the Pope's request, and was deported to Turkey in June 2000. Let us now compare Jean Valjean's story and the Pope's forgiveness of his assassin to the childish behavior of our President. (04/07/19)

Lose a tooth while chewing tofu.
두부 먹다 이 빠진다.

[186]

However processed into a dish, tofu is one of the softest food ingredients one can imagine. And yet, the above proverb tells us that you can crack and lose a tooth while you are enjoying a meal made of tofu. It implies that, quite often, what you assume to be harmless can surprise you in the most unexpected way. Your own dog bites you while you are feeding him or stepping on a rake the wrong way to get hit in the face. We cannot and should not live on edge all the time, but being over-complacent toward a seemingly innocuous circumstance can create a disaster. It can be a direct result of bad luck, ignorance, negligence, overlooking, or wrong assumption. See also Entry #60, "Is this stone bridge sturdy enough to cross

In an Aesop's fable, the tortoise wins the footrace against the hare because the latter assumes he is a shoo-in winner. Arrogance thus results in embarrassing consequence once in a while. In the 2018 National Collegiate Athletic Association (NCAA) basketball playoff, the No. 1 seeded Virginia Cavaliers in one of the four Divisions lost with a lopsided score of 74-54 in the first round to No. 16 team, the University of Maryland, Baltimore County. This was the first time in the NCAA tournament history that a No. 1 seed lost to a No. 16. I doubt that the Cavaliers let their guard down during the game, but still such perception prevailed. Incidentally, the Cavaliers won the 2019 national championship, beating Texas Tech in overtime. It was the first time in their university history. Speaking of redemption, this was it.

Cinderella stories abound in the arena of sport. Daniel Brown's historic account, *The Boys on the Boat,* describes how the obscure nine oar crew from the University of Washington won the gold medal in the 1936 Berlin Olympics. The story was already introduced in Entry #142, "A mad dog can kill a tiger." By the time the Winter Olympic Games were held in Lake Placid in upstate New York, in 1980, the Soviet Union had won the gold medal in five of the six previous ice hockey tournaments. Their team, consisting of experienced professionals, was once again the favorites to win it all. In contrast, the U.S. team was made exclusively of amateurs, and the youngest team in the tournament history. In what has been known since then as the "Miracle on Ice," the U.S. team upset the Soviet Union with three period scores of 2-2, 2-3, and 4-3. The U.S. then beat another power house Finland team, in the final, to claim the gold medal. The victory over the Soviets was something no one who watched the game on TV will ever forget, especially considering the cool relationship between the two countries.

Disguised identity, which is revealed later at a critical juncture, is the climax of many stories involving the good and the evil. According to the French version of Cinderella, a young girl with unparalleled kindness and sweet temper is forced into servitude by her cruel stepmother and jealous stepsisters. Cinderella was able to attend a royal ball, held by the Prince, only with the help of a Fairly Godmother, who transforms not only Cinderella to a beautiful young lady with a delicate pair of glass slippers but also "a pumpkin to a golden carriage, mice to horses, a rat to a coachman, and lizards into footmen." At the ball, the entire court, especially the Prince, is entranced by Cinderella's beauty and disposition. At the second ball next evening, Cinderella almost forgets to leave the festivities by midnight. That is when her Godmother's spell breaks. During her hasty retreat, she loses one of her glass slippers. The Prince tries the glass slipper he found at his palace on every young girl in his kingdom until he finally found Cinderella.

In "playing possum," an animal pretends to be dead as a means of defense in a dire situation. Assuming a dead prey, a predator may relax, rendering the death-feigning animal with an escape opportunity. Albeit passive, this line of strategies among weaker animals has apparently survived testing times and apparently still in use. Any attempt to resemble the surrounding background is the major purpose of camouflage; ranging from that of chameleons and octopuses to military camouflage. Luring fish with man-made bait would be another area of deception being used to our advantage. These are instances where the softest tofu could crack your teeth. (04/21/19)

Cracking noise from a demon munching rice seeds.
귀신 씨나락 까먹는 소리.

[187]

As the sun rises earlier and the day light gets longer in the spring, Korean farmers become busier preparing to sow rice. Rice seeds from the previous year are first put into a seedbed or nursery. Typically, early April is the time they prepare the nursery. It may take 40 to 45 days to raise the seedlings. Sometime in May, farmers begin the labor-intense back-breaking planting, in the prepared rice paddy. Maintaining shallow water throughout the summer mandates proper water control, in terms of not only dam systems but also water ways. This is in addition to protecting the seedlings from various diseases and pests as well as fertilizing them. Harvest then takes place around September.

Almost all Korean meals offer steamed rice as the main dish, regardless of the time of day: at least it used to be that way when I grew up. As such, cultivating rice is a serious business. The storing of rice seeds for several months, after the harvest in the fall but before sowing the next spring, is considered one of the most sacred steps. There are many dos and don'ts, some likely based on century-old superstition, but farmers won't change their tradition. Why rock the boat when it has survived the test of time? As a kind of sacrificial ritual, porcelain pots containing the seed are "protected" from evil spirits or demons by salt spread around the jars. Likewise, if seeds are stored in a straw sack, they are covered with pine twigs. A person who has witnessed, not to mention committed, injustice or wrongdoings, is not allowed to see the seeds, as it could lead to infertile seedlings. Folks in the Southern region of Korea refer to the seed as *sinarak* or 씨나락.

In the dead of night, a farmer hears some strange noise coming from the pantry, where he has kept *sinarak* for the following spring. He then comes across a most disturbing scene: a demon is consuming the seeds! The strange noise he heard earlier was, in fact, the crunching noise that the demon made as he was chewing the seeds. This is a most outrageous and unexpected event. How did such a thing happen with all the rituals he took to keep the seed well preserved?

The proverb describes the above scene as a phrase, not in a clause. It depicts an unthinkable and utterly ridiculous incident. How can we use such a description? Any shocking "noise" or news will justify its use. The proverb likens to the first time I heard an outrageous lie from President Trump: he claimed that former President, Barack Obama, was born in Kenya and not in Hawaii. It is a sad acknowledgment that I am no longer hearing "the demon's noise," as I have become immune to a new and significantly lower moral and ethical standard displayed by the man. Nowadays, some ominous "noises" we hear more often may include: the ever-widening gap of wealth between the rich and the poor, the ever-increasing atmospheric carbon dioxide level and its consequences; the dire need of potable water in various regions of the world; the size of student loans in the nation; the polluted air of major cities; the national debt, which exceeded $22 trillion and still counting; and so on and so forth.

Filtering unfounded or outlandishly distorted stories, rampant in social media nowadays, is absolutely necessary so we can ignore them for the sake of sanity. We have just learned that a five-year old boy missing since last week, who made headlines on national TV, had been in fact murdered by his own parents. I sure wish that such "noise" will never reach my ears from now on. When we were selling our previous home, one offer we received was about half the listing price. We ignored the offer completely, thinking it did not deserve our counter-offer.

The city mayor of South Bend, Indiana, Pete Buttigieg, is running for the Democratic presidential nomination. At this writing, the 37-year old man, seemingly out of nowhere, is in the leading group of more than 20 candidates. Because he is gay, he has been receiving some flak from Trump's cronies, who are comparing him to Jussie Smollett, the gay actor who was accused of staging a hate crime on himself. Mayor Pete's response was: "I'm not a master fisherman, but I know bait when I see it, and I'm not going to take it." (04/24/19)

Morning enlightenment is for peaceful evening death.
아침에 도를 들으면 저녁에 죽어도 좋다.

Neither Buddhism nor Hinduism vigorously denies the existence of a god or gods. This does not mean that they actively promote worshiping them either. The fact is, the Buddha himself did not believe in a creator god. Instead, spiritual liberation has been the focus of Buddhism. Many of us are not outright atheists and yet from the depth of our minds we may believe in "something" spiritual, while struggling with the question of how to establish the existence of a god or gods. These agnostics may not go to a church or temple regularly, but seek "personal" enlightenment at some quiet corner of an office building, in the midst of a noisy and breakneck modern life: that is, without distraction from the external "forced" belief in a universal and eternal god. The paramount importance of spiritual enlightenment in life is thus the main theme of this proverb: "If you listened to (들으면) and understood the truth, *doh* (도), about our own existence this morning, you can depart this world peacefully this evening."

The so-called Four Noble Truths, or Four *Sacca* in Buddhist principles, are stages of progress one is to ultimately go through for attaining the Buddhist Way of life. The First is concerned with recognition of imperfect existence; mainly dealing with suffering, pain, illness, etc. The Second Principle questions why and how the imperfections happen. At the Third stage, having passed the first two, one may attain freedom in perfect existence. The Fourth Principle is the Path through which one finally progresses toward Enlightenment. This last Principle is the meditation ability that a person acquires from practicing the other principles. The person is to maintain it throughout his or her life. I am taking the liberty of defining *doh* (도) in the proverb as this ultimate stage of Enlightenment. The proverb seems to imply that attaining the final stage of enlightenment is the goal as well as the purpose of life.

"I Raised Two CEOs and a Doctor. These Are My Secrets to Parenting Successful Children" was the title of an article that I was reading this morning on my mobile phone, while waiting for my weekly allergy injection. It was from the web-based, April 26, 2019, issue of *TIME* magazine. An early paragraph reads: "What everyone wants to know is how to help our children live good lives – to be both happy and successful, and to use their talents to make the world a better place." The author, a mother of three most successful daughters, goes on to provide practical advices to aspiring parents. It is imbedded in what she calls TRICK: Trust, Respect, Independence, Collaboration, and Kindness. No, her TRICK does not address individual self-enlightenment or wisdom of the "one life" given to each of us.

There is only so much one can learn from others about the true meaning of life. Regardless who your mentor might be, at some point, we all have to actively jump onto the fray of finding our own voice on the subject. As the remaining days of my life are numbered, I am wondering if it is too late to tackle the task. As in a football game, as your team approaches the end zone, the playing field becomes more crowded with players from both teams, and thus renders it more difficult to score a touchdown. Wouldn't it be better to devise a play to score a touchdown when our offensive is far away from the end zone? Why can't parents teach children the true meaning of life early on? The difficulty here is, of course, that children hardly understand what life, not to mention death, is. When they are young adults, success in the practical world predominates their time, say, learning TRICK, etc. It is at best a prescription on "how": it seldom guides young people to "what."

The 14th, and thus current, Dalai Lama was born in 1935 as one of 16 children to a humble family of farmers in a remote part of Tibet. In 1939, a Tibetan regent received a clear vision of a house with turquoise roof tiles among others, which led to the discovery of the four-year old boy, Tenzin Gyatso, as the reincarnation. This story and the follow-up life-long meditation and prayer by the Dalai Lama seems to resonate quite well with the birth and life of Jesus Christ. In both cases, their spiritual lives, dedicated to fellow humans, began at quite an early age. I doubt very much that their lives could have used the advice involving TRICK. (04/29/19).

Lend the money and lose a friend.
돈 빌려주면 돈도 잃고 친구도 잃는다.

[189]

Mark Twain (1835 - 1910) said the same: "The holy passion of friendship is so sweet and steady and loyal and enduring in nature that it will last through a whole lifetime, if not asked to lend money." In Shakespeare's (1564 - 1616) Hamlet, we read: "Neither a borrower nor a lender be." I also found the following proverbs from various cultures: "Do not lend your money to a great man." "Money borrowed is soon sorrowed." "Money lent, an enemy made." "Would you know the value of money go borrow some." A direct translation of this Korean proverb is, "You will lose both money and friend if you lend money to your friend." I doubt that our Korean ancestors copied the wisdom from Shakespeare, Mark Twain, or other countries. That is to say, the wisdom therein must be deeply true, independent of both time and place.

There are two ways to lose a friend after you lend money. In the first case, the man who had borrowed money from you, after profusely begging and promising, never had any intention to pay you back from the very beginning. This example is bona fide fraud, and you did not realize that he was not a true "friend" until much later, when nothing happened to the repayment of money. He will avoid you "forever" in every social gathering. He will avoid the awkward moment of an accidental encounter, where he will have to invent some excuse for the delayed payment of the debt. The net result is, you have just paid a sum of money to discover what kind of a man the borrower really is. No matter, he's gone, the money is gone, and you wish you could have given the money to a panhandler on the street.

The second possibility is exactly opposite to the above case. Here, the borrower is sincerely trying to return your money, but he has been unsuccessful in doing so. Even if you try to tell your friend honestly that he can forget about the debt and that you can comfortably survive without that portion of your wealth, he cannot face your kindness out of shame and guilt. You and your once-dear friend are simply not on equal footing any more. You may interact with your friend the same way as before, but he has now become quite sensitive to what you say and how you behave. He may over-analyze everything you do. You cannot get mad or angry with him, as you had in the past, even on trivial matters, lest he might think that you are angry because of his debt to you. You cannot be overly-generous to him either because he may think he is on the receiving end of your generosity due to his financial struggle. The friendship you used to have is no longer in play.

When we were children, in an eight-sibling family, our mother used to warn us that friends and siblings remain close, only so long as everyone becomes comparatively equal in wealth, education, and social status. How right she was.

A corollary of the above old saying is that we should be awfully careful in developing a joint venture in business. If you do not have to, don't. When the venture flourishes, everything is fine and dandy. Trouble always rears its ugly head when the business is not moving along well or when a break-up is inevitable. A man who was once a friend, close enough to become a business partner, has now becomes a foe. Each side points fingers at the failed business, and tries to explain their discontent to mutual friends whenever an opportunity arises. It is a fertile ground of hearsay and gossip and we, the mutual friends, are left in a strange place, without knowing what to say or to whom. One can simply shrug off saying, "Money will do that," and walk away from it all. What a pity. Such problems seem to be less frequent, at least on the face of it, when your business partner is your son or brother, as we frequently see business names like, "Johnson & Sons" or "Ringly Brothers."

Money, money, money··· They sure do strange things. See these additional proverbs: "A man without money is a bow without an arrow." "Give me money, not advice." "If you have money, take a seat." "Money answers all." "Money does all." "Money is a universal language, speaking any tongue." "Money is power." "Money makes dogs dance." "Money rules the world," and "Money is the god of the world." Oh, really? And ironically, I also found this: "Much money, many friends." (04/29/'19)

Plant trees if you wish to watch birds.
새가 보고 싶거든 나무를 심어라.

[190]

Presently, my wife and I live in a city built on a vast desert valley in southern Nevada. We moved to this town about a year ago from the green pastures of North Carolina. Our home in North Carolina was on one-acre of land and had a wooded area full of wild animals such deer, snakes, possums, raccoons, squirrels, box turtles, snails, and chipmunks. Birds we used to feed and enjoyed watching included blue birds, woodpeckers, doves, golden finches, chickadees, thrashers, hummingbirds, sparrows, swallows, chimney swifts, Baltimore orioles, even hawks once in a while. Others, I could not identify. The animals we disliked most and tried to avoid as much as we could were spiders, some of which were quite nasty, and mosquitoes. These are what we left behind, some two thousands mile away. It would be difficult to imagine any greater difference in weather and terrain than what we have gone through with the move.

Early in the morning, on the day the movers were to deliver furniture to our new home, we introduced ourselves to a small jack rabbit staring at us from a corner of a stamp-size, barren backyard. It was the only creature who was welcoming us. We had yet to encounter a scorpion or rattler. There was nothing that was moving, including the desert hot air of mid-May. Even the rabbit disappeared for good a few days later. It took more than a month to have hummingbirds visit the nectar we set out. Now, almost a year later, plumb trees, oleanders, various bushes, and the chaste trees we planted last fall, are bursting to grow with a brand new spring. Curious birds I cannot identify have started to appear in our backyard. We are also anxiously looking forward to seeing butterflies on the chaste trees. Indeed, with trees and bushes, the backyard has begun to show some sign of life.

The state bird of North Carolina is the northern cardinal. It is quite common and we had a lot of them around the house, especially on top of the side mirrors of our cars. It is a mid-sized songbird, with a body length of about eight inches, or 20 cm. The male is a vibrant red, just like those cardinals in Vatican City, while the female is a reddish olive color. They eat mainly grain and seed, but also feed on insects and fruit. We used to see them "kissing" on our patio. As it turns out, it is the male feeding seeds to the female, beak-to-beak, during courtship. Here, in Nevada, the state bird is the mountain bluebird, which is slightly smaller than the cardinal. They have light underbellies and black eyes. Adult males have thin bills and are bright turquoise-blue with somewhat lighter shades underneath. The ones in North Carolina showed a brownish underside and they banged into windows in early spring, as they thought they saw rivals in reflection on the glass. Cleaning the mess they left on the upstairs window was a pain, but they were beautiful birds to watch.

The almighty, powerful homeowners association (HOA) of our community strongly discourages feeding birds, because they leave a mess. In fact, there is a list of bushes and trees that we are allowed to plant in our backyard. It excludes all those fruit-bearing trees such as apple, pear, plum, cherry, etc. The plum tree we planted was called a purple-leaf plum, which apparently does not bear plum. The artificially manicured greens and royal palm trees surrounding our neighbors look pleasing, but are too sterile to my taste. Yes, we have many songbirds that I have not yet been acquainted with. Interestingly, the HOA does not seem to care about the mess that Canada geese make around the pond and fallen plums on the walk path. Their plum trees are those bearing fruit. In short, there are not many birds visiting our backyard, even if we wanted to lure them with trees. One of our neighbors, a few houses away, has put up a hawk decoy on top of their wall to keep small birds away. So much for bird-watching!

The above proverb simply says that you will have to invest your time and effort, if you really want something. "There is no free lunch." Fair enough, but if you do not wish to exert so much labor and want to look for a short cut, there is always web-based advice: "7 (not 'seven') ways to happiness," "5 ways to have people love you," and "3 ways to get rid of your girl friend," etc. No one seems to promote hard work any more. (04/30/19)

The very ghost at your home will carry you away.
집안 귀신이 사람 잡아간다.

[191]

According to what I understood from a scholarly article on Korean mythology, a person who has lived an honest life becomes *shin* (신) after death. This word may be equivalent to Lord, God, or Almighty. In contrast, a person who has lived a questionable life will become a *gui-shin* (귀신), a ghost or demon. Both can function as if they were alive, with intact emotions of love and hatred as well as passion and apathy, but with extraordinary capability and capacity. It is thus natural that they are sought after by descendants in prayer at a ritual known as *jesa* (제사), where the ancestors are remembered. To *shin*, people pray for happiness, prosperity, a long life, and the well-being of extended family. To *gui-shin,* they pray for preventing tragic events from happening. A nuanced difference between these two concepts is that the former represents goodness while the latter, evil.

Many various versions of *gui-shin* (귀신) exist at a given time at various places. The above proverb says that: "It is the ghost in your home, not those far away, that will take you away," presumably from this world to the next one. It is trying to tell us that more harm is done to you and more frequently by those who are close to you (backstabbing, that is); like your spouse, friends, siblings, relatives, or colleagues. A dead woman, often pregnant (!), found after seeming foul play immediately brings the attention of police detectives to her boy friend or husband. Next, the detectives will look into people close to the victim through other relationships. This hunch is about right. Unless it is a random murder, what is the probability for a person to get killed by a total stranger? Likewise, we can ask ourselves why some *gui-shin,* unrelated to the victim, would care about the fate of the victim?

Judas Iscariot identified Jesus by kissing him in front of the crowd who came to arrest Jesus. Remember that Judas was one of the original Twelve Disciples of Jesus

Christ. He was as close to Jesus as anyone. Why did Judas betray Jesus? The Gospel of Matthew said that Judas did so for "thirty pieces of silver" (Matthew 26:15). Later, the same Gospel also stated that Judas hung himself after he had attempted to return the silver upon hearing that Jesus would be soon crucified (Matthew 27:1-10). In contrast, according to Peter, as quoted in the Acts of the Apostles (Acts 1:18), Judas "bought a parcel of land with the wages of his iniquity, and falling headlong, he burst open in the middle, and all his insides spilled out." In short, why Judas betrayed Jesus and what happened to him later have never been clearly established. This uncertainty in itself is not really relevant to the discussion on the above proverb. Fact is that he, a close disciple of Jesus, was disloyal to his mentor.

Another betrayal, in equally biblical scale, is undoubtedly that by the current U.S. President Trump to his nation and people. According to Chris Cillizza, the editor-in-large of CNN's *The Point,* as of April 29, 2019, the President has surpassed 10,000 lies during his 827 days in office, which is about 12 lies a day. Just yesterday, *The New York Times* revealed that Mr. Trump lost over one billion U.S. dollars from 1985 till 1994. His response on Twitter was that it was all by his brilliant design of "losses for tax purposes." We do not know if his propensity to lying during that 10-year period was greater or lower than now. If we assume it to be equal to the current rate, he must have lied about 45,000 times. Even with this many lies, he was still able to lose over one billion dollars, which may mean only one thing: he must have a pea-sized brain, not to mention pea-sized morals and ethics.

His pathological lying and cheating, vulgarity toward handicapped people and foreign countries, misogynistic behavior in public, lack of intellectual capacity required for leading this nation, etcetera, all pale when we consider his impact on many generations to come. He has reset, or lowered to be exact, the standard by which these issues are gauged not only for those people who blind-faithfully voted for him into the presidency but also the rest of the nation. We, as well as future generations of this nation, are all duped by our own ghost, or *gui-shin* (귀신). (05/08/19)

Water to lower ground, criminals to jail.
죄는 지은 데로 가고 물은 트는 데로 흐른다.

[192]

Unless one inputs some energy, as in an electric water pump, water cannot travel upward. It is a matter of gravity, which even a child understands. During a flood, a river spills over the compromised levee at the lowest place to the surrounding farm land. Just like this phenomenon, a criminal goes to jail. That is what the above provers says. No one would dispute the first half of the proverb that deals with water flow. However, the second part involving criminals getting punishment can be a controversial subject with two levels of questions. First, do criminals always go to jail? The key word in this question is "always." This demands a yes or no answer. If no is the answer, the follow-up discussion can become a tome dealing with social justice, corruption, etc. This may well be where we are now. If the answer is yes, then the accompanying second question is concerned with punishment. In an ideal society, the answers would be "yes" and "appropriately," respectively.

Once a verdict and final sentence are made to the public, people could react in at least three different ways. First, some may feel that justice was well served by the legal system. The second group may feel that the sentence was too harsh for the crime. According to the third group, the defendant received too lenient a punishment, really just a reprimand. If and when most of us feel that the final outcome was about right and just, there won't be any widespread follow-up discontent. It is the second and third cases that will divide the nation, or even sow hatred among the opposing factions. There can be public demonstrations of their displeasure. People, at the peak of a heated discussion, can confront each other with physical altercations on the street. If the police force gets involved, journalists and photographers will have a field day, spin doctors will open their mouths, and the family dinner table can become a battle ground.

One of our neighbors just received a traffic ticket, along with a fine of $100, from our homeowners association (HOA), for having committed a so-called "California stop" at a stop sign. Just like many other drivers around here, he failed to practice a full stop. He was understandably hopping mad and immediately appealed the case. But, soon he realized that he was on the losing end when the HOA showed the videotape. Then, he changed his tune, by submitting a letter begging for clemency. We composed his letter together. It was full of praising adjectives for the HOA: how much he appreciates their outstanding work for the safety of the community, for which he is "eternally grateful," blah, blah⋯ Speaking of a harsh penalty, on March 10, 2017, the eight members of the Korean Constitutional Court unanimously agreed to impeach President Park Geun-Hye, the first female president in Korean history. As far as I can tell, the only crime she committed was having a dubious associate, Ms. Choi Soonsil.

One of the greatest running backs in National Football League history, O.J. Simpson (born in 1947), was arrested and charged in 1994, 15 years after retirement, with the murders of his ex-wife, Nicole Brown, and her friend Ron Goldman. He was acquitted by a jury, after a lengthy and widely broadcasted trial, under a heavy tone of racial tension. For most African Americans it was a moment of eureka: finally justice shined on them. The rest of the country did not share the same sentiment. Later, in 1997, he was convicted in a civil court for the wrongful deaths. Less than a million dollars of the awarded $35 million was recovered by the plaintiffs, because Simpson was broke at that time. All in all, the majority of people felt Simpson walked away from the murder scot free.

Simpson's saga with the law did not end here. In 2008, he was sentenced to 33 years of imprisonment for the felonies of armed robbery and kidnapping. This sentence certainly appeared to be too harsh, and yet nobody seemed to complain. People felt that his previous evasion from the law was now finally fully paid. Both of Simpson's cases provide a perfect example of the above proverb. (05/14/19)

A wooden roller thrusts out in the dark.
아닌 밤중에 홍두깨다.

[193]

First, let me explain what *hong-doo-kae* (홍두깨) is. It is a wooden roller, of approximately one foot long, and about an inch thick. In the good old days, Korean folks used it in smoothing cloth, by wrapping cloth around it, and beating it on a flat surface. It looks like a dough roller, but thinner. Now, in the middle of the deadest, darkest night, a *hong-doo-kae* appears out of nowhere. It is an expression of something unexpected happening. This incident report to Dean C. describes a day in my life in 1995.

Dear Dean C. :

This is what happened. Forget about what anyone else says. They were not here when it happened. I am the only one to survive the occasion to tell you as it really happened. November the 9th, THE Thursday: it all began innocently enough for me to fall right into my comfortable dozing posture at my desk, just after two computer service guys, Ernie and Hal, left without succeeding in fixing my PC. My mouse was dead with his balls facing the sky. I cleaned it with acetone but to no avail. Ernie kept saying that a cat got inside. Hal said the same problem happened in Miller Hall (implying that a traveling ghost was responsible). Half dozing, half composing the second midterm exam for PHAR 52, I was suddenly jolted by a screeching sound coming from my left and above. I saw the right hand side of the ceiling breaking off, releasing an (estimated) 50-pound light fixture. This immediately prompted a downswing of the four-fluorescent-bulb-eight-foot assembly, moving right-to-left and plunging to certain destruction. But a few milliseconds prior to the expected crash, the left support line broke off (refer to the

50-pound estimate). The immediate result was a counterbalancing left-to-right force, which caused a straight downward fall of the light fixture. Net result was the entire assembly dropped straight down, without breakage of any of the four eight-foot-long light bulbs. Can you believe it? I mean, one minute, it's a normal office, the next minute this thing is standing by itself on the floor?

It made a tremendous sound at impact! I walked out of my office to see if anyone else might have heard the crash. it was about 9:47 AM but nobody was around, which irritated me greatly for I needed, then and there, some sort of sympathy, empathy, condolence, and maybe envy too. Then, Dr. K., a professor in the Biology Department, showed up and noticed how dark my office was. He couldn't close his mouth for ten minutes after my account of the event. But, I have to admit, he was the one who noticed that there was only one bracket on the floor, after the fall. He offered a hypothesis that the initial breakage of the right-hand side support wire, was due to the absence of the bracket intended to keep the 25-pound, right-half in the air, and a respectable distance above anybody's head. He is either terribly smart, or watches too much TV. People from the Physical Plant came out this morning and completed the re-hanging of the same, once-fallen, eight-foot light fixture.

As a footnote, Dean C. had rather mixed feelings about this episode. Had I been extinguished for good, he could have sued somebody for the exact sum of money needed to construct our annex building. It was about $15 million and with attorney's fees it may have become a $30-million lawsuit. He was a fair man, and I am sure he would have named the building after me. No, I wouldn't mind at all. As far as the building supervisor is concerned, he said he was very remorseful that he was away and missed this exciting episode. After all was said and done, I think the people responsible for Wilson Hall were very lucky. What if I had been walking across my office to photocopy old exam questions at that particular moment, instead of dosing at my desk, and trying to compose new questions? May their luck last forever, and mine too. (05/14/19)

Messengers on a one-way journey.
함흥차사

[194]

The Joseon dynasty (1392 - 1897) was founded by Tae-jo (태조), previously known as Yi Seong-gye (이성계), after he toppled the much troubled Goryeo dynasty (918 - 1392) without much bloodshed. Not only was the name of the nation changed, but the capital city was also moved to Seoul, which has remained as such since then. Yi had two wives, from whom a total of eight sons were born. Inevitably, family skirmishes ensued among the siblings as to who would be enthroned after Yi abdicates. Yi was so disgusted with what appeared to be endless feuds and conspiracies among his sons that he decided to leave the capital, once and for all, for Hamheung, a small town in the Northeast Korean peninsula. That's where he was born and raised till he became a young adult. Eventually, Tae-jong, the fifth son from his first wife, became the third king of the dynasty. (The second king doesn't play a role in this story.) Throughout his tenure as king, Tae-jong felt ashamed of, and repented deeply for, the way he had become king. To seek forgiveness from his self-exiled father, Tae-jong kept sending a messenger to bring his father back to Seoul. This special convoy was called *cha-sa* (차사).

Yi, on the other hand, flatly refused to be any part of the awful business happening in the capital. In fact, Yi would order his men to kill each and every messenger from Tae-jong, even before they could enter the town of Hamheung: usually, a volley of arrows would meet them at the entrance gate to the town. This repeated refusal from Yi did not stop Tae-jong from sending messengers, although his men began to avoid the job as much as they could. This was considered a journey of no-return. In the end, a loyal senior official, Park Soon, who used to be a bosom buddy of Yi, when they were young "revolutionaries," volunteered to become the messenger. Tae-jong tried to stop Park's plea, saying that he was one of a few senior ministers in his kingdom, and thus he could not sacrifice another loyal subordinate. Park wore the king out and took off for Hamheung.

It was a long and difficult trek from Seoul to Hamheung, with many rivers and mountains to cross. Although Yi killed all messengers from the capitol, 차사 *(cha-sa)*, he had been in deep turmoil all along, having had remorse for his cruel acts. When he was told that his old friend Park was at the gate, wanting to visit with him, he rushed up a tower to see. Yi noticed Park riding a horse and he brought along a colt. With the baby horse tied to a tree, neighing loudly and continuously in desperation, Park, still on horseback, approached Yi. When soldiers asked Yi if they ought to kill Park, as in the past, Yi was in an unenviable quandary. The old king Yi told the soldiers, "Let him enter my castle. He is, after all, a dear friend of mine. I would like to share a drink with him first. What difference does it make if he dies after spending some time with his old friend?"

As they reminisced about the old days, Yi asked Park why he brought the colt all the way from Seoul. Park replied: "As you saw, the baby was crying his heart out, as he was separated from his mother. How can children survive without parents? Please come back to Seoul." Yi scolded Park, saying: "No! I will never go back to Seoul. This is where I was born, and thus will die here! Don't ever utter such nonsense, now hurry back home. In the past, I had all messengers killed, but how can I kill you, my dear friend?" As Park was leaving, Yi's men urged him not to sway from killing Park, merely out of old sentimental emotion. Indeed, Yi had promised his men to kill Park after the feast. Finally, the old king allowed his men to kill Park, if and only if, he had not yet crossed a river skirting the south of Hamheung. Yi thought that a sufficient time had passed so that his friend would have been safely across the river. As the soldiers rushed to the river, Park was about to get aboard a small ferry crossing the river. He was summarily killed. The legend has it that the news broke the heart of the old king Yi.

Once again, Hamheung is the name of a small town in North Korea. It so happened that I was also born in that town. Cha-sa means a special messenger. Taken together, Hamheung *cha-sa* refers to a person who has left home but never came back again, just like me. (05/15/19)

True stories from a drunken man.
취중에 진담 나온다.

[195]

"The gibberish uttered by a drunken man still carries some truth," is my translation of the above proverb. Although this man is hopelessly drunk and much nonsense comes out of his mouth, if we listen to his slurred speech carefully, we can learn much about him as well as many other possible lessons. Because the man speaks incoherently in a stupor and with unsteady posture, we tend to ignore what he is mumbling. It is quite a natural response to such a situation, and to some extent, similar to the case of hearing a joke. As there must be some hidden message behind any jokes your friend throws at you, including underlying cynicism, it is the listener's choice to decipher what the drunken man is trying to convey. Instead, we often walk away saying, "Oh he's drunk again. Just leave him alone. He will sober up soon." Most likely he would say that he was not always like this and try to explain how he's ended up in this sad state of affairs. He may also describe lost opportunities of love, wealth, career, and even religion. There must be some lessons that all of us can learn from his narrative, but we are usually not patient enough to take advantage of the occasion.

Alcohol, ethanol or ethyl alcohol, is a unique chemical in that it freely passes through the transport barrier existing between the blood stream and the central nervous system or brain. The gate-keeper of the brain is referred to as the blood-brain barrier, which allows passage only for those nutrients that the brain needs. This difficult passage of foreign substances is the main reason why chemotherapy fails to treat brain tumors. Most medicines that freely travel in our body cannot penetrate the blood-brain barrier. Ethanol is small in size, so it moves faster. It shows affinity toward the surface of cells comprising tissues and organs, including the blood-brain barrier. Therefore, its physiological effect, for most of us is governed mainly by the absorption rate from the gut and the extent of metabolism in the liver. Needless to say, alcohol enjoys a long history of love affairs with humans. It lowers the guard in all of us and lessens the inhibitions we usually maintain.

Alcohol emboldens us in behavior and speech, especially in expressing our emotions and feelings. Li Bai (701 - 762), or *Yi Baik* (이백) in Korean pronunciation, was one of the greatest Chinese poets during the Tang dynasty. While he was drinking, his romantic poems often dealt with the moon. Legend has it that Li Bai drowned in a river when he reached out to grasp for the moon's reflection. Reproduced below is part of his famous poem, *Drinking Alone by Moonlight* (月下獨酌).

花間一壺酒	A cup of wine, under the flowering trees;
獨酌無相親	I drink alone, for no friend is near.
舉杯邀明月	Raising my cup to beckon the bright moon,
對影成三人	For he, with my shadow, will make three men.

What people, especially politicians, say in public under the pretense of formal politeness and diplomacy can be quite different from what they truly believe or feel. During the G20 Meeting in 2011, French President Nicolas Sarkozy said to Barrack Obama that Israeli Prime Minister Benjamin Netanyahu "is a liar. I can't stand him." In response, Obama told him, "You are tired of him. What about me? I have to deal with him every day." What they did not realize was that the microphone was still on. In 2005, during a filming of Access Hollywood, Donald Trump said to the program host privately that "When you're a star, women let you do it. You can do anything ... grab them by the pussy." This recorded conversation was made public by *the Washington Post*, during the 2016 presidential election, but Trump still managed to win the election. They should drink more often so we, the average citizens, can grasp their true feelings more directly. (05/21/19)

A watermill never freezes.
부지런한 물방아는 얼 새도 없다.

[196]

A small stream of mountain water shows signs of having a cold temperature when ice forms along its edge. This is not so much because the ground is colder than in the middle of stream, but because water flows more slowly at the periphery. The stream would experience much more resistance because of the friction with its sides as well as its shallow bottom. Turbulent water just doesn't have chance to become viscous enough to get solidified. Likewise, the "diligent" watermill will not freeze so long as the water flows through it. A nuanced interpretation of the proverb may well be that people who are busy all the time will not become corrupt or will not have a chance to go astray. In this sense, a similar Korean proverb would be; "A busy dog always has the nose bruised and banged up," or Entry #94, "A rolling stone gathers no moss."

Being busy is presented here, in a favorable connotation. On the other hand, the great American philosopher, Henry David Thoreau (1817 - 1862), went one step further, asking, "It is not enough to be busy. So are the ants. The question is: What are we busy about?" We are busy with many different activities for living: farming, fishing, teaching, researching for new knowledge and technology, conspiring for fraudulent business, starting a war, relieving pain from the sick, saving lives, interpreting laws, etc. These are activities we are engaged in on a daily basis, perhaps not so much with pleasure but out of necessity. Thoreau's question is more concerned with how one maintains a balance between what is necessary in earning a life and non-vocational activities such as meditating for enlightenment, gazing at the night sky, getting drunk, looking for entertainment, and even chasing women, etc. We all know the importance of taking a break for recreation, as in the old saying "All work and no play makes Jack a dull boy." But neither this American proverb nor Thoreau tells us what we ought to be doing right now, as we are maintaining our busy lives at a frantic pace. Rightly so, because it is a subjective matter, but we could always read about how others have lived their lives as a sort of reference.

There are so many inspirational and amazing biographies out there, it is difficult to select even a few. I am compelled though to present Truman by David McCullough as my first choice. Harry S. Truman (1884 - 1972), the 33rd President of this country, was introduced earlier in Entry #41, "Clean upstream begets clean water downstream." Truman was born on a farm in a small town in Missouri as the oldest of three children. Even when he was a small child, he was always occupied with "things" to do and apparently quite studious in piano, reading history, and learning skills such as shorthand, bookkeeping, and typing. The diligence he acquired early in his life served him quite well later on. As president, he helped Western Europe rebuild their economy after the Second World War with the Marshall Plan; developed what is now known as the Truman Doctrine as well as NATO.

What is most remarkable about this man was that he did what he believed in, regardless public opinions. He fired General Douglas MacArthur, right when he was the most admired national hero and a commander of the U.N. forces during the Korean War, all simply because MacArthur failed to "respect the authority of the President." He was equally firm about the use of atomic bombs on Japan to expedite the end to the Second World War. After he retired to Independence, Missouri, he refused to go after any financial opportunities that may have compromised the presidency. He and his wife Bess lived in frugality, as he had no personal savings at that waning point of their lives. He did not blame anybody else but himself when things did not proceed favorably. Sitting on his table, in his White House office, was the famous sign, "The Buck Stops Here." It was not only proclaiming his assertiveness, but also taking full responsibility for his actions. As a businessman, Donald Trump was notably litigious. By 2016, when he was running for President, *USA Today* reported that he had been involved in 3,500 lawsuits and was the plaintiff in nearly 2,000 of them. Yes, he has been very busy also, but with what though. (05/25/19)

None of the fingers are alike.
한날한시에 난 손가락도 길고 짧다.

[197]

All of the ten fingers we are born with are of different lengths and shapes, although they were all "born" at the same time, on the same day, and the same year. This finding is in spite of many structural commonalities they share in terms of bone, muscle, and skin. We are so accustomed to our fingers that we do not think about their differences and do not imagine any other forms of fingers or hands. As usual, the above proverb describes a simple observation, but does not tell what the variations actually mean. I suppose that different types of fingers allow for different functions, which could not be achieved with identical fingers. Normally, humans have five fingers: thumb, index finger, middle finger, ring finger, and little finger or pinkie. Each participates in a given manipulation with varying contributions. Opening a bottle cap is usually done by thumb and index finger. A wedding ring is placed on the ring finger of the left hand. It is the pinkie that digs out snot or ear wax. The middle finger is raised when you want to express disgust. A thumb-up means "okay" or is a sign of approval. Typing usually employs all ten fingers for speed. Shadow figures on the wall usually calls for the cooperation of hands as well as fingers. See also Entry #38, "Each and every finger would feel pain if bitten."

What the above proverb is trying to convey is that there are no identical beings on this planet, in both the plant and animal kingdoms: just like fingerprints, human faces, or 10 siblings in a family. Once we accept this unavoidable fact, we are bound to respect and protect the diversity and individualism involved. From the perspective of controlling a population, diversity or individualism could be the worst nightmare. "How can we control thousands of individuals, with more than thousands of different ideas? Just put them in uniform and make one mass march toward the destination I have chosen. Shoot down anyone who is out the line in my campaign!" This will be the order of the day from a dictator. Individual citizens may cry for freedom. Needless to say, much social unrest and political turmoil stems from this conflict between the opposing desires of rulers and citizens. See also Entry #61, "I can't find my sword in somebody else's scabbard."

Three Identical Strangers, a 2018 documentary film directed by Tim Wardle, introduces identical triplets, who were born in 1961 and immediately released to an adoption agency by their young single mother. Just six months after birth, the babies were separated and intentionally raised by three families of different economic levels: blue-collar, middle-class, and affluent. The separation upon birth was part of a scientific research on "nature versus nurture." They were indeed ideal "samples" for studying how different environments, or nurture, influenced genetically identical siblings to become different beings. The study was sponsored by the Jewish Board of Guardians and run by two psychiatrists. David Kellman, Eddy Galland, and Bobby Shafran did not know they had identical brothers until it was discovered, rather accidentally, when they were 19 years old.

Their encounters in serendipity as young adults as well as their unparalleled resemblance in appearance, personality, behaviors, and taste, was widely publicized and much talked about during the early 1980s. One cannot imagine any higher degree of similarity and closeness among three individuals than these triplets: they even had the same taste in women. Following their fame in the mass media, they opened a steak house called Triplets, in SoHo, New York. It was a financially lucrative venture for a few years. However, all the publicity frenzy blurred the subtle differences they must have had.

In 1995, Eddy Galland committed suicide. In their late 20s, Bobby and David met their biological mother, who they believed was having serious emotional problems. Likewise, it had been known for a while that all of them had suffered from mental illness, and yet there was a subtle but significant difference in dealing the mental disorders between the triplets, possibly reflecting the influence of nurture. In short, even identical triplets can still show differences, supporting the theme of the above proverb. (05/26/19)

Can you fly even without hair?
털도 안 난 것이 날기부터 하려 한다.

[198]

In the INTRODUCTION of *The Tongue Can Break Bones*, it was pointed out that many English words are missing from the Korean vocabulary. As a few examples, I said that both small krill and jumbo shrimp are referred to as 새우, or *saewoo*. Tangerine and orange are both 귤, or *gule*. Here is another example: 털, or *teol*, means not only hair, as in human or dog, but also the fur of animals such as mink and sheep, and even the feathers on a bird. Yes, it covers a wide range of animals. Another proverb says, "This immature thing (*gut*, 것), even without *teol*, is trying to fly." I do not know which *teol* it refers to here. If it is meant to be feather, then the narrative is straightforward: "This chick is trying to fly, even though she doesn't have any mature wings." If it was supposed to mean hair or fur, then my translation would be: "This creature (것) is trying to fly without even hair, let alone feather." I prefer the latter, as it touches upon a broader scope.

Either way, that is what we often notice in this world: ill-qualified people embarking on an important project, often with disastrous results. As far as I am concerned, it wouldn't matter that much to me personally, if a project's outcome does not affect me one way or another. Many first-time home owners, usually young and ambitious couples but not experienced, follow a DIY (do it yourself) spirit to try and remodel their homes themselves. In many instances, they end up hiring a contractor, perhaps spending more money, but they do acquire some experience they can use in the future.

These sorts of episodes are all "a fire beyond the river" so-to-speak. But there are certain cases where my emotions inevitably get involved. Just the other day, I saw a cop issuing a ticket to a driver on the I-215 Beltway around Las Vegas. This was the same reckless driver who, only a few minutes earlier, zipped through heavy traffic at a high rate of speed, with sudden and frequent lane changes. And now, I felt that my earlier anger and cursing were well validated and wished that this guy had to pay a hefty fine and a raised insurance premium. Whichever way one looked at it, it was a very satisfactory outcome. But more importantly, how was this punk allowed to drive in the first place anyway? Where did he obtain his driver's license, at Walmart?

Prior to retirement, at the age of 70, my primary interaction with people was all in academic settings: professors, administrators, students in a professional program, as well as PhD students in my lab and in our department. Compared with the general population, they were better educated, intelligent, ambitious, efficacious, and courteous (most of them, anyway). In addition, being their teacher offered some degree of leverage on matters of mutual interest, like their academic performance, or research progress. Because of this "luxurious" situation, I must have developed a high expectation from people and a thorough criticism of their performance, which might have been perceived too analytical and often too harsh. This is to justify why I have become less accommodating a person than one may expect at my age. I am afraid I might have become more cantankerous.

To me, this world is full of mediocre people: nothing seems to be working as it was supposed to and nobody seems to know what they are doing. Whenever I ask for help, I seldom receive satisfactory response even when, or particularly when, I pay for their service. In many instances, I have to talk to their superiors, but they can be worse. "The Peter Principle is a concept in management, developed by Laurence J. Peter, which observes that people in a hierarchy, tend to rise to their level of incompetence." This is basically because one skillset at a given position does not necessarily translate to another position. One most pitiful observation I have made during my long life is that these people do not know that they are incapable of the very job they are holding, and yet ask for promotions. My inclination to this resignation is largely from the naysayers about global climate change. (05/27/19)

Speak louder, win the argument.
남대문 본 놈과 안 본 놈이 다투면, 안 본 놈이 이긴다.

[199]

With the birth of the Joseon Dynasty in 1392, the capital city was established in Hanyang, the old name of Seoul. As commonly found during that particular period of time, the city was protected by stone walls, interrupted only by four strategically located Great Gates, or *dae-mun*. They are: *Nam-dae-mun*, meaning South Gate (남대문, also called *Sung-rye-mun*, or 숭례문), the East Gate (동대문, or *Dong-dae-mun*), the West Gate (서대문, or *Seo-dae-mun*), and the North Gate (숙정문, or *Suk-jeong-mun*). Of these, 남대문 (South Gate) is historically one of the most cherished sites in the nation. The structure is, in fact, designated as National Treasure Number One. Tourists from rural areas must see the Gate, almost as an obligation. When they go back home, they can describe what they saw to friends, neighbors, colleagues, and others who have yet to visit Seoul. Visiting 남대문 (South Gate) is like visiting the National Mall in Washington, DC. It offers them a bragging right.

So, at a social gathering, after you come back home, you are telling a crowd what you've seen in Seoul with a great deal of enthusiasm, and perhaps a bit of exaggeration here and there. Then, a guy, out of nowhere, starts to tell the same audience how he saw the South Gate, which might be slightly different from yours. The fact is, this guy has never even been to Seoul, but he was book-smart and elegant enough in his speech to effectively steal the thunder from right under your nose. The whole gathering has now become mesmerized by his story. He is asking you if you saw this and that, followed by, "Man, oh man, you missed the most interesting part. What a shame!" By now, people don't even look at you, no matter how hard you try to attract their attention. In the end, you just lick your wounds and leave the gathering with a sour taste in your mouth.

The above proverb is describing exactly the scene presented above: "When two guys argue about the South Gate, the guy who has never been to Seoul wins the argument." He could have been a smooth talker, better looking, well-dressed, excellent in pleasing the ladies, etc. Even if you knew he had never been to Seoul, you cannot declare it, lest you sound like a loser. You have already lost the battle. An interesting word used here is 놈, pronounced *nom*. I translated the word to "guy" but it can be "son of bitch," "rascal," or even a "man." The word is not necessarily insulting or deleterious. It is commonly used, often in an affectionate manner: several proverbs introduced in *The Tongue Can Break Bones* contain the same word.

We are in a troubled society if the wrong people win over the right, the fake prevails the truth, vanity overrides reality, appearance matters more than content, the ugly outshine the beauty, apathy rules over compassion, science is pushed away by fantasy, politics is more important than the national interest, fraud appears as legitimate, and so on and so forth. Having listed these phenomena, it sure looks like describing the current world we live in. With xenophobic ideals, fueled by nationalism, populists seem to lead the immigration issue further away from what basic humanity is demanding. This selfish me-first philosophy, coupled with the ugly underside of capitalism, creates an ever-increasing gap in wealth, not only between the rich and the poor but also among nations. Walls are built between neighboring nations as well as the perimeter of gated communities. It is them versus us.

The only thing that leaders, often demagogues really, seem to understand well is "divide and conquer." Establishing a common enemy is the easiest way to control a disgruntled mass. "Lock them up!" then all will be okay. "There is no climate change. It is all a hoax! We, including endangered species, will successfully adapt to the change, as natural history attest to." This is all such sweet talk to the ears of those who practice "active ignorance" that they accept wholeheartedly what they are hearing. The real danger lies in the possibility that these folks honestly do not know that they are ignorant. They are true believers, in a truest sense. Now read the above proverb again. (05/28/19)

Flexibility over rigidity.
꺾이느니 보다 차라리 굽히는 편이 낫다.

[200]

This summer, we have been following the trade war between the United States and China, with fascination on one hand and a great deal of apprehension on the other hand. It is fascinating as the two economically strongest nations in the world engage in what appears to be the initial stage of a cockfight. They are circling each other to see if there is an opportunity for a fatal attack. It is also frightening as the feud can cause another global, economic meltdown, like the one in 2008. So far, neither side shows any willingness to repair the current rift. On-and-off talks between the negotiators do not seem to go anywhere. Both sides behave as if they were two steel balls colliding each other.

Since elected in 2017, President Moon of Korea has maintained a foreign policy that deviates dramatically from the past. He has been downgrading the relationship with Japan and complaining about Japan's ill treatment of Koreans during their 35-year occupation of the Korean peninsula beginning 1910. This constant nagging, together with Moon's friendly approach towards North Korea and China, has not been sitting very well with Abe government of Japan. In recent months, Japan banned the export to Korea of certain materials essential in the manufacture of semiconductors, televisions, and smartphones. The Korean government retaliated against Japan in kind. Then, both countries removed the other party from their list of most-trusted trading partners. Mutual tourism has precipitously declined. Boycotts against Japanese products and culture have become everyday occurrence throughout Korea.

Moon does not want to be the first to suggest diplomatic conversations with Abe of Japan as he could be perceived as the a weaker of the two. This is politically not acceptable. Abe must be in the same situation. Has any friendly gestures towards North

Korea, China, and Russia from Moon brought any goodwill from them? Hardly. Can then Korea continuously rely on support from the United States? The problem with this question is that Donald Trump is not the most reliable person on this planet. Most of the well-informed Koreans have already realized that Korea can no longer trust the U.S. As of this writing, August 12, 2019, Korea appears completely isolated from historically friendly nations such as Japan and the United States. The dire situation between China and the U.S. as well as the dilemma Korea is facing now in the world stage could have been avoided, had the leaders involved learned the simple lesson from the above proverb. (08/12/19)

INDEX

A

Abe • 200
active ignorance • 114, 199
Acts (1:18) • 191
acupuncture • 184
ae-jeong (애정) • 153
Aesop's fable • 130, 169, 171, 179, 186
Affordable Care Act • 120, 171
Afghanistan, war in • 160
Ağca, Mehmet Ali • 185
alcohol • 156, 195
alcoholic liver disease • 164
al-Qaeda • 154
altered state of mind • 142
American Civil War • 163
amoxicillin • 183
amphiphilic (substances) • 175
Antoinette, Marie • 170
Appalachian Trail • 106
Apple • 114, 157
astronomer • 102
Atkinson, Kate • 135
atomic bombs • 133
9/11 attack • 138
Axis of Germany, Italy, and Japan • 116
Azalea Flowers (진달래꽃) • 153

B

Baekdudaegan Trail (백두대간) • 146
Baekdu-san (백두산) • 146
Bagje • 116
baik-jeong (백정) • 155
Baker, Jim • 101
Barr, Bob • 115
Basilica in Barcelona • 160
Battle of Stalingrad • 122
big-bang theory • 106
bilirubin • 164
Bill and Melinda Gates Foundation • 112
bin Laden, Osama • 154
birth rate • 122
blood-brain barrier • 195
Bobbitt, Lorena • 170
Bolton, Elmer • 152
bong (봉 ; phoenix) • 172
Boston Marathon • 104
Bounty, Royal Navy HMS • 137
Brady, Tom • 121
Brown, Daniel James • 142, 186
BTS • 107, 121
Buddhism • 188
Buddhist • 103, 126, 178, 188
Bundy, Ted • 132

100 Korean Proverbs

Burmese python • 102
Burton, Dan • 155
Busan, Korea • 144
Buttigieg, Pete • 187

C

Cain, Burl • 132
calcium ion • 148
California stop • 192
cannibalism • 122
cardiovascular system • 141
Carnal Payer Mat, The • 103
Carothers, Wallace Hume • 152
Carson, Johnny • 102
Carter, Forrest • 174
Catch 22 • 169
Cato at Liberty • 114
Cavendish, Henry • 143
centipede grass • 117
charity foundation • 112
cha-sa (차사) • 194
cheon-min (천민) • 155
Chernow, Ron • 110
Chicago Bears • 163
Cups • 104

chloride (ion) • 148
Chok-han (촉한) • 124
choo-suk (추석) • 151
Choon-hyang • 104
Chung-Cheong Province • 181
Churchill, Winston • 116, 176
Cillizza, Chris • 191
Cinderella • 104, 186
Cleveland Browns • 130
climate change • 104, 112, 141, 198, 199
Clinton, Bill • 101, 115
color association • 138
Comey, James • 135
Condit, Gary • 115
Confederate soldier, a statue of • 163
Confucianism • 155
Conway, Kellyanne • 135
Crazy Rich Asians • 123
cremation • 129, 182
Crowley, Joseph • 104, 110
Cuomo, Andrew • 120
Curry, Stephen • 128

D

daily exercise • 113
Dalai Lama • 188
dang-sin (당신) • 127
Davis, Adelle • 132
DDT • 124
Dean, James • 119, 155
Debt to Penny clock • 143
deep vain thrombosis (DVT) • 141
DMV (Department of Motor Vehicles) • 108
doenjang (된장) • 135
doh (도) • 188
Domenici, Pete • 115
dong-jeong (동정) • 153
donkey • 111
Do-Not-Call Registry • 184
doru-meggy (도루메기) • 162
dual circulatory system • 141
duck boat • 106
Duterte, R. • 132
Duvall, Robert • 129

E

Education of Little Tree • 174
egalitarian (philosophy) • 110, 143
Eisenhower, Dwight D. • 110, 152
Einstein, Albert • 124, 131, 185
Emperor of China • 166
eobo (여보) • 127
eo-pyun-ne (여편네) • 127
Ephesian (5:21, 24, 25) • 145
Esquivel, Laura • 151
E.T. • 116

F

Facebook • 114
false humility • 143
Faye, Tammie • 101
Federal Emergency Management Agency • 134
feet on snake • 184
Fiddler on the Roof • 173
field of view • 109
Fisherian Runaway • 159
Forrest Gump • 171
Four Noble Truths • 188
French Revolution • 168
Friendship Bridge • 146

G

Gang-nam bus terminal • 126
Gang-nam Style • 107
Gaudi, Antoni • 160
GDP (Gross Domestic Product) • 139
Genesis (2:24) • 145
Gingrich, Newt • 101, 114
glycated hemoglobin (A1C) • 164
goat • 111
Goat, Billy • 170
GoFundMe website • 180
Goguryo • 116
Golden State Warriors • 128
Grant Ulysses S. • 110
Grassley, Charles • 113
Great Santini • 129
Greek tragedies • 111
grits • 171
gui-shin (귀신) • 191
Gun Violence Archive • 154
gwa-go (과거) • 104

H

haan (한) • 170
haak (학; flamingo) • 172
Hahn, Jessica • 101
Hamheung • 194
Hamlet • 189
Han River • 120, 179
hanbok (한복) • 140
Hanh, Thich Nhat • 147
Han-yang (한양) • 162, 199
Hart, Gary • 101
HDL (high-density lipoprotein) • 125
Heller, Joseph • 169
Helsinki Summit • 107
hierarchical reductionism • 161
Hinduism • 188
Hitler, Adolf • 114, 142, 175
Holy Land • 122
homeowners association • 128, 190, 192
homee (호미) • 113
hong-doo-kae (홍두깨) • 193
Hope Diamond • 170
Hudson, Rock • 155
Hughes, Howard • 143
Hugo, Victor • 185
hurricane Sandy • 122

hurricane Florence and Michael • 141
Hyde, Henry • 115
hydrogen bonding • 125
hyo-ja (효자) • 127
Hyoja-dong (효자동) • 140
hyung-sik (형식) • 177

I

illegal interrogation • 140
imjin-oeran (임진왜란) • 162
industrial revolution • 125
in-jeong (인정) • 153
Innocents, The • 164
Italian operas • 111

J

Jackson, Stonewall • 163
jaet-mool (잿물) • 136
Jagger, Mick • 121
James, LeBron • 128
Jegal-liang (제갈량) • 124
jeon (전), 121
jeong (정) • 127, 153
Jeremiah (17: 7) • 172

jesa (제사) • 108, 191
Jesus • 185, 188, 191
Jiri-san (지리산) • 146
Johnny Walker Blue • 119
Johnson & Johnson • 113
Jones, Alex • 114
Jones, Jim • 142
Jordan, Jim • 102
Joseon Dynasty of Korea • 121, 155, 162
Judas Iscariot • 191

K

Kalamazoo, Michigan • 144
karate chop • 181
Keller, Helen • 168
Kennedy, John F. • 115, 170
Kerr, Steve • 128
Kilimanjaro in Tanzania • 122
kimchi (김치) • 182
Kim, Jong-un • 116, 142, 176
Kim, Sowal (김소월) • 153
Kipling, Rudyard, 114
Koi fish, 157
kong (콩), 152

100 Korean Proverbs   230

Korean
    as conformists • 177
    chaebols • 112
    Culture Center • 175
    immigrants • 167
    National Assembly • 172
    peninsula • 107, 108, 116, 122, 131, 146, 159, 176, 178, 194, 200
    Town • 175
    War • 110, 116, 119, 133, 144, 168, 176
K-pop • 107, 119
Kumgang-san (금강산) • 122
Kung Fu master Wei • 177
Kwan, Kevin • 123
5·18 Kwangju Massacre • 168

L

Las Vegas Strip • 154
LaTourette, Steven • 115
LDL (low-density lipoprotein) • 125
Lee, Robert E. • 163
Lemon, Don • 128
Les Misérables • 185
Lewinsky, Monica • 101, 115
Li, Bai • 195
Life in Foreign Land (타향살이) • 147
lips and teeth • 145
Livingston, Robert • 115
log rolling • 165
Louis XVI, King • 170
Louisiana State Penitentiary • 132
Luke (6:37) • 185
lyophilization • 108

M

MacArthur, Douglas • 196
Maclean, Norman • 148
mag-geol-li (막걸리) • 147
magnesium (ion) • 148
Manchurian territory • 116
Mann Gulch tragedy • 148
manura (마누라) • 127
mapo tofu • 148
Markle, Meghan • 158
Matthew
    (18:21-22) • 185
    (26:15) • 191
    (27:1-10) • 191
MBA • 152, 169
McCabe, Andrew • 185
McCullough, David • 196
McVeigh, Timothy • 102

Mecca • 122
Medal of Honor • 142
meju (메주) • 135
Mencius • 119, 171
Menéndez brothers • 158
Merchant of Venice, The • 171
5·16 Military Coup • 168
military spending • 113
Mills, Wilbur • 101
Miracle on Ice • 186
monkey(s) • 101, 102, 119, 180
Monroe, Marilyn • 115
monsoon season • 183
moo-dang (무당) • 155, 170
Moon, J., President • 136, 176, 200
More, Hannah • 170
Mother Teresa • 118
Mount Fuji • 122
Mount Vesuvius • 156
Murphy's Laws • 104, 106

N

Nam-dae-mun, South Gate • 199
national debt • 187
National Institute of Cancer • 108
National Mall • 199
NATO • 116, 196
nature versus nurture • 197
Navy SEAL team • 154
NCAA basketball playoff • 186
Netanyahu, Benjamin • 195
Netherlands, the • 113
Nicholson, Jack • 181
nicotine withdrawal symptoms • 137
Nielson, Kirstjen • 134
nom (놈) • 118, 159, 199
1965 Northeast Blackout • 122
nyang (냥) • 121

O

Obama, Barack • 120, 134, 187, 195
Ocasio-Cortez, Alexandria • 104, 110, 136
on-dol-bang (온돌방) • 138
OxyContin • 183
oxygen • 125, 141

P

paat (팥) • 135, 152

pacifist constitution of Japan • 168

Paddock, Stephen • 154

Paris Agreement • 104

Park, Geun-Hye • 120, 133, 168, 192

Park, J. H. • 107, 133, 137, 172

Park, Soon • 194

Pauling, Linus • 131

Pearl Harbor • 109, 154

Peter, Laurence J. • 198

Philadelphia Eagles • 163

pine trees • 160

Pittsburg Steelers • 130

playing possum • 186

polygraph • 102

Pompeo, Mike • 104

poon (푼) • 121, 179

Pope John Paul II • 185

Powerball • 157

Project Tango • 183

pronunciation (of English and Korean) • 173

Prum, Richard O. • 145

Purdue Pharma • 183

Putin, Vladimir • 107

R

Rants, Joe, 142

red blood cells • 125, 129

4·19 Revolution • 168

Rhee, Syngman • 133

Ringer's Solution • 129

Roger, Aaron • 117, 158

Rohingya refugees • 132

Roman Empire • 156

Roosevelt, Franklin D. • 116, 176

Russo-Japanese War • 116

Ryan, Paul • 151

S

sake • 148, 150

Sampoong Department Store • 179

Sanders, Sarah Huckabee • 135

sang-min (상민) • 155

Sarkozy, Nicolas • 195

Schrodinger, Erwin • 131

Schweitzer, Albert • 118

Second Amendment • 154

Segeum-jung (세금정) • 140

seo-bang (서방) • 161

Seoul Summer Olympics • 107

Seongsu Daegyo • 179

Sessions, Jeff • 185

Seven Wonders of the World • 122

Shilla • 116

shin (신) • 191

Silent Sam • 163

Simpson, O.J. • 192

sinarak or (씨나락) • 187

Singer sewing machine • 162

Sino-Japanese War • 116

smell of fear • 114

Smokejumpers • 148

Socrates • 127, 176

soju • 108, 147

Son, Heung-min (손흥민) • 121

Soros, George • 112

sot (솥) • 138

Spielberg, Steven • 116

Spieth, Jordan • 158

Stalin, Joseph • 116, 176

St. Andrews College • 174

St. Augustine • 103, 171

St. Ignatius • 103

Stern, Ken • 112

Stormy Daniels • 101, 141

student loans • 139, 187

stunt-kites • 139

su-jeong-gwa (수정과) • 130

sulfate (ion) • 148

surface tension • 175

SWAT team • 124

Syrus, Publilius • 170

T

talcum powder • 113

Tang Dynasty • 116, 156, 178

tannins • 130

Taylor, Elizabeth • 155

temporary insanity • 102

Ten Military Classics (of ancient China) • 128

testosterone • 109, 115, 118

Thoreau, Henry David • 196

Three Identical Strangers • 197

Three wise monkeys • 102, 180

time, definition of • 160

trade war • 200

Transition State Theory • 142

TRICK • 188

Truman, Harry S. • 134, 145, 196

Trump, Donald • 101, 107, 114, 117, 128, 134, 135, 139, 141, 143, 148, 175, 176, 180, 185, 187, 191, 195, 196, 200

TSP • 136
Twain, Mark • 188
Tyndall Effect • 143

U
Unabomber • 102
United States Forest Service • 148

V
Valjean, Jean • 185
Virginia Cavaliers • 186
Vitter, David • 115

W
Wallace, George • 174
walleye pollack (명태) • 108
Walton, Sam • 179
Warsaw Pact • 116
wavelength • 131
wee-gey (위기) • 176
Western Axis • 109
what-ifs • 178
white supremacists • 117

Whittaker, Jack • 157
Wikipedia • 109, 115, 139
1980 Winter Olympic Games • 186
Wolitzer, Meg • 103
world population • 151
World War II • 107, 109, 114, 164, 168, 176, 178, 196

X
Xi Jinping • 132

Y
Yalta Conference • 116, 176
Yalu River • 146
Yamamoto, Isoroku • 109
yang (양) or nyang (냥) • 179
yang-ban (양반) • 155
Yi, Seong-gye (이성계) • 194
YouTube • 114